# Flutter for Beginners

An introductory guide to building cross-platform mobile
applications with Flutter and Dart 2

**Alessandro Biessek**

**BIRMINGHAM - MUMBAI**

# Flutter for Beginners

**Commissioning Editor:** Amarabha Banerjee
**Acquisition Editor:** Larissa Pinto
**Content Development Editor:** Akhil Nair
**Technical Editor:** Sachin Sunilkumar
**Copy Editor:** Safis Editing
**Project Coordinator:** Manthan Patel
**Proofreader:** Safis Editing
**Indexer:** Pratik Shirodkar
**Production Designer:** Jyoti Chauhan

First published: September 2019

Production reference: 1120919

Published by Packt Publishing Ltd.
Livery Place
35 Livery Street
Birmingham
B3 2PB, UK.

ISBN 978-1-78899-608-2

www.packt.com

*To my mother, Antonina, and my father, Euclides, for their sacrifices and for exemplifying the power of determination*

*– Alessandro Biessek*

`mapt.io`

Subscribe to our online digital library for full access to over 7,000 books and videos, as well as industry leading tools to help you plan your personal development and advance your career. For more information, please visit our website.

# Why subscribe?

- Spend less time learning and more time coding with practical eBooks and Videos from over 4,000 industry professionals

- Improve your learning with Skill Plans built especially for you

- Get a free eBook or video every month

- Fully searchable for easy access to vital information

- Copy and paste, print, and bookmark content

# Packt.com

Did you know that Packt offers eBook versions of every book published, with PDF and ePub files available? You can upgrade to the eBook version at `www.packt.com` and as a print book customer, you are entitled to a discount on the eBook copy. Get in touch with us at `customercare@packtpub.com` for more details.

At `www.packt.com`, you can also read a collection of free technical articles, sign up for a range of free newsletters, and receive exclusive discounts and offers on Packt books and eBooks.

# Contributors

## About the author

**Alessandro Biessek** was born in the beautiful city of Chapecó, in the state of Santa Catarina, southern Brazil, in 1993. He is currently working on mobile application development for Android and iOS in his hometown. He has more than 7 years of experience in development, from desktop development with Delphi to backend with PHP, Node.js, Golang, mobile development with Apache Flex, and Java/Kotlin. Most of his time is devoted to the development of Android apps. Always interested in new technologies, he has been following the Flutter framework for a long time, evidencing its growth and adoption in recent months.

*Firstly, thanks to the Flutter team for their incredible tool that is helping the developer community to help other people.*
*I am grateful to all of those with whom I have had the pleasure to work with during this project, all the reviewers, and the entire Packt team who helped me in this work.*
*I'd like to thank my friends, coworkers and family, especially my mother Antonina, my father Euclides, my sister Hellen and my brother Alan, for being supportive and were holding the fort while I worked hard on the book. Also, thanks to my graduation teachers, who encouraged me to face challenges like this book in a more natural and brave way.*
*Finally, I'd like to thank you, the reader. Your support of books such as this, through your purchase, makes it possible for everyone who wants to share their experiences to continue.*

# About the reviewer

**Ugurcan Yildirim** is an enthusiast of Android and Flutter mobile application development frameworks. He graduated as valedictorian with a BSc degree in Computer Science from Bilkent University, Ankara. Since 2015, he has been working as an Android Engineer at Accenture Industry X.0, Istanbul. With Flutter's promising uptrend that started in 2018, he began to concern himself with the peculiarities of Flutter and experiment with them. Since then, he has contributed to the open source community of Flutter by writing articles on Medium (@ugurcany) and giving presentations. His latest contribution is to review this book, which he believes should be consulted and referenced by Flutter developers of any level.

*I would like to thank Packt for giving me the opportunity to contribute to the ever-expanding Flutter universe by reviewing one of the first and most comprehensive Flutter books published. I would also like to thank my parents and my wife, Karsu, for their support and patience over the course of reviewing this book.*

# Packt is searching for authors like you

If you're interested in becoming an author for Packt, please visit authors.packtpub.com and apply today. We have worked with thousands of developers and tech professionals, just like you, to help them share their insight with the global tech community. You can make a general application, apply for a specific hot topic that we are recruiting an author for, or submit your own idea.

# Table of Contents

# Preface

*Flutter for Beginners* helps you to enter the Flutter framework world and build awesome mobile applications. I'll take you from an introduction to the Dart language to an in-depth exploration of all the Flutter blocks needed to make a high-level app. Together, we will build a fully featured app. With clear code examples, you will learn about how to start a small Flutter project, add some widgets, apply styles and themes, connect with remote services such as Firebase, get user input, add some animations to improve user experience, and more. In addition, you will learn how to add advanced features, map integrations, work with platform-specific code with native programming languages, and create fantastic UIs with personalized animations. In short, this book will prepare you for the future of mobile development with this amazing framework.

## Who this book is for

This book is for developers looking to learn Google's revolutionary framework, Flutter from scratch. No knowledge of Flutter or Dart is required. However, basic programming language knowledge will be helpful.

## What this book covers

Chapter 1, *An Introduction to Dart*, introduces the basics of the Dart language.

Chapter 2, *Intermediate Dart Programming*, looks at object-oriented programming features and advanced concepts from Dart, libraries, packages and asynchronous programming.

Chapter 3, *An Introduction to Flutter*, introduces you to the world of Flutter.

Chapter 4, *Widgets: Building Layouts in Flutter*, looks at how to build layouts in Flutter.

Chapter 5, *Handling User Input and Gestures*, shows you how to handle user input with Flutter widgets.

Chapter 6, *Theming and Styling*, teaches you how to apply different styles to Flutter widgets.

Chapter 7, *Routing: Navigating between Screens*, explores how to add navigation to app screens.

Chapter 8, *Firebase Plugins*, covers how to use Firebase plugins in Flutter apps.

Chapter 9, *Developing Your Own Flutter Plugin*, explains how to create your own Flutter plugins.

Chapter 10, *Accessing Device Features from the Flutter App*, dives into how to interact with device features such as cameras and contact lists.

Chapter 11, *Platform Views and Map Integration*, shows you how to add map views to Flutter applications.

Chapter 12, *Testing, Debugging, and Deployment*, delves into Flutter tools for improving productivity.

Chapter 13, *Improving User Experience*, explores how to improve user experience using features such as background Dart execution and internationalization.

Chapter 14, *Widget Graphic Manipulations*, gets into how to create unique visuals with graphic manipulations.

Chapter 15, *Animations*, gives you an insight into how to add animations to Flutter widgets.

# To get the most out of this book

You will be introduced to the requirements as we move through the chapters. To get started, you need to have access to a browser so you can access the DartPad website and play with Dart code.

To professionally develop and publish iOS apps, you need a developer license (paid annually), a Mac, and at least one device to test the applications. All this is not strictly necessary for the purpose of learning Flutter, but it might be useful to you.

The entire installation process and the requirements of the Flutter environment are available on the official website (`https://flutter.dev/docs/get-started/install`), but do not worry: you can start with the bare minimum and install any extras only when necessary.

# Download the example code files

You can download the example code files for this book from your account at `www.packt.com`. If you purchased this book elsewhere, you can visit `www.packtpub.com/support` and register to have the files emailed directly to you.

You can download the code files by following these steps:

1. Log in or register at `www.packt.com`.
2. Select the **Support** tab.
3. Click on **Code Downloads**.
4. Enter the name of the book in the **Search** box and follow the onscreen instructions.

Once the file is downloaded, please make sure that you unzip or extract the folder using the latest version of:

- WinRAR/7-Zip for Windows
- Zipeg/iZip/UnRarX for Mac
- 7-Zip/PeaZip for Linux

The code bundle for the book is also hosted on GitHub at `https://github.com/PacktPublishing/Flutter-for-Beginners`. In case there's an update to the code, it will be updated on the existing GitHub repository.

We also have other code bundles from our rich catalog of books and videos available at `https://github.com/PacktPublishing/`. Check them out!

# Download the color images

We also provide a PDF file that has color images of the screenshots/diagrams used in this book. You can download it here: `https://static.packt-cdn.com/downloads/9781788996082_ColorImages.pdf`.

# Conventions used

There are a number of text conventions used throughout this book.

`CodeInText`: Indicates code words in text, database table names, folder names, filenames, file extensions, pathnames, dummy URLs, user input, and Twitter handles. Here is an example: "It evaluates and returns the value of `expression2`: `expression1 ?? expression2`."

A block of code is set as follows:

```
main() {
  var yeahDartIsGreat = "Obviously!";
  var dartIsGreat = yeahDartIsGreat ?? "I don't know";
  print(dartIsGreat); // prints Obviously!
}
```

When we wish to draw your attention to a particular part of a code block, the relevant lines or items are set in bold:

```
main() {
  var someInt = 1;
  print(reflect(someInt).type.reflectedType.toString()); // prints: int
}
```

Any command-line input or output is written as follows:

```
dart code.dart
```

**Bold**: Indicates a new term, an important word, or words that you see onscreen. For example, words in menus or dialog boxes appear in the text like this. Here is an example: "Also, the floating action button at the bottom end should redirect you to the **Request a favor** screen."

 Warnings or important notes appear like this.

 Tips and tricks appear like this.

# Get in touch

Feedback from our readers is always welcome.

**General feedback**: If you have questions about any aspect of this book, mention the book title in the subject of your message and email us at customercare@packtpub.com.

**Errata**: Although we have taken every care to ensure the accuracy of our content, mistakes do happen. If you have found a mistake in this book, we would be grateful if you would report this to us. Please visit www.packtpub.com/support/errata, selecting your book, clicking on the Errata Submission Form link, and entering the details.

**Piracy**: If you come across any illegal copies of our works in any form on the Internet, we would be grateful if you would provide us with the location address or website name. Please contact us at copyright@packt.com with a link to the material.

**If you are interested in becoming an author**: If there is a topic that you have expertise in and you are interested in either writing or contributing to a book, please visit authors.packtpub.com.

# Reviews

Please leave a review. Once you have read and used this book, why not leave a review on the site that you purchased it from? Potential readers can then see and use your unbiased opinion to make purchase decisions, we at Packt can understand what you think about our products, and our authors can see your feedback on their book. Thank you!

For more information about Packt, please visit packt.com.

# Section 1: Introduction to Dart

In this section, you will gain an understanding of the core of the Flutter framework, explore the basics of the Dart language, learn how to set up your own environment, and finally, learn how to get started with it.

The following chapters are included in this section:

- Chapter 1, *An Introduction to Dart*
- Chapter 2, *Intermediate Dart Programming*
- Chapter 3, *An Introduction to Flutter*

# An Introduction to Dart 1

The Dart language is present at the core of the Flutter framework. A modern framework such as Flutter requires a high-level modern language to be capable of providing the best experience to the developer and making it possible to create awesome mobile applications. Understanding Dart is fundamental to working with Flutter; developers need to know the origins of the Dart language, how the community is working on it, its strengths, and why it is the chosen programming language to develop with Flutter. In this chapter, you will review the basics of the Dart language and be provided with some links to resources that can help you on your Flutter journey. You will review Dart built-in types and operators and how Dart works with **object-oriented programming (OOP)**. By understanding what the Dart language provides, you will be able to comfortably experiment with the Dart environment by yourself and expand your knowledge.

We will be covering the following topics in this chapter:

- Getting to know the principles and tools of the Dart language
- Understanding why Flutter uses Dart
- Learning the basics of the Dart language structure
- Introducing OOP with Dart

## Getting started with Dart

The Dart language, developed by Google, is a programming language that can be used to develop web, desktop, server-side, and mobile applications. Dart is the programming language used to code Flutter apps, enabling it to provide the best experience to the developer for the creation of high-level mobile applications. So, let's explore what Dart provides and how it works so we can later apply what we learn in Flutter.

Dart aims to aggregate the benefits of most of the high-level languages with mature language features, including the following:

- **Productive tooling**: This includes tools to analyze code, integrated development environment (**IDE**) plugins, and big package ecosystems.
- **Garbage collection**: This manages or deals with memory deallocation (mainly memory occupied by objects that are no longer in use).
- **Type annotations** (optional): This is for those who want security and consistency to control all of the data in an application.
- **Statically typed**: Although type annotations are optional, Dart is type-safe and uses type inference to analyze types in runtime. This feature is important for finding bugs during compile time.
- **Portability**: This is not only for the web (transpiled to JavaScript), but it can be natively compiled to ARM and x86 code.

# The evolution of Dart

Unveiled in 2011, Dart has been evolving ever since. Dart saw its stable release in 2013 with major changes included in the release of Dart 2.0 toward the end of 2018:

- **It was focused on web development in its conception, with the main aim of replacing JavaScript**: However, now Dart is focused on mobile development areas as well as on Flutter.
- **It tried solving JavaScript's problems**: JavaScript doesn't provide the robustness that many consolidated languages do, so Dart wanted to bring a mature successor to JavaScript.
- **It offers the best performance and better tools for large-scale projects**: Dart has modern and stable tooling provided by IDE plugins. It's been designed to get the best possible performance while keeping the feel of a dynamic language.
- **It is molded to be robust and flexible**: By keeping the type annotations optional and adding OOP features, Dart balances the two worlds of flexibility and robustness.

Dart is a great modern cross-platform, general-purpose language that continually improves its features, making it more mature and flexible. That's why the Flutter framework team chose the Dart language to work with.

# How Dart works

To understand where the language's flexibility came from, we need to know how we can run Dart code. This is done in two ways:

- Dart **Virtual Machines (VMs)**
- JavaScript compilations

Have a look at the following diagram:

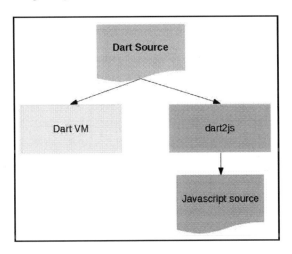

# Dart VM and JavaScript compilation

Dart code can be run in a *Dart-capable environment*. A Dart-capable environment provides essential features to an app, such as the following:

- Runtime systems
- Dart core libraries
- Garbage collectors

The execution of Dart code operates in two modes—**Just-In-Time (JIT)** compilation or **Ahead-Of-Time (AOT)** compilation:

- A JIT compilation is where the source code is loaded and compiled to native machine code by the Dart VM on the fly. It is used to run code in the command-line interface or when you are developing a mobile app in order to use features such as debugging and hot reloading.

- An AOT compilation is where the Dart VM and your code are precompiled and the VM works more like a Dart runtime system, providing a garbage collector and various native methods from the Dart software development kit (**SDK**) to the application.

 Dart contributes to Flutter's most famous feature, hot reload, which is based on the Dart JIT compiler, allowing fast interactions with live code swaps. See the *Understanding why Flutter uses Dart* section for details.

# Hands-on Dart

The way Flutter is designed is heavily influenced by the Dart language. So, knowing this language is crucial for success in the framework. Let's start by writing some code to understand the basics of the syntax and the available tools for Dart development.

# DartPad

The easiest way to start coding is to use the DartPad tool (`https://dartpad.dartlang.org/`). It is a great online tool to learn and experiment with Dart's language features. It supports Dart's core libraries, except for VM libraries such as `dart:io`.

This is what the tool looks like:

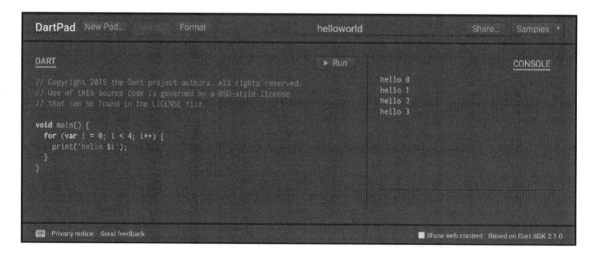

# Dart development tools

DartPad is a perfect way to start experimenting with the language without any extra effort. Since you will soon want to learn advanced things such as writing on files or using custom libraries, you'll need to have a development environment configured for that.

 Flutter is based on Dart and you can develop Dart code by having a Flutter development environment. To find out how to configure a Flutter development environment, just refer to the official website for the installation tutorial (`https://dart.dev/tools/sdk#install`).

The most common IDEs used for Dart and Flutter development are Visual Studio Code or VS Code (for the web and Flutter) and Android Studio or any JetBrains IDE such as WebStorm (which is web-focused). All of the Dart functionalities of these IDEs are based on official tools, so it doesn't matter what you choose—the provided tools will be mostly the same. The Dart SDK provides specialized tools for each development ecosystem, such as web and server-side programming.

The standalone Dart SDK ships with the following tools:

- `dart` (`https://dart.dev/tools/dart-vm`): This is the standalone Dart VM; this executes Dart code. To execute a Dart script, run the following command:

    **dart code.dart**

- `dart2js` (`https://dart.dev/tools/dart2js`): This is the original Dart-to-JavaScript compiler.
- `dartanalyzer` (`https://github.com/dart-lang/sdk/tree/master/pkg/analyzer_cli#dartanalyzer`): This statically analyzes code (as a typical linter), helping to catch errors early.

 Lint, or a linter, is a tool that analyzes source code to flag errors, bugs, stylistic errors, and suspicious constructs.

- `dartdoc` (`https://github.com/dart-lang/dartdoc#dartdoc`): This generates the API reference documentation.
- `pub` (`https://dart.dev/tools/pub/cmd`): This is a package manager. It is a tool that can be used for the management of libraries and packages.
- `dartfmt` (`https://github.com/dart-lang/dart_style#readme`): This applies style guidelines to Dart code.

For web development, Dart adds some tools (with additional installations steps at `https://dart.dev/tools`):

- `webdev` (`https://dart.dev/tools/webdev`) and `build_runner` (`https://dart.dev/tools/webdev`): Both of these tools are used for building and serving web apps, with `build_runner` being used in testing or when more configuration is required than `webdev` provides.

- `dartdevc` (`https://dart.dev/tools/dartdevc`): This is powered for `dev` Dart-to-JavaScript compiler-like integration with Chrome tools.

 `dart2js` is also a web-focused tool, although it ships with the standard SDK. For server-side development, the standard SDK tools are the only ones we need.

All of the IDE plugins use these tools behind the scenes, so you can take advantage of the full toolset for Dart development.

## Hello world

The following code is a basic Dart script, so let's take a look:

```
main() { // the entrypoint of an Dart app
    var a = 'world'; // declaring and initializing variable
    print('hello $a'); // call function to print to display output
}
```

This code contains some basic language features that need highlighting:

- Every Dart app must have an entry point top-level function (you can refer to Chapter 2, *Intermediate Dart Programming*, for more information on top-level functions), that is, the `main()` function.

 If you choose to run this code locally on your preconfigured machine with Dart SDK, save the contents to a Dart file, and then run it with a Dart tool in a Terminal, for example, `dart hello_world.dart`. This will execute the `main` function of the Dart script.

- As we have seen before, although Dart is type-safe, type annotations are optional. Here, we declare a variable with no type and assign a `String` literal to it.

- A `String` literal can be surrounded with single or double quotes, for example, `'hello world'` or `"hello world"`.
- To display output on the console, you can use the `print()` function (which is another top-level function).
- With the string interpolation technique, the `$a` statement inside a `String` literal resolves the value of the `a` variable. Dart calls the object's `toString()` method.

 We'll explore more about string interpolation later in this chapter, in the *Dart types and variables* section, when we talk about the string type.

- We can use the `//comment` syntax to write single-line comments. Dart also has multiline comments with the `/* comment */` syntax, as follows:

```
// this is a single line comment

/*
    This is a long multiline comment
*/
```

Note the return type of the `main` function; as it was omitted in the example, it assumes the special `dynamic` type, which we will explore later.

# Understanding why Flutter uses Dart

The Flutter framework aims to be a game-changer in mobile app development, providing all of the tools needed for the developer to make awesome applications with no drawbacks in performance and scalability. Flutter has, in its core structure, multiple concepts focused on app performance and the user interface. To deliver the best of the development world with high performance that compares to the of official native SDKs, Flutter uses the support of Dart to provide tools that contribute to developer productivity in the development phase and to build applications optimized for publication.

As we have seen before in the *Getting started with Dart* section, Dart is mature enough and robust with many tools that contribute to Flutter's success. Let's understand why Dart was the perfect choice for the Flutter framework.

# Adding productivity

Dart is not only a language, not in concept at least. The Dart SDK comes with a set of tools (seen in the previous *Dart development tools* section) that Flutter benefits from to help with common tasks during the development phase, such as the following:

- The Dart JIT and AOT compilers
- Profiling, debugging, and logging with the Dart DevTools and Observatory (more in `Chapter 12`, *Testing, Debugging, and Deployment*).
- Static code analysis with its built-in analyzer: `https://dart.dev/guides/ language/analysis-options`

# Compiling Flutter apps and hot reload

When you're writing or debugging code, you will be using the Dart VM with JIT. This helps to utilize features such as profiling tools, hot reloading (you can refer to `Chapter 3`, *An Introduction to Flutter*), and more.

When building your app for release, the code will be compiled in AOT and your app will ship with a tiny version of the Dart VM (which is more like a runtime library) with Dart SDK capabilities such as core libraries and garbage collectors.

This difference, at first, does not seems to be important from the developer's point of view, as we want to simply write and run the app, right? However, when it comes to productivity, this becomes one of the most fundamental Dart strengths used by Flutter.

Flutter's **hot reload** is one of its most famous features and shows the promised productivity in action. It relies on JIT compilation to make live Dart code swaps while running the app, so we can change our application code and see the result almost in real time. With IDE plugins, this becomes even faster as, after saving a change, the plugin dispatches the reload and the result is seen quickly.

 In `Chapter 3`, *An Introduction to Flutter*, we will check out hot reload and other features in more detail.

No image can describe the potential of this incredible feature. So, after checking out `Chapter 3`, *An Introduction to Flutter*, I suggest you run the Flutter starter project to have first contact with this incredible feature.

Another very cool Dart tool is the Dart analyzer:

```
//The type of temperature is inferred to be int.
var temperature = 25;

// Static code analysis catches errors early.
temperature = 'Freezing';
                        A String can't be assigned to an 'int'

// Customizable code style checks
class weather{}
        [dart] Name types using UpperCamelCase
```

This tool helps to figure out potential problems with types and the recommended syntax before running the code.

 DevTools also adds an important value to the productivity offered by the Flutter framework; find out more information in Chapter 12, *Testing, Debugging, and Deployment.*

# Easy learning

Dart is a new language for many developers, and learning a new framework and a new language at the same time can be challenging. However, Dart makes this task simple by not reinventing concepts, just fine-tuning them and trying to make them as effective as possible for designated tasks.

Dart is inspired by many modern and mature languages such as Java, JavaScript, C#, Swift, and Kotlin, as you can see here:

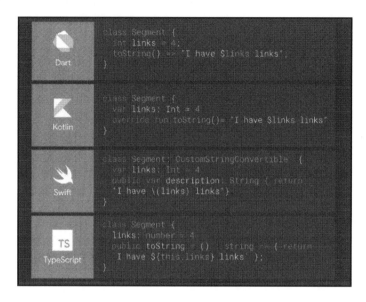

With this in mind, reading Dart code, even without knowing the language deeply, is possible. Also, take a look at the official documentation start page:

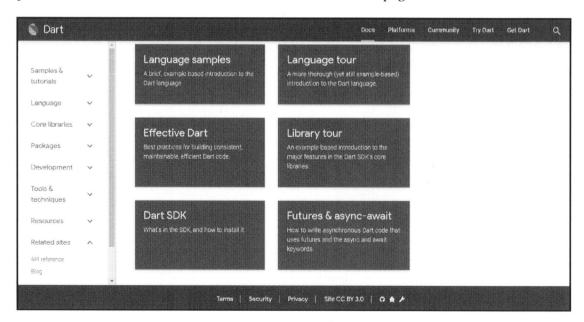

The provided documentation and guides are very clean materials and informative, also, the awesome community helps the developer to be able to learn with no headache.

 Check out the official Dart guides on learning: `https://dart.dev/guides`.

# Maturity

Despite being a relatively new language, Dart is not poor or lacking in resources. On the contrary, in version 2, it already has various modern language resources that help the developer to write effective high-level code.

One perfect feature to exemplify this is the **async-await** feature:

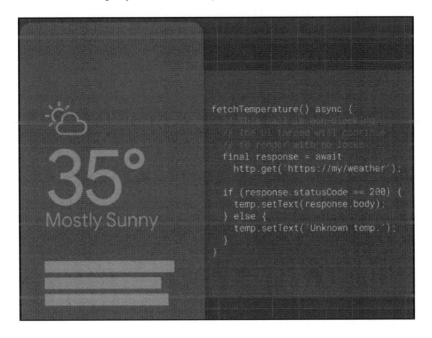

This enables the developer to write non-blocking calls with a very simple syntax, allowing the application to continue to render with no drawbacks.

As Dart focuses on the developer, another important thing for mobile and web developers is building user interfaces. With this in mind, the Dart syntax is easy to understand when you think in UI terms. Let's see an example:

```
TabBar build(BuildContext context) {
    return TabBar(tabs: [
        Tab(text: 'Shoes'),
        Tab(text: 'Pants'),
        Tab(text: 'Shirts'),
        if (promoActive) Tab(text: 'Outlet'),
    ]);
}
```

Shopping

Shoes    Pants    Shirts    Outlet

 These screenshots are taken from the official Dart website: `dart.dev`.

The **collection if** operator that can be seen in the preceding screenshot is one great example of a new feature that is easy to understand even if you are new to Dart.

Dart is evolving alongside Flutter, and these are only some of the important strengths the language provides to the framework. As long as you realize Dart is easy to learn and how much it contributes to Flutter power, the challenge of learning a new language together with a new framework becomes easier and even enjoyable.

In this book, we are not going to dive too deep into the details of the Dart syntax. You can check the source code of this chapter on GitHub for syntax examples and use this as a study guide or a learning path for the language. Later, you can explore specific syntax or features while you advance in your Flutter framework journey.

# Introducing the structure of the Dart language

If you already know some programming languages inspired by the old C language or have some experience of JavaScript, much of the Dart syntax will be easy for you to understand. Dart provides the most typical operators for manipulating variables. Its built-in types are the most common ones found in high-level programming languages, with a few particularities. Also, control flows and functions are very similar to typical ones. Let's review some of the structure of the Dart programming language before diving into Flutter.

If you already know Dart, you can use this section as a review of the Dart syntax; otherwise, you can check out this introduction and refer to the Dart language tour for a quick and easy learning guide on Dart: `https://dart.dev/guides/language/language-tour`.

## Dart operators

In Dart, operators are nothing more than methods defined in classes with a special syntax. So, when you use operators such as `x == y`, it is as though you are invoking the `x.==(y)` method to compare equality.

 As you might have noted, we are invoking a method on `x`, which means `x` is an instance of a class that has methods. In Dart, everything is an `Object` instance; any type you define is also an `Object` instance. There's more on that in the *Introduction to OOP in Dart* section.

This concept means that operators can be overridden so that you can write your own logic for them. Again, if you have some experience in Java, C#, JavaScript, or similar languages, you can skip most of the operators, as they are very similar in several languages.

 We are not going to go into every specific Dart syntax detail in this book. You can refer to the source code on GitHub for many examples on the Dart syntax.

Dart has the following operators:

- Arithmetic
- Increment and decrement
- Equality and relational
- Type checking and casting
- Logical operators
- Bits manipulation
- Null-safe and null-aware (modern programming languages provide this operator to facilitate null value handling)

Let's look at each one in more detail.

## Arithmetic operators

Dart comes with many typical operators that work like many languages; this includes the following:

- +: This is for the addition of numbers.
- −: This is for subtraction.
- *: This is for multiplication.
- /: This is for division.
- ~/: This is for integer division. In Dart, any simple division with / results in a `double` value. To get only the integer part, you would need to make some kind of transformation (that is, type cast) in other programming languages; however, here, the integer division operator does this task.
- %: This is for modulo operations (the remainder of integer division).
- -expression: This is for negation (which reverses the sign of `expression`).

Some operators have different behavior depending on the left operand type; for example, the + operator can be used to sum variables of the `num` type, but also to concatenate strings. This is because they were implemented differently in the corresponding classes as pointed out before.

 Dart also provides shortcut operators to combine an assignment to a variable after another operation. The arithmetic or assignment shortcut operators are +=, −=, *=, /=, and ~/=.

# Increment and decrement operators

The increment and decrement operators are also common operators and are implemented in number type, as follows:

- ++var or var++ to increment *1* into var
- --var or var-- to decrement *1* from var

The Dart increment and decrement operators don't have anything different to typical languages. A good application of increment and decrement operators is for count operations on loops.

# Equality and relational operators

The equality Dart operators are as follows:

- ==: For checking whether operands are equal
- !=: For checking whether operands are different

For relational tests, the operators are as follows:

- >: For checking whether the left operand is *greater than* the right one
- <: For checking whether the left operand is *less than* the right one
- >=: For checking whether the left operand is *greater than or equal to* the right one
- <=: For checking whether the left operand is *less than or equal to* the right one

 In Dart, unlike Java and many other languages, the == operator does not compare memory references but rather the content of the variable.

# Type checking and casting

Dart has optional typing, as you already know, so type checking operators may be handy for checking types at runtime:

- is: For checking whether the operand has the tested type
- is!: For checking whether the operand does not have the tested type

The output of this code will be different depending on the context of the execution. In DartPad, the output is true for the check of the double type; this is due to the way JavaScript treats numbers, and, as you already know, Dart for the web is precompiled to JavaScript for execution on web browsers.

There's also the `as` keyword, which is used for typecasting from a supertype to a subtype, such as converting `num` into `int`.

 The `as` keyword is also used to specify a prefix for the libraries, using imports (you can read more about this in `Chapter 2`, *Intermediate Dart Programming*).

## Logical operators

Logical operators in Dart are the common operators applied to bool operands; they can be variables, expressions, or conditions. Additionally, they can be combined with complex expressions by combining the results of the expressions. The provided logical operators are as follows:

- `!expression`: To negate the result of an expression, that is, `true` to `false` and `false` to `true`
- `||`: To apply logical OR between two expressions
- `&&`: To apply logical AND between two expressions

## Bits manipulation

Dart provides bitwise and shift operators to manipulate individual bits of numbers, usually with the `num` type. They are as follows:

- `&`: To apply logical AND to operands, checking whether the corresponding bits are both 1
- `|`: To apply logical OR to operands, checking whether at least one of the corresponding bits is 1
- `^`: To apply logical XOR to operands, checking whether only one but not both of the corresponding bits is 1
- `~operand`: To invert the bits of the operand, such as $1_s$ becoming $0_s$ and $0_s$ becoming $1_s$

- <<: To shift the left operand in $x$ bits to the left (this shifts $0_s$ from the right)
- >>: To shift the left operand in $x$ bits to the right (discarding the bits from the left)

Like arithmetic operators, the bitwise ones also have shortcut assignment operators, and they work in the exact same way as the previously presented ones; they are <<=, >>=, &=, ^=, and |=.

## Null-safe and null-aware operators

Following the trend on modern OOP languages, Dart provides a null-safe syntax that evaluates and returns an expression according to its null/non-null value.

The evaluation works in the following way: if `expression1` is non-null, it returns its value; otherwise, it evaluates and returns the value of `expression2: expression1 ?? expression2`.

In addition to the common assignment operator, =, and the ones listed in the corresponding operators, Dart also provides a combination between the assignment and the null-aware expression; that is, the `??=` operator, which assigns a value to a variable only if its current value is `null`.

Dart also provides a null-aware access operator, `?.`, which prevents accessing `null` object members.

## Dart types and variables

You probably already know how to declare a simple variable, that is, by using the `var` keyword followed by the name. One thing to note is that when we did not specify the variable's initial value, it assumed `null` no matter its type.

## final and const

A variable will never intend to change its value after it is assigned, and you can use the `final` and `const` ways for declaring this:

```
final value = 1;
```

The `value` variable cannot be changed once it's initialized:

```
const value = 1;
```

Just like the `final` keyword, the `value` variable cannot be changed once it's initialized, and its initialization must occur together with a declaration.

In addition to this, the `const` keyword defines a compile-time constant. As a compile-time constant, the `const` values are known at compile time. They also can be used to make object instances or `Lists` immutable, as follows:

```
const list = const [1, 2, 3]
// and
const point = const Point(1,2)
```

This will set the value of both variables during compile time, turning them into completely immutable variables.

# Built-in types

Dart is a type-safe programming language, so types are mandatory for variables. Although types are mandatory, type annotations are optional, which means that you don't need to specify the type of a variable when declaring it. Dart performs type inference, and we will examine more of this in the *Type inference – bringing dynamism to the show* section.

Here are the built-in data types in Dart:

- Numbers (such as `num`, `int`, and `double`)
- Booleans (such as `bool`)
- Collections (such as lists, arrays, and maps)
- Strings and runes (for expressing Unicode characters in a string)

## Numbers

Dart represents numbers in two ways:

- **Int**: 64-bit signed non-fractional integer values such as $-2^{63}$ to $2^{63}$-1.
- **Double**: Dart represents fractional numeric values with a 64-bit double-precision floating-point number.

Both of them extend the `num` type. Additionally, we have many handy functions in the `dart:math` library to help with calculations.

In JavaScript, numbers are compiled to JavaScript Numbers, and allow the values $-2^{53}$ to $2^{53}-1$.

Additionally, note that `num`, `double`, and `int` types cannot be extended or implemented.

## BigInt

Dart also has the `BigInt` type for representing arbitrary precision integers, which means that the size limit is the running computer's RAM. This type can be very useful depending on the context; however, it does not have the same performance as `num` types and you should consider this when deciding to use it.

JavaScript has the concept of safe integers, which Darts follows when transpiling to it. However, as JavaScript uses double-precision to represent even integers, we do not have an overflow when doing (`maxInt * 2`).

Now, you might consider putting `BigInt` everywhere you would use integers to be free of overflows, but remember, `BigInt` does not have the same performance as `int` types, making it unsuitable for all contexts.

Additionally, if you want to know how Dart VM handles numbers internally, take a look at the *Further reading* section at the end of this chapter.

## Booleans

Dart provides the two well-known literal values for the `bool` type: `true` and `false`.

Boolean types are simple truth values that can be useful for any logic. One thing you may have noticed, but that I want to reinforce, is about expressions.

We already know that operators, such as > or ==, for example, are nothing more than methods with a special syntax defined in classes, and, of course, they have a return value that can be evaluated in conditions. So, the return type of all these expressions is `bool` and, as you already know, Boolean expressions are important in any programming language.

## Collections

In Dart, lists are considered to be the same as arrays in other programming languages with some handy methods to manipulate elements.

Lists have the [index] operator to access elements at the given index and, additionally, the + operator can be used to concatenate two lists by returning a new list with the left operand followed by the right one.

Another important thing about Dart lists is the *length* constraint. This is in the way we define the preceding lists, making them grow as needed by using the add method, which will grow to append the element.

Another way to define the list is by setting its length on creation. Lists with a fixed size cannot be expanded, so it's the developer's responsibility to know where and when to use fixed size lists, as it can throw exceptions if you try to append or access invalid elements.

Dart **Maps** are dynamic collections for storing values on a key basis, where the retrieval and modification of a value is always performed by using its associated key. Both the key and value can have any type; if we do not specify the key-value types, they will be inferred by Dart as Map<dynamic, dynamic>, with its keys and values of the dynamic type. We'll explain more about dynamic types later.

## Strings

In Dart, strings are a sequence of characters (UTF-16 code) that are mainly used to represent text. Dart strings can be single or multiple lines. You can match single or double quotes (typically for single lines), and multiline strings by matching triple quotes.

We can use the + operator to concatenate strings. The string type implements useful operators other than the plus (+) one. It implements the multiplier (*) operator where the string gets repeated a specified number of times, and the [index] operator retrieves the character at the specified index position.

## String interpolation

Dart has a useful syntax to interpolate the value of Dart expressions within strings: ${}, which works as follows:

```
main() {
  String someString = "This is a String";
  print("The string value is: $someString ");
   // prints The string value is: This is a String

  print("The length of the string is: ${someString.length} ");
   // prints The length of the string is: 16
}
```

As you may have noticed, when we are inserting just a variable and not an expression value into the string, we can omit the braces and just add `$identifier` directly.

Dart also has the **runes** concept to represent UTF-32 bits. For more details, check out the Dart language tour: `https://dart.dev/guides/language/language-tour`.

## Literals

You can use the `[]` and `{}` syntaxes to initialize variables such as lists and maps, respectively. These are some examples of literals provided by the Dart language for creating objects of the provided built-in types:

| Type | Literal example |
|---|---|
| int | `10`, `1`, `-1`, `5`, and `0` |
| double | `10.1`, `1.2`, `3.123`, and `-1.2` |
| bool | `true` and `false` |
| String | `"Dart"`, `'Dash'`, and `"""multiline String"""` |
| List | `[1,2,3]` and `["one", "two", "three"]` |
| Map | `{"key1": "val1", "b": 2}` |

A literal is a notation to represent a fixed value in programming languages. You have likely already used some of these before.

# Type inference – bringing dynamism to the show

In the previous examples, we demonstrated two ways of declaring variables: by using the type of the variable, such as `int` and `String`, or by using the `var` keyword.

So, now you may be wondering how Dart knows what type of variable it is if you don't specify it in a declaration.

From the Dart documentation (https://dart.dev/guides/language/effective-dart/documentation), consider the following statement:

> *"The analyzer can infer types for fields, methods, local variables, and most generic type arguments. When the analyzer doesn't have enough information to infer a specific type, it uses the dynamic type."*

This means that, when you declare a variable, the Dart analyzer will infer the type based on the literal or the object constructor.

Here is an example:

```
import 'dart:mirrors';

main() {
  var someInt = 1;
  print(reflect(someInt).type.reflectedType.toString()); // prints: int
}
```

As you can see, in this example we have only the var keyword. We didn't specify any type, but as we used an int literal (1), the analyzer tool could infer the type successfully.

Local variables get the type inferred by the analyzer in the initialization. In the preceding example, trying to assign a string value to someInt would fail.

So, let's consider the following code:

```
main() {
  var a; // here we didn't initialized var so its
         // type is the special dynamic
  a = 1; // now a is a int
  a = "a"; // and now a String

  print(a is int); // prints false
  print(a is String); // prints true
  print(a is dynamic); // prints true
  print(a.runtimeType); // prints String
}
```

As you may have noticed, a is a String type and a dynamic type. dynamic is a special type and it can assume any type at runtime; therefore, any value can be cast to dynamic too.

Dart can infer types for fields, method returns, and generic type arguments; we'll explore each one in more detail in their respective sections in this book.

The Dart analyzer also works on collections and generics; for the map and list examples in this chapter, we used the literal initializer for both, so their types were inferred.

# Control flows and looping

We've reviewed how to use Dart variables and operators to create conditional expressions. To work with variables and operators, we typically need to implement some control flow to make our Dart code take the appropriate direction in our logic.

Dart provides some control flow syntax that is very similar to other programming languages; it is as follows:

- `if-else`
- `switch/case`
- Looping with `for`, `while`, and `do-while`
- `break` and `continue`
- `asserts`
- Exceptions with `try/catch` and `throw`

The Dart syntax for these control flows does not have any important particularity that needs to be reviewed in detail. Please refer to the official language tour on control flows for details: `https://dart.dev/guides/language/language-tour#control-flow-statements`.

# Functions

In Dart, `Function` is a type, like `String` or `num`. This means that they can also be assigned to fields or local variables or passed as parameters to other functions; consider the following example:

```dart
String sayHello() {
  return "Hello world!";
}

void main() {
  var sayHelloFunction = sayHello; // assigning the function
                                   // to the variable
  print(sayHelloFunction()); // prints Hello world!
}
```

In this example, the `sayHelloFunction` variable stores the `sayHello` function itself and does not invoke it. Later on, we can invoke it by adding `()` to the variable name just as though it was a function.

 Trying to invoke a non-function variable could result in a compiler error.

The function return type can be omitted as well, so the Dart analyzer infers the type from the `return` statement. If no `return` statement is provided, it assumes `return null`. If you want to tell it that it doesn't have a return, you should mark it as `void`:

```
sayHello() { // The return type stills String
  return "Hello world!";
}
```

Another way to write this function is by using the shorthand syntax, `() => expression;`, which is also called the `Arrow` function or the `Lambda` function:

```
sayHello() => "Hello world!";
```

You cannot write statements in place of `expression`, but you can use the already known `conditional` expressions (that is, `?:` or `??`).

 In this example, the `sayHello` function is a top-level function. In other words, it does not need a class to exist. Although Dart is an object-oriented language, it is not necessary to write classes to encapsulate functions.

# Function parameters

A function can have two types of parameters: **optional** and **required**. Additionally, as with most modern programming languages, these parameters can be named on call to make the code more readable.

The parameter type doesn't need to be specified; in this case, the parameter assumes the **dynamic** type:

- **Required parameters**: This simple function definition with parameters is achieved by just defining them in the same way as most other languages. In the following function, both name and additionalMessage are required parameters, so the caller *must* pass them when calling it:

  ```
  sayHello(String name, String additionalMessage) => "Hello $name.
  $additionalMessage";
  ```

- **Optional positional parameters**: Sometimes, not all parameters need to be mandatory for a function, so it can define optional parameters as well. The optional positional parameter definition is done by using the [ ] syntax. Optional positional parameters must go after all of the required parameters, as follows:

  ```
  sayHello(String name, [String additionalMessage]) => "Hello $name.
  $additionalMessage";
  ```

If you run the preceding code without passing a value for additionalMessage, you will see null at the end of the returned string. When the optional parameter is not specified, the default value is null unless you specify default values for them:

```
void main() {
  print(sayHello('my friend')); // Hello my friend. null
  print(sayHello('my friend', "How are you?"));
  // prints Hello my friend. How are you?
}
```

To define a default value for a parameter, you add it after the = sign right after the parameter definition:

```
sayHello(String name, [String additionalMessage = "Welcome to Dart
Functions!" ]) => "Hello $name. $additionalMessage";
```

Not specifying the parameter results in printing the default message, as follows:

```
void main() {
  var hello = sayHello('my friend');
  print(hello);
}
```

- **Optional named parameters**: The optional named parameter definition is done by using the { } syntax. They must also go after all of the required parameters:

```
sayHello(String name, {String additionalMessage}) => "Hello $name.
$additionalMessage";
```

The caller must specify the name of the optional named parameter, as follows:

```
void main() {
  print(sayHello('my friend'));
  // it stills optional, prints: Hello my friend. null

  print(sayHello('my friend', additionalMessage: "How are you?"));
  // prints: Hello my friend. How are you?
}
```

Named parameters are not exclusive to optional parameters; to make a named parameter a required parameter, you can mark it with @required:

```
sayHello(String name, {@required String additionalMessage}) =>
"Hello $name. $additionalMessage";
```

Again, the caller must specify the name of the required named parameter:

```
void main() {
  var hello = sayHello('my friend', additionalMessage:"How are
    you?");
  // not specifying the parameter name will result in a hint on
  // the editor, or by running dartanalyzer manually on console

  print(hello); // prints "Hello my friend. How arc you?"
}
```

- **Anonymous functions**: Dart functions are objects and they can be passed as parameters to other functions. We already saw this when using the forEach() function of the iterable.

An anonymous function is a function that doesn't have a name; it is also called *lambda* or *closure*. The forEach() function is a good example of this; we need to pass a function to it that will be executed with each of the list collection elements:

```
void main() {
  var list = [1, 2, 3, 4];
  list.forEach((number) => print('hello $number'));
}
```

Our anonymous function receives an item but does not specify a type; then, it just prints the value received by the parameter.

- **Lexical scope**: The Dart scope is determined by the layout of the code using curly braces like many programming languages; the inner functions can access variables all the way up to the global level:

```
globalFunction() {
  print("global/top-level function");
}

simpleFunction() {
  print("simple function");
  globalFunction() {
    print("Not really global");
  }

  globalFunction();
}

main() {
  simpleFunction();

  globalFunction();
}
```

If you examine the preceding code, `globalFunction` function from `simpleFunction` will be used instead of the global version, because it is defined locally on its scope.

In the `main` function, in contrast, the global version of `globalFunction` function is used, because, in this scope, the internal `globalFunction` function from `simpleFunction` is not defined.

# Data structures, collections, and generics

Dart provides multiple kinds of structures to manipulate a of values. Dart lists are widely used even in the most simple use cases. Generics are an concept when working with collections of data tied to a specific type, such as `List` or `Map`, for example. They ensure a collection will have homogeneous values by specifying the type of data it can hold.

# Generics

The < .. > syntax is used to specify the type supported by a collection. If you look at the previous examples of lists and maps, you will notice that we have not specified any type. This is because they are optional, and Dart can infer the type based on elements during the collection initialization.

 Check this chapter's source code on GitHub for examples on collections and generics. Remember, if the Dart analyzer tool cannot infer the type, it assumes the dynamic type.

## When and why to use generics

The use of generics can help a developer to maintain and keep collection behavior under control. When we use a collection without specifying the allowed element types, it is our responsibility to correctly insert the elements. This, in a wider context, can become expensive, as we need to implement validations to prevent wrong insertions and to document it for a team.

Consider the following code example; as we have named the variable avengerNames, we expect it to be a list of names and nothing else. Unfortunately, in the coded form, we can also insert a number into the list, causing disorganization or confusion:

```
main() {
  List avengerNames = ["Hulk", "Captain America"];
  avengerNames.add(1);
  print("Avenger names: $avengerNames");
  // prints Avenger names: [Hulk, Captain America, 1]
}
```

However, if we specify the string type for the list, then this code would not compile, avoiding this confusion:

```
main() {
  List<String> avengerNames = ["Hulk", "Captain America"];
  avengerNames.add(1);
  // Now, add() function expects an 'int' so this doesn't compile
  print("Avenger names: $avengerNames");
}
```

## Generics and Dart literals

If you check out this chapter's list and map examples, you will see we used the `[]` and `{}` literals to initialize them. With generics, we can specify a type during the initialization, adding a `<elementType>[]` prefix for lists and `<keyType, elementType>{}` for maps.

Take a look at the following example:

```dart
main() {
  var avengerNames = <String>["Hulk", "Captain America"];
  var avengerQuotes = <String, String>{
    "Captain America": "I can do this all day!",
    "Spider Man": "Am I an Avenger?",
    "Hulk": "Smaaaaaash!"
  };
}
```

Specifying the type of list, in this case, seems to be redundant as the Dart analyzer will infer the string type from the literals we have provided. However, in some cases, this is important, such as when we are initializing an empty collection, as in the following example:

```dart
var emptyStringArray = <String>[];
```

If we have not specified the type of the empty collection, it could have any data type on it as it would not infer the generic type to adopt.

To learn how Dart plays with the generics concept and the additional data structures provided by the language, you can refer to the official language tour for details: https://dart.dev/guides/language/language-tour#generics.

# Introduction to OOP in Dart

In Dart, everything is an object, including the built-in types. Upon defining a new class, even when you don't extend anything, it will be a *descendant of an object*. Dart implicitly does this for you.

Dart is called a **true object-oriented** language. Even functions are objects, which means that you can do the following:

- Assign a function as a value of a variable.
- Pass it as an argument to another function.
- Return it as a result of a function as you would do with any other type, such as `String` and `int`.

This is known as having **first-class functions** because they're treated the same way as other types.

Another important point to note is that Dart supports *single inheritance* on a class, similar to Java and most other languages, which means that a class can inherit directly from only a single class at a time.

 A class can implement multiple interfaces and extend multiple classes using mixins, which we will cover later in this chapter.

Here are the main OOP artifacts that are presented in the Dart language (we will delve deeper into each throughout this chapter):

- **Class**: This is a blueprint for creating an object.
- **Interface**: This is a contract definition with a set of methods available on an object. Although there is no explicit interface type in Dart, we can achieve the interface purpose with abstract classes.
- **Enumerated class**: This is a special kind of class that defines a set of common constant values.
- **Mixin**: This is a way of reusing a class's code in multiple class hierarchies.

# Dart OOP features

Every programming language can provide the OOP paradigm in its own way, with partial or full support, by applying some or all of the following principles:

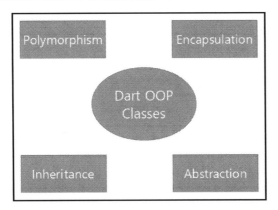

Dart applies many of the principles with many particularities. So, let's reinforce the available OOP techniques and structures to use this paradigm in the Dart language.

 The subjects indicated here may sound new to you. They are covered in greater depth in the next sections of this chapter. Feel free to revisit this section later if you find it helpful.

## Objects and classes

The starting point of OOP, objects, are instances of defined classes. In Dart, as has already been pointed out, everything is an object, that is, every value we can store in a variable is an instance of a class. Besides that, all objects also extend the Object class, directly or indirectly:

- Dart classes can have both instance members (methods and fields) and class members (static methods and fields).
- Dart classes do not support constructor overloading, but you can use the flexible function argument specifications from the language (optional, positional, and named) to provide different ways to instantiate a class. Also, you can have named constructors to define alternatives.

# Encapsulation

Dart does not contain access restrictions explicitly, like the famous keywords used in Java—protected, private, and public. In Dart, encapsulation occurs at the library level instead of at the class level (this will be discussed further in the following chapter). The following also applies:

- Dart creates implicit getters and setters for all fields in a class, so you can define how data is accessible to consumers and the way it changes.
- In Dart, if an identifier (class, class member, top-level function, or variable) starts with an underscore( _ ), it's private to its library.

 We will check out the definition of *libraries* in Chapter 2, *Intermediate Dart Programming*. Here, we will also cover in more detail how privacy works in Dart.

# Inheritance and composition

Inheritance allows us to extend an object to specialized versions of some abstract type. In Dart, by simply declaring a class, we are already extending the Object type implicitly. The following also applies:

- Dart permits single direct inheritance.
- Dart has special support for mixins, which can be used to extend class functionalities without direct inheritance, simulating multiple inheritances, and reusing code.
- Dart does not contain a final class directive like other languages, that is, a class can always be extended (have children).

# Abstraction

Following inheritance, **abstraction** is the process whereby we define a type and its essential characteristics, moving to specialized types from parent ones. The following also applies:

- Dart contains abstract classes that allow a definition of *what* something does/provides, without caring about *how* this is implemented.
- Dart has the powerful **implicit interface** concept, which also makes every class an interface, allowing it to be implemented by others without extending it.

# Polymorphism

**Polymorphism** is achieved by inheritance and can be regarded as the ability of an object to behave like another; for example, the `int` type is also a `num` type. The following also applies:

- Dart allows overriding parent methods to change their original behavior.
- Dart does not allow **overloading** in the way you may be familiar with. You cannot define the same method twice with different arguments. You can simulate overloading by using flexible argument definitions (that is, optional and positional, as seen in the previous *Functions* section) or not use it at all.

# Summary

We have finished our introduction to the Dart language, and I hope you liked what you have read so far. In this first chapter, we presented the available tools to start your Dart language studies, discovered what a basic Dart program looks like, and learned about the basic Dart code structure.

We demonstrated how the Dart SDK works and the tools it provides that help with Flutter app development and make the Flutter framework succeed in its objectives.

We reviewed some important concepts of the Dart language with useful links to the official language guides to support the developer. Additionally, we reviewed functions and parameter specifications, such as named/positional and optional/required, and introduced Dart OOP.

In the next chapter, we will advance toward the OOP concept of programming in the Dart language and its particularities. We will also examine several important advanced Dart features for development, especially when talking about Flutter development, such as `async` programming with `Futures`, unit testing and packages & libraries concept, which is perhaps the most important in terms of serving as the basis for Flutter app development. So, check out the next chapter for more advanced Dart topics.

# Further reading

In addition to this chapter's content, you can check the following materials for further reference:

- For more information about integer number representations in Dart, you can read the following article, which may help you to understand how the language treats numbers internally: `https://www.dartlang.org/articles/dart-vm/numeric-computation`.
- You can read more about generics syntax here: `https://github.com/dart lang/sdk/blob/master/pkg/dev_compiler/doc/GENERIC_METHODS.md`.

# Intermediate Dart Programming $2$

In this chapter, you will learn the core concept of objects in Dart, for example, how to create object-oriented code in Dart by using its concepts, such as interfaces, implicit interfaces, and abstract classes, as well as mixins, to add a behavior to a class.

If you are an experienced programmer or already familiar with Java or similar languages, you can skip some parts of this chapter, as it has many similarities with the typical OOP concepts, such as inheritance and encapsulation. Some ideas, in particular, are important to verify, even if you are already familiar with the majority of OOP features, such as implicit interfaces and mixins, as they may introduce you to new concepts.

You will also learn how to use third-party libraries to accelerate a project's development, gain an understanding of the advanced features of the Dart language to start developing multithreading apps by using callbacks and futures, and learn how to unit test your Dart code.

This chapter covers the following topics:

- Dart class definition syntax
- Abstract classes, interfaces, and mixins
- Understanding Dart libraries and packages
- Adding dependencies with `pubspec.yaml`
- Introducing async programming with Futures and Isolates
- Introducing unit tests

# Dart classes and constructors

Dart classes are declared by using the `class` keyword, followed by the class name, ancestor classes, and implemented interfaces. Then, the class body is enclosed by a pair of curly braces, where you can add class members, that include the following:

- **Fields**: These are variables used to define the data an object can hold.
- **Accessors**: Getters and setters, as the name suggests, are used to access the fields of a class, where `get` is used to retrieve a value, and the `set` accessor is used to modify the corresponding value.
- **Constructor**: This is the creator method of a class where the object instance fields are initialized.
- **Methods**: The behavior of an object is defined by the actions it can take. These are the object functions.

Refer to the following small class definition example:

```
class Person {
    String firstName;
    String lastName;

    String getFullName() => "$firstName $lastName";
}

main() {
  Person somePerson = new Person();
  somePerson.firstName = "Clark";
  somePerson.lastName = "Kent";
  print(somePerson.getFullName()); // prints Clark Kent
}
```

Now, let's take a look at the `Person` class declared in the preceding code and make some observations:

- To instantiate a class, we use the `new` (*optional*) keyword followed by the constructor invocation. As we advance in this book, you will notice that this keyword is used less.
- It does not have an ancestor class explicitly declared, but it does have one, the object type, as already mentioned, and this inheritance happens implicitly in Dart.
- It has two fields, `firstName` and `lastName`, and a method, `getFullName()`, which concatenates both by using string interpolation and then returns.

- It does not have any `get` or `set` accessor declared, so how did we access `firstName` and `lastName` to mutate it? A default `get`/`set` accessor is defined for every field in a class.
- The *dot* `class.member` notation is used to access a class member, whatever it is—a method or a field (get/set).
- We have not defined a constructor for the class, but, as you may be thinking, there's a default empty constructor (no arguments) already provided for us.

# The enum type

The `enum` type is a common type used by most languages to represent a set of finite constant values. In Dart, it is no different. By using the `enum` keyword, followed by the constant values, you can define an `enum` type:

```
enum PersonType {
    student, employee
}
```

Note that you define just the value names. `enum` types are special types with a set of finite values that have an `index` property representing its value. Now, let's see how it works.

First, we add a field to our previously defined `Person` class to store its type:

```
class Person {
  ...
  PersonType type;
  ...
}
```

Then, we can use it just like any other field:

```
main() {
  print(PersonType.values); // prints [PersonType.student,
                            //PersonType.employee]
  Person somePerson = new Person();
  somePerson.type = PersonType.employee;
  print(somePerson.type); // prints PersonType.employee
  print(somePerson.type.index); // prints 1
}
```

You can see that the `index` property is zero, based on the declaration position of the value.

Also, you can see that we are calling the `values` getter on the `PersonType` enum directly. This is a static member of the `enum` type that simply returns a list with all of its values. We will examine this further soon.

# The cascade notation

We've seen that Dart provides the dot notation to access a class member. In addition to that, we can also use the double dot/cascade notation, **syntactic sugar**, which allows us to chain a sequence of operations on the same object:

```
main() {
  Person somePerson = new Person()
    ..firstName = "Clark"
    ..lastName = "Kent";

  print(somePerson.getFullName()); // prints Clark Kent
}
```

The result is the same as when employing the typical approach. It's just a good way to write succinct and legible code.

 The cascade syntax works by getting the first expression return value (`new Person()`, in this case) and always operates in this value, ignoring the next expression return values.

Next, we are going to delve deeper as regards each of the class components mentioned previously to understand how they can be used to extend a class to all of our needs.

# Constructors

To instantiate a class, we use the `new` keyword, followed by the corresponding constructor with parameters, if required. Now, let's change the `Person` class and define a constructor with parameters on it:

```
class Person {
    String firstName;
    String lastName;

    Person(String firstName, String lastName) {
      this.firstName = firstName;
      this.lastName = lastName;
    }
```

```
      String getFullName() => "$firstName $lastName";
}

main() {
  // Person somePerson = new Person(); this would not compile as we
  //defined mandatory parameters on constructor
  Person somePerson = new Person("Clark", "Kent");
  print(somePerson.getFullName());
}
```

The constructor is also a function in Dart and its role is to initialize the instance of the class properly. As a function, it can have many of the characteristics of a common Dart function, such as arguments—required or optional and named or positional. In the preceding example, the constructor has two mandatory arguments.

If you look in our constructor body, it uses the `this` keyword. Furthermore, the constructor parameter names are the same as the field ones, which could cause ambiguity. So, to avoid this, we prefix the object instance fields with the `this` keyword during the value assign step.

Dart provides another way to write a constructor like the one provided in the example, by using a shortcut syntax:

```
// ... class fields definition

// shortcut initialization syntax
Person(this.firstName, this.lastName);
```

We can omit the constructor body as it only sets the class field values without any additional setup applied to it.

# Named constructors

Unlike Java and many other languages, Dart does not have overloading by redefinition, so, to define alternative constructors for a class, you need to use the named constructors:

```
// ... class fields definition
// other constructors

Person.anonymous() {}
```

A named constructor is how you define alternative constructors for a class. In the preceding example, we defined an alternative constructor for a `Person` class without a name.

The only difference compared with a simple method is that constructors do not have a `return` statement, as the only thing they have to do is to initialize the object instance properly.

We will see named constructors in action in the chapters on Flutter, as the framework uses these a lot to initialize widget definitions.

# Factory constructors

Another useful syntax in Dart is the factory constructor, which helps to apply the `factory` pattern, a creation technique that allows classes to be instantiated without specifying the exact resulting object type. Suppose we have the following descendants of the `Person` class:

```
class Student extends Person {
  Student(firstName, lastName): super(firstName, lastName);
}

class Employee extends Person {
  Employee(firstName, lastName): super(firstName, lastName);
}
```

As you can observe, the descendant classes are still almost the same as the `Person` class, as they do not yet add any specific functionalities.

We can define a factory constructor on the `Person` class to instantiate the corresponding class based on the required `type` argument:

```
class Person {
  String firstName;
  String lastName;

  Person([this.firstName, this.lastName]);

  factory Person.fromType([PersonType type]) {
    switch (type) {
      case PersonType.employee:
        return new Employee();
      case PersonType.student:
        return new Student();
    }
    return Person();
  }
}
```

```
    String getFullName() => "$firstName $lastName";
}

enum PersonType { student, employee }
```

The `factory` constructor is specified by adding the `factory` keyword, followed by the constructor definition, typically in a base class or abstract class type. In our case, the `Person` class defines a factory-named constructor based on `PersonType` specified in the argument. If no type is passed, it creates a simple `Person` class by using its default constructor.

Another important thing to note is that the factory constructor *does not* replace the default class constructor. Hence, it and its descendants can still be instantiated directly by the caller.

# Field accessors – getters and setters

As mentioned previously, getters and setters allow us to access a field on a class, and every field has these accessors, even when we do not define them. In the preceding `Person` example, when we execute `somePerson.firstName = "Peter"`, we are calling the `firstName` field's `set` accessor and sending `"Peter"` as a parameter to it. Also in the example, the `get` accessor is used when we call the `getFullName()` method on the person, and it concatenates both names.

We can modify our `Person` class to replace the old `getFullName()` method and add it as a getter, as demonstrated in the following code block, for example:

```
class Person {
  String firstName;
  String lastName;

  Person(this.firstName, this.lastName);

  Person.anonymous() {}

  String get fullName => "$firstName $lastName";
  String get initials => "${firstName[0]}. ${lastName[0]}.";
}

main() {
  Person somePerson = new Person("clark", "kent");

  print(somePerson.fullName);  // prints clark kent
  print(somePerson.initials);  // prints c. k.
```

```
    somePerson.fullName = "peter parker";
    // we have not defined a setter fullName so it doesn't compile
  }
```

The following important observations can be made regarding the preceding example:

- We could not have defined a getter or setter with the same field names: firstName and lastName. This would give us a compile error, as the class member names cannot be repeated.
- The initials getter would throw an error for a person instantiated by the anonymous named constructor, as it would not have firstName and lastName values (equates to null).
- We do not need to always define the pair, get and set, together, as you can see that we have only defined a fullName getter and not a setter, so we cannot modify fullName. (This results in a compilation error, as indicated previously.)

We could have also written a setter for fullName and defined the logic behind it to set firstName and lastName based on that:

```
class Person {
  // ... class fields definition
  set fullName(String fullName) {
    var parts = fullName.split(" ");
    this.firstName = parts.first;
    this.lastName = parts.last;
  }
}
```

This way, someone could initialize a person's name by setting fullName and the result would be the same. (Of course, we have not carried out any checks to establish whether the value passed as fullName is valid, that is, not empty, with two or more values, and so on.)

# Static fields and methods

As you already know, fields are nothing more than variables that hold object values, and methods are simple functions that represent object actions. In some cases, you may want to share a value or method between all of the object instances of a class. For this use case, you can add the static modifier to them, as follows:

```
class Person {
  // ... class fields definition

  static String personLabel = "Person name:";
```

```
  String get fullName => "$personLabel $firstName $lastName";
  // modified to print the new static field "personLabel"
}
```

Hence, we can change the static field value directly on the class:

```
main() {
  Person somePerson = Person("clark", "kent");
  Person anotherPerson = Person("peter", "parker");

  print(somePerson.fullName); // prints Person name: clark kent
  print(anotherPerson.fullName); // prints Person name: peter park

  Person.personLabel = "name:";

  print(somePerson.fullName); // prints name: clark kent
  print(anotherPerson.fullName); // prints name: peter parker
}
```

The static fields are associated with the class, rather than any object instance. The same goes for the `static` method definitions. We can add a `static` method to encapsulate the name printing, as demonstrated in the following code block, for example:

```
class Person {
  // ... class fields definition
  static String personLabel = "Person name:";

  static void printsPerson(Person person) {
    print("$personLabel ${person.firstName} ${person.lastName}");
  }
}
```

Then, we can use this method to print a `Person` instance, just like we did before:

```
main() {
  Person somePerson = Person("clark", "kent");
  Person anotherPerson = Person("peter", "parker");

  Person.personLabel = "name:";

  Person.printsPerson(somePerson); // prints name: clark kent
  Person.printsPerson(anotherPerson); // prints name: peter park
}
```

We could modify the `fullName` getter on the `Person` class to not use the `personLabel` static field, to make more sense and obtain distinct results according to our requirements:

```
class Person {
  // ... class fields definition

  String get fullName => "$firstName $lastName";
}

main() {
  Person somePerson = Person("clark", "kent");
  Person anotherPerson = Person("peter", "parker");

  print(somePerson.fullName); // prints clark kent
  print(anotherPerson.fullName); // prints peter parker

  Person.printsPerson(somePerson); // prints Person name: clark kent
  Person.printsPerson(anotherPerson); // prints Person name: peter park
}
```

As you can see, static fields and methods allow us to add specific behaviors to classes in general.

# Class inheritance

In addition to the implicit inheritance to the `Object` type, Dart allows us to extend defined classes by using the `extends` keyword, where all of the members of the parent class are inherited, except the constructors.

Now, let's check out the following example, where we create a child class for the existent `Person` class:

```
class Student extends Person {
  String nickName;

  Student(String firstName, String lastName, this.nickName)
      : super(firstName, lastName);

  @override
  String toString() => "$fullName, also known as $nickName";
}

main() {
  Student student = new Student("Clark", "Kent", "Kal-El");
```

```
    print(student); // same as calling student.toString()
    // prints Clark Kent, also known as Kal-El
}
```

The following observations can be made regarding the preceding example:

- Student: The Student class defines its own constructor. However, it calls the Person class constructor, passing the required parameters. This is done with the super keyword.
- @override: There's an overridden toString() method on the Student class. This is where inheritance makes sense—we change the behavior of a parent class (Object, in this case) on the child class.
- print(student): As you can see in the print(student) statement, we are not calling any method; the toString() method is called for us implicitly.

## The toString() method

A great common example of overriding parent behavior is the toString() method. The objective of this method is to return a String representation of the object:

```
class Student extends Person {
  // ... fullName(from Person class) and other fields
  @override
  String toString() => "$fullName, also known as $nickName";
}

main() {
  Student student = new Student("Clark", "Kent", "Kal-El");

  print("This is a student: $student");
  // prints: This is a student: Clark Kent, also known as Kal-El
  // will also call the toString() of student implicitly
}
```

As you can see, this makes the code cleaner, and we provide a good textual representation of the object that can aid in understanding logs, text formatting, and more.

# Interfaces, abstract classes, and mixins

In Dart, abstract classes and interfaces are closely related to one another. This is because Dart implements interfaces in a subtly different way from most typical languages.

Let's take a look at abstract classes first before linking them to the topic of implicit interfaces.

# Abstract classes

In OOP, abstract classes are classes that cannot be instantiated, which makes a lot of sense, depending on the context and the level of abstraction in a program.

For example, our `Person` class could be abstract if we want to make sure that it only exists in the context of the program if it is a `Student` instance or another subtype:

```
abstract class Person {
  // ... the body was hidden for brevity
}
```

The only thing we need to change here is the beginning of the class definition, marking it as abstract:

```
main() {
  Person student = new Student("Clark", "Kent", "Kal-El"); // works as
          //we are instantiating the subtype
  // Person p = new Person();
  // abstract classes cannot be instantiated

  print(student);
}
```

As you can see, we can no longer instantiate a `Person` class, just its subtype, `Student`.

An abstract class may have abstract members without an implementation, allowing it to be implemented by the child types that extend them:

```
abstract class Person {
  String firstName;
  String lastName;

  Person(this.firstName, this.lastName);

  String get fullName;
}
```

The `fullName` getter from the preceding `Person` class is now abstract, as it does not have an implementation. It is the responsibility of the child to implement this member:

```
class Student extends Person {
  //... other class members

  @override
  String get fullName => "$firstName $lastName";
}
```

The `Student` class implements the `fullName` getter because, if it did not, we would not be able to compile the code.

# Interfaces

Dart does not have the interface keyword but does allow us to use interfaces in a subtly different way from what you may be used to. All class declarations are themselves interfaces. This means that, when you are defining a class in Dart, you are also defining an interface that may be *implemented* and not only *extended* by other classes. This is called **implicit interfaces** in the Dart world.

On this basis, our previous `Person` class is also a `Person` interface that could be implemented, instead of extended, by the `Student` class:

```
class Student implements Person {
  String nickName;

  @override
  String firstName;

  @override
  String lastName;

  Student(this.firstName, this.lastName, this.nickName);

  @override
  String get fullName => "$firstName $lastName";

  @override
  String toString() => "$fullName, also known as $nickName";
}
```

Note that, in general, the code does not change too much, except inasmuch as the members are now defined in the `Student` class. The `Person` class is just a *contract* that the `Student` class adopted and must implement.

> If you want to declare an explicit interface, you just need to make an abstract class without any implementation on it, just member definitions, and it will be a pure interface, ready to be implemented.

# Mixins – adding behavior to a class

In OOP, mixins are a way to include functionalities on a class without the need for associations between the parts, such as inheritance.

The most common contexts where mixins can be used are in places where multiple inheritances may be needed, as it is an easy way for classes to use common functionality.

In Dart, there are several ways in which to declare a mixin:

- By declaring a *class* and using it as a mixin, allowing it to also be used as an object
- By declaring an *abstract class*, allowing it to be used as a mixin or to be inherited, but not instantiated
- By declaring it as a *mixin*, allowing it to be used only as a mixin

> No matter how you declare a mixin, it can also be used as an interface, since it exposes members, and that is the premise behind all of it.

Now, let's check an example of declaring a functionality that our previous `Person` class could have.

For example, let's think about the professions a person could have. Some persons may have specific skills and common ones, and mixins can be ideal for this use case because we can add the skills to a profession without the need to make them extend a common, more generic class or implement an interface in each one. As the implementation would probably be the same, it would cause code duplications:

```
// Person class definition

class ProgrammingSkills {
```

```
  coding() {
    print("writing code...");
  }
}

class ManagementSkills {
  manage() {
    print("managing project...");
  }
}
```

In the preceding example, we created two profession skills classes, `ProgrammingSkills` and `ManagementSkills`. Now, we can use them by adding the `with` keyword to the class definition, for example:

```
class SeniorDeveloper extends Person with ProgrammingSkills,
ManagementSkills {
    SeniorDeveloper(String firstName, String lastName) : super(firstName,
lastName);
}

class JuniorDeveloper extends Person with ProgrammingSkills {
    JuniorDeveloper(String firstName, String lastName) : super(firstName,
lastName);
}
```

Both classes will have the `coding()` method without the need to implement it in each class, as it is already implemented in the `ProgrammingSkills` mixin.

As mentioned previously, there are multiple ways of declaring a mixin. In the preceding example, we used a simple class definition. This way, the `ProgrammingSkills` class can be extended like a normal class or even implemented as an interface (losing the mixin property):

```
class AdvancedProgrammingSkills extends ProgrammingSkills {
  makingCoffee() {
    print("making coffee...");
  }
}
```

Writing `AdvancedProgrammingSkills` in this way does not make it a mixin. Mixin classes must extend the `Object` class and declare no constructor.

Another way of writing a mixin is by using the `mixin` keyword:

```
mixin ProgrammingSkills {
  coding() {
    print("writing code...");
  }
}

mixin ManagementSkills {
  manage() {
    print("managing project...");
  }
}
```

Writing mixins in this way prevents unwanted behavior because mixins cannot be extended and are intended to be used properly. The profession classes that use mixins remain the same.

Another thing we can do is to limit the classes that can use a certain mixin. To do so, we need to specify the superclass required by using the `on` keyword:

```
mixin ProgrammingSkills on Developer {
  coding() {
    print("writing code...");
  }
}
```

 Mixins limited by the `on` keyword require the target class to have a no-arguments constructor.

# Callable classes, top-level functions, and variables

Dart is very flexible in terms of letting the developer take control of all of the pieces of code and, unlike many languages, there's no single way of doing something.

As Dart proposes to combine the benefits of modern OOP concepts with traditional ones, you can always choose when and where to apply different approaches.

# Callable classes

In the same way that Dart functions are nothing more than objects, Dart classes can behave like functions too, that is, they can be invoked, take some arguments, and return something as a result. The syntax for emulating a function in a class is as follows:

```
class ShouldWriteAProgram { // this is simple class
    String language;
    String platform;

    ShouldWriteAProgram(this.language, this.platform);

    // this special method named 'call' makes the class behave as a function
    bool call(String category) {
      if(language == "Dart" && platform == "Flutter") {
        return category != "to-do";
      }
      return false;
    }
  }

main() {
  var shouldWrite = ShouldWriteAProgram("Dart", "Flutter");

  print(shouldWrite("todo")); // prints false.
  // this function is invoking the ShouldWriteAProgram callable class
  // resulting in a implicit call to its "call" method
}
```

As you can see, the `shouldWrite` variable is an object, an instance of the `ShouldWriteAProgram` class, but can also be called as a normal function passing a parameter and using its return value. This is possible because of the existence of the `call()` method defined in the class.

The `call()` method is a special method in Dart. Every class that defines it can behave as a normal Dart function.

> If you assign a callable class to a function type variable, it will be implicitly converted into a function type and behave just like a normal function.

## Top-level functions and variables

In this chapter, we have seen that functions and variables in Dart can be tied to classes as members—class fields and methods.

The top-level way of writing functions is also already known from Chapter 1, *An Introduction to Dart*, where we wrote the most famous Dart function: the entry point of every application, main(). For variables, the way of declaring is the same. We just leave it out of any function scope, so that it's accessible globally on the application/package:

```
var globalNumber = 100;
final globalFinalNumber = 1000;

void printHello() {
  print("""Dart from global scope.
    This is a top-level number: $globalNumber
    This is a top-level final number: $globalFinalNumber
    """);
}

main() {
  // the most famous Dart top level function
  printHello(); // prints the default value

  globalNumber = 0;
  // globalFinalNumber = 0; // does not compile as this is a final variable

  printHello(); // prints the new value
}
```

As you can see, variables and functions do not need to be bound to a class to exist. This is the flexibility proposed by the Dart language, bringing to the developer the ability to write simple and consistent code, without forgetting the patterns and features of modern languages.

# Understanding Dart libraries and packages

Libraries are a way to structure a project based on modularity, which allows the developer to split the code over multiple files and to share some *piece of code* or *module* with other developers.

Many programming languages use libraries to provide this modularity to the developer, and Dart is no different. In Dart, these libraries also have another important role besides code structuring. That is, they determine what is visible or not to other libraries.

Before we get into the Dart package, we need to understand the smallest unit that the library consists of. First, let's explore how to use a library inside our package and, following this, learn how to define a library in Dart.

# Importing and using a library

In Chapter 1, *An Introduction to Dart*, in the *Functions* section, we imported the meta library to use the @required annotation on some parameters. Now, let's explore the import statement in more detail.

To define a library, we simply create a Dart file with some code in it.

 Take a look at the example_1_importing example for a clearer visualization of the libraries and import statements. You can find the source code of this chapter on GitHub.

In this example, we defined a simple library with the Person, Student, and Employee classes alongside the PersonType enum:

```
// person_lib library - the Classes contents were truncated for brevity

class Person {
  String firstName;
  String lastName;
  PersonType type;

  Person([this.firstName, this.lastName]);

  String get fullName => "$firstName $lastName";
}

enum PersonType { student, employee }

class Student extends Person {
  Student([firstName, lastName]): super(firstName, lastName) {
    type = PersonType.student;
  }
}
```

```
class Employee extends Person {
  Employee([firstName, lastName]): super(firstName, lastName) {
    type = PersonType.employee;
  }
}
```

To import it, we can just add the `import library_path;` statement at the beginning of the file and before any code:

```
import 'person_lib.dart';

void main() {

  Person person = Person("Clark", "Kent");
  // omitted the optional 'new' keyword

  Person student = Student("Clark", "Kent");

  print("Person: ${person.fullName}, type: ${person.type}");
  print("Student: ${student.fullName}, type: ${student.type}");
}
```

As the files are in the same directory, the import path is just the filename. After adding the `import` statement, we can use any available code from it—in the same way that we did with the `Person` and `Student` classes.

## Importing show and hide

If you take a look at the preceding example, you will notice that we have not used all of the available classes from the `person_lib` library. To make the code cleaner and less susceptible to errors and naming conflicts, we can use the `show` keyword, which allows us to import only the identifiers that we want to use effectively in our code:

```
// import 'person_lib.dart' show Person, Student;
```

We can also specify the identifiers we explicitly don't want to import by using the `hide` keyword. In this case, we will be importing all of the identifiers from the library except the ones after the `hide` keyword:

```
// import 'person_lib.dart' hide Employee;
```

# Importing prefixes to libraries

In Dart, there's no namespace definition or something that uniquely identifies a library in the context that it is used, so conflicts may happen when creating identifier names, that is, libraries may define a top-level function or even a class with the same name. Although we can use the `show` and `hide` modifiers to explicitly set what members we want to import from a library, this is not sufficient for solving the issue because, sometimes, we may be interested in some class or top-level function with the same name in different libraries:

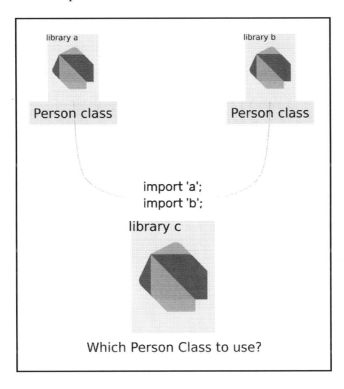

Fortunately, Dart has a way to work around this. The `as` keyword can be added after an `import` statement to set a prefix to all of the identifiers from the imported library:

```
import 'a.dart' as libraryA;
import 'b.dart' as libraryB;

void main() {

  libraryA.Person personA = libraryA.Person("Clark", "Kent");

  print("Person A: ${personA.fullName}");
```

```
    libraryB.Person personB = libraryB.Person(); // 'b' Person does not
                                                  // have any field
    print("Person B: ${personB}");
}
```

As you can see, without this prefix, we don't have a way to identify which `Person` class to use. The same applies to any public library identifier, such as a function or a variable. After specifying the prefix, we need to add it to every call to a member of that library, not only the conflicting ones.

 You can find the source code of this chapter on GitHub.

 If you remember from `Chapter 1`, *An Introduction to Dart,* the `as` keyword is also used for typecasting from a supertype to a subtype.

# Importing path variants

In the previous examples, we imported a local file library that lives in the same directory as the library customer, so we just specified the filename.

However, that's not the case for when you are using third-party Dart packages. In this case, the files will not exist in the same directory, so let's take a look at how we can import an outer package Dart library.

There are several ways to specify library paths in the `import` statement, and we have already used two of them: relative file import and importing from a *package.* Now, let's take a look at all of them in more detail.

Let's assume that we have a package directory of a small `foo` package containing two files: `a.dart` and `b.dart`. To import them, we can use multiple approaches:

- **A relative file path**: This is similar to the method that we used in the previous example, as the libraries were in the same folder. We can just put the relative path to the library file we want to import, as follows:

    ```
    import 'foo/a.dart';
    import 'foo/b.dart';
    ```

- **An absolute file path**: We can add the absolute path on the computer to a library file by adding the `file://` URI prefix to the import path:

```
import "file:///c:/dart_package/foo/a.dart";
import "file:///c:/dart_package/foo/b.dart";
```

 Although possible, absolute importing is not recommended and it is a bad way to import libraries as, in distributed development environments, it will likely cause problems when locating files.

- **A URL over the web**: In the same way as using an absolute file path, we can add the URL of a website containing the source code of a library directly over the `http://` protocol:

```
import "http://dartpackage.com/dart_package/foo/a.dart";
```

- **A package**: This is the most common way to import a library. Here, we specify the library path from the `package` root. We will explore the packages definition later in this chapter; in the case of importing a local library, it goes *from the root of the package, down the source tree until the library file*:

```
import 'package:my_package/foo/a.dart';
import 'package:my_package/foo/b.dart';
```

The `package` method is the recommended way to import libraries, as it works well with *local libraries* (that is, your project's local files and libraries) and is the way to use the provided libraries from third-party packages.

 Feel free to revisit the example of the package after you learn what a package is in the Dart context. You can find the source code of this chapter on GitHub.

# Creating Dart libraries

A Dart library can be composed of a single file or multiple files. In the most common and recommended way, when you create a file, you create a small library. But, if you prefer, you can split a library definition into multiple files. Although less common, it can be useful depending on the context, especially when working with very interdependent classes, for example.

The decision for splitting is important, not only for encapsulation but also for how library customers will import and use them. Let's say, for example, that we have two tightly coupled classes that need to live together for them to work. Dividing them into different libraries will force customers to import both libraries. This is not the most practical way, so it's very important to be careful of library splitting when creating open source libraries.

Before we get into alternative ways of defining a library, we need to take a look at library privacy; this helps with encapsulation, making it easier to understand why we need to properly split a library into multiple files or not.

## Library member privacy

The most common way to control privacy (code *encapsulation*), in most languages, happens at the class level. This is by adding some specific keyword that identifies the member level of access, such as `protected` and `private` in the Java language, for example; consider the following diagram:

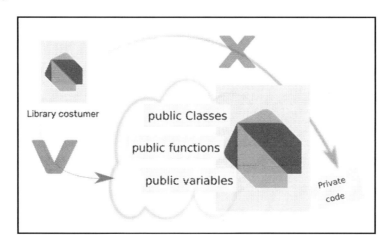

In Dart, every identifier, by default, is accessible from any place, inside and outside the library, except if it is prefixed with an _ (underscore) character. This means that it becomes private to the declaring libraries, preventing it from being accessible from the outside. Take a look at the next example, where we have used the _ prefix.

The Dart meta package provides the `@protected` annotation. When added to a class member, it indicates the member should be used only inside the class or its subtypes.

Additionally, note that this part of Dart is very likely to change in future versions, as a portion of the Dart community has been influenced by Java and other object-oriented languages, where the privacy control takes place at the class level.

# The library definition

Dart has a keyword to define a library—`library`, as you may expect. Although optional, this keyword is very useful when creating multiple file libraries or to create documentation for libraries before publishing them as APIs.

 Dart has the `dartdoc` tool for generating HTML documentation for Dart packages. To use this tool, we have to write comments in a specific way, and we will explore this further in the following examples.

Let's take a look at how to define a library using this keyword, and the multiple approaches that can be taken when creating libraries to make the correct encapsulation and to make library usage more concise.

## A single-file library

The most simplistic way to define a library is by adding all the interrelated code, that is, classes, top-level functions, and variables into one single file. For example, our previous `Person` library is as follows:

```dart
class Person {
  String firstName;
  String lastName;
  PersonType _type;

  Person({this.firstName, this.lastName});

  String toString() => "($_type): $firstName $lastName";
}

enum PersonType { student, employee }

class Student extends Person {
  Student({firstName, lastName})
      : super(firstName: firstName, lastName: lastName) {
    _type = PersonType.student;
  }
}
```

```
class Programmer extends Person {
  Programmer({firstName, lastName})
      : super(firstName: firstName, lastName: lastName) {
    _type = PersonType.employee;
  }
}
```

There is nothing new to note here in the file definition, just the following two observations:

- The file, by itself, is a library, so we do not need to declare anything explicitly.
- The _type field is private to the library, that is, it's only accessible by code from this same library.

Let's say that we try to use these classes from another library, as follows:

```
main() {
  Programmer programmer = Programmer(firstName: "Dean", lastName: "Pugh");

  // we cannot access the _type property as it is private to the
  // single_file library programmer._type = PersonType.employee;

  print(programmer);
}
```

As you can see, we have access to all of the public identifiers from the previously defined library. We cannot access the _type property to set the value, although, in the toString() method of the Person class, its value is exposed.

Although it is tempting to define all of the related code in just one file, it may become harder to maintain, as the code and its complexity grow over time. Instead, use this for simple types of definitions that are unlikely to change over time.

## Splitting libraries into multiple files

We have seen the single-file approach to define a library, so now let's explore how to split the library definition into multiple files to allow us to organize the project in small, reusable pieces (which is the real purpose of using libraries).

To define a multiple-file library, we can use the combined `part`, `part of`, and `library` statements:

- `part`: This allows a library to specify that it's composed of small library parts.
- `part of`: The small library part specifies which library it helps to compose.
- `library`: This is for using the preceding `part` statements, as we need to relate `part` files with the `main` part of the library.

Let's examine what the preceding example looks like by using the `part` statements:

```
// the 'main' part of the library, person_library.dart
// defined using the library keyword and listing parts below

library person;

part 'person_types.dart';
part 'student.dart';
part 'programmer.dart';

class Person {
  String firstName;
  String lastName;
  PersonType _type;

  Person({this.firstName, this.lastName});

  String toString() => "($_type): $firstName $lastName";
}
```

Let's make some observations about the preceding code, as follows:

- The `library` keyword is followed by the library identifier, `person`, in this case. It's good practice to name the identifier by using only lowercase characters and the underscore character as a separator. Our example could be called anything such as `person_lib` or `person_library`.
- The library parts are listed just below the library definition.
- The code itself does not change anything.

The `part` syntax is defined as follows:

- The `PersonType` part is defined in the `person_types.dart` file:

```
part of person;

enum PersonType { student, employee }
```

- The `Student` part is defined in the `student.dart` file:

```
part of person;

class Student extends Person {
  Student({firstName, lastName})
      : super(firstName: firstName, lastName: lastName) {
    _type = PersonType.student;
  }
}
```

- The `Programmer` part is defined in the `programmer.dart` file:

```
part of person;

class Programmer extends Person {
  Programmer({firstName, lastName})
      : super(firstName: firstName, lastName: lastName) {
    _type = PersonType.employee;
  }
}
```

The implementation by itself does not change anything; the only difference is the `part of` statement at the beginning of the file.

Additionally, as you can see, the `_type` property is also accessible in the `part` files, as it's private to the `person` library and all of the files are in the same library.

If the `part` files had some fields, classes, or top-level functions and variables prefixed with _, they would be accessible to the `main` library file and other parts as well; remember, they are all in the same library.

Let's take a look at the following code, which uses the `person` library:

```
import 'person_lib/person_library.dart';

main() {
  // access the Programmer class is allowed, part of the person_library
  Programmer programmer = Programmer(firstName: "Dean", lastName: "Pugh");

  // cannot access the _type property, it is private to person library
  // programmer._type = PersonType.employee;

  print(programmer);
}
```

Take a look at the preceding code; the `person` library customer does not need to change anything, as the modifications we made are in the library's inner structure.

> The `part` syntax is changing and is a candidate to be discontinued in the next Dart release. If this occurs, the most likely change will be the creation of new syntax to replace it.

## A multiple-file library – the export statement

The preceding approach is not the ideal way of splitting a Dart library, as already mentioned. This is because the syntax of the `part` statement is likely to change in future versions. Additionally, you may have found it a little overdone and difficult to use if you just want to control the visibility of library members.

We can choose to simply not create the library parts and just split the library into small individual libraries. For the previous examples, this would result in some important changes during implementation.

We have the previous parts as three individual libraries: `person_library`, `programmer`, and `student`. Although related, they behave as individual libraries and do not know anything except the public members of each other:

```
// person library defined in person_library.dart
class Person {
  String firstName;
  String lastName;
  final PersonType type;

  Person({this.firstName, this.lastName, this.type});
```

```
    String toString() => "($type): $firstName $lastName";
}

enum PersonType { student, employee }
```

The `person` library does not need the library identifier in this case.

The `programmer` library imports the `person` library to access its `Person` class:

```
// programmer library defined in programmer.dart

import 'person_library.dart';

class Programmer extends Person {
 Programmer({firstName, lastName})
 : super(firstName: firstName, lastName: lastName, type:
PersonType.employee);
}
```

In the same way, the `student` library imports the `person` library:

```
// student library defined in student.dart

import 'person_library.dart';

class Student extends Person {
  Student({firstName, lastName})
      : super(
          firstName: firstName,
          lastName: lastName,
          type: PersonType.student,
        );
}
```

You can see the following from the preceding code:

- The `programmer` and `student` libraries need to import the `person` library to extend it.
- Additionally, the `type` property from the `Person` class was made public by removing the _ prefix. This means that it can be accessed by the other libraries. As the `type` property, in this case, is not intended to change and it is initialized in the constructor, we have made it `final` as well.

Let's take a look at the library customer, as follows:

```
import 'person_lib/programmer.dart';
import 'person_lib/student.dart';
```

```
main() {
    // we can access the Programmer class as it is part of the person_library
    Programmer programmer = Programmer(firstName: "Dean", lastName: "Pugh");
    Student student = Student(firstName: "Dilo", lastName: "Pugh");

    print(programmer);
    print(student);
}
```

The person library customer will have a small change, as now the library is split into multiple parts, so we will need to import each library we want to use individually.

This is not a big deal when talking about small libraries, but try to think about a more complex library structure, where importing all of the interrelated libraries individually would add difficulty to its usage.

This is where the export statement comes in. Here, we can select the main library file and, from there, export all of the smaller libraries related to it. In this way, the customer only needs to import a single library and all of the smaller libraries will be available alongside it.

In our example, the best choice for using this could be the person library:

```
export 'programmer.dart';
export 'student.dart';

class Person { ... }

enum PersonType { ... }
```

In this way, the library customer would be as follows:

```
import 'person_lib/person_library.dart';

main() {
    // we can access the Programmer and Student class as they are exported
    // from the person_library
    Programmer programmer = Programmer(firstName: "Dean", lastName: "Pugh");
    Student student = Student(firstName: "Dilo", lastName: "Pugh");

    print(programmer);
    print(student);
}
```

Notice that only the import statement changes. We can use the classes from the small libraries normally as they are exported from person_library.

After gaining an understanding of the Dart library concept, we can now examine how to combine these pieces of code into something shareable and reusable: the Dart package.

# Dart packages

A Dart package is the starting point of any Dart project. In previous examples, we did not bother about it as we were using single-file syntax examples; however, in the real world, we will be always working with *packages*:

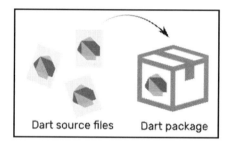

The main benefit of using and creating packages is that the code can be reused and shared. In the Dart ecosystem, this is done by the `pub` tool, which allows us to pull and send dependencies to the `pub.dartlang.org` website and repository.

The use of a library package in a project makes it an *immediate* dependency, and the used library may have its own dependencies, called **transitive** dependencies.

 If you are playing with DartPad, it's time to change; now, you will need a proper Dart development environment configured, as we will start to work with packages.

In general, there are two kinds of Dart package: **application packages** and **library packages**.

## Application packages versus library packages

Not all packages are meant to be shareable; an application itself is also a package. These packages can have dependencies on library packages normally, but they are not intended to be used as a dependency in other projects.

On the other hand, library packages are the ones that contain some useful code that may be helpful in many projects. These types can be used as a dependency and have dependencies on others too.

Put simply, the recommended structure of a Dart package does not differ too much between an application and a library package—their purpose and usage are different from each other.

# Package structures

The first important thing to point out about a Dart package project structure is that its validity is asserted by the presence of a `pubspec.yaml` file; that is, if there's a `pubspec.yaml` file in your structure, then there is a package and this is where you properly describe it—without it, there's no package at all. This is what a typical package looks like:

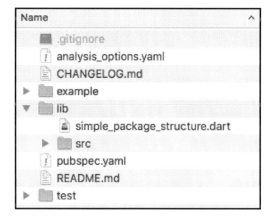

 This example package was generated by using the *Stagehand* tool. You can refer to the following section for more details.

For application packages, there is no required project layout to adopt (as it's not intended to be published to the `pub` repository); however, as it is evolving, there's already several recommended ways and conventions to follow. Let's take a look at the common structure of a general Dart package. Most of the structure is conventional and depends on your project complexity and whether you want to share its code in some way.

Let's take a look at the role of each file and directory in a typical Dart package structure:

- `pubspec.yaml`: As already pointed out, this is the fundamental package file and it describes the package to the pub repository. We will be examining the full structure of this file in more detail later.
- The `lib/` and `lib/src/` directories: These are the places where the package library source code lives. As you already know, a simple `.dart` file is a *small* library, so everything you put in the `lib` directory is publicly available to other packages. This is known as the package public API.
  The `src` subdirectory contains, by convention, all of the internal package code, that is, the private source code of the package that is not meant to be directly imported by others.

> Although it is possible to import a library placed in the `src` subdirectory, this is not recommended, as it's intended to be an internal library implementation and not part of the library's public API. It may change and break the customer code.

- `lib/simple_package_structure.dart`: A common practice is to add a single, or a few, top-level files that export (remember the `export` statement) the local `src/`libraries. The name of this file is typically the same as the package. If there is more than one library, then the name must be simple enough to identify the general purpose of the exported libraries.
- `test/`: Unit tests and benchmark analysis are conventionally put inside the `test` and `benchmark` directories, respectively. Additionally, the source code inside the test folder is typically postfixed with the `_test` identifier.

> You can refer to the *An introduction to unit testing with Dart* section to understand how to write unit tests.

- `README.md`, `CHANGELOG.md`, and `LICENSE`: These are markdown files typically present in packages that are intended to be published in some public repository, such as the Dart pub. These files are also very common in open source projects. The `LICENSE` file, which specifies the source code copyright information, is also sometimes present.
- `example/`: This is important in published packages and can demonstrate how the package can be used.
- `analysis_options.yaml`: This is a useful file to customize the lint checks, style analysis, and other precompile checks.

You can check the analysis customization tutorial on the Dart website at `https://www.dartlang.org/guides/language/analysis-options`.

Some additional files depend on the purpose of the project, including the following:

- `tools/`: This is a directory containing scripts that can be used during development, including utilities to manipulate images, raw files, and any kind of script that is private to the package and useful to the developer.
- `doc/` and `doc/api`: This is where you can add some useful information about the project. `api/ subdirectory` is where the `dartdoc` tool (presented in Chapter 1, *An Introduction to Dart*) generates the API documentation based on code comments.

In web packages, some new files and directories are included; they are as follows:

- The `lib/` folder is the typical destination of static web resource files, such as images or `.css` files.
- `web/` is a directory used in web application projects. Unlike the `lib/` folder, which is meant to be library code, this code is meant to have the web application source code and entry points (that is, the `main()` function).

In command-line packages, the `bin` directory is included:

- The `bin/` directory is meant to have some script that can run directly from the command line; the Stagehand tool described next is an example of the command-line library tool.

 The Flutter project structure has some similarities to Dart packages and we will learn about this structure in the following chapter.

# Stagehand – the Dart project generator

Starting a new Dart project requires a few simple steps: create an empty folder, add a `pubspec.yaml` file to it, and describe the package with a name, version, and so on. Afterward, you add the necessary files gradually.

In general, most of the files and their structures do not change from package to package, so creating the whole Dart package structure every time can be tedious. This is why the Stagehand tool was created—to generate Dart scaffolding projects.

To run the Stagehand tool, we first need to install it on our system. In a properly configured Dart environment, run the following `pub` command in a Terminal to install it:

```
pub global activate stagehand
```

 The pub tool is present in the Dart SDK. If you have a Dart or Flutter environment ready, you can use this tool. Otherwise, take another look at `Chapter 1`, *An Introduction to Dart*.

This command downloads a package (Stagehand, in this case) from the `pub` repository and installs it in the Dart packages cache directory in your system. This varies according to your operating system: `$HOME/.pub-cache/bin` on Linux-based systems and `AppData\Roaming\Pub\Cache\bin` on Windows.

To run Stagehand and any other global activated package tool from the command line, you can use one of two ways:

- The first is by preceding the tool command with the following:

  ```
  pub run global
  ```

- The second is by adding the Dart global packages cache directory into the operating system path.

After properly installing and configuring the Stagehand tool, you can start generating Dart projects:

1. First, create an empty folder with the desired package name.

 Take a look at the `name` field description in *The pubspec file* section to understand how to properly name your package.

2. Then, inside the created folder, generate the package structure using the following command:

```
pub run global stagehand <template>
```

Alternatively, if you have your path properly configured, you can use stagehand <template>, where <template> is the desired Stagehand template to use.

You can check the available project templates on the project page of the Dart pub website at https://pub.dartlang.org/packages/stagehand.

# The pubspec file

The pubspec file is in the heart of a Dart package, and to understand how to properly describe the package, we need to understand how this file is structured. This file is based on the yaml syntax, a common format used for configuration files, with a structure that is easy to read and follow. The pubspec file is as follows:

```
name: simple_package_structure
description: A simple package example
version: 1.0.0
homepage: https://www.example.com
author: Alessandro Biessek <alessandrobiessek@gmail.com>

environment:
  sdk: '>=2.0.0 <3.0.0' # check the dependencies section
                        # below to understand deps versioning

dependencies:
  json_serializable: ^2.0.1

dev_dependencies:
  test: ^1.0.0
```

Flutter projects also contain a pubspec file with some specific available fields. For more information, you can refer to Chapter 3, *An Introduction to Flutter*.

The file specifies the package metadata information, which is useful if you want to publish the package. It also defines the package's third-party dependencies and the Dart SDK version. Let's examine the `pubspec` fields in more detail:

- `name`: This is the identifier of the package. It is *required* and should contain *only* lowercase letters and digits, plus the _ character; additionally, it should be a valid Dart identifier (that is, it cannot start with digits and cannot be a reserved word). This is a very important property if you want to publish the package in the `pub` repository, and it is good to check the existing package names to avoid duplication.
- `description`: While this is an optional field, it is required if you intend to publish the package, describing in simple words the purpose of the package.
- `version`: This is also optional for personal packages, but it is required for publication to the `pub` repository. It's important to maintain consistency in the versioning of a package that will be usable by the community.
- `homepage`: For `pub` packages, this will be linked to the package's page on the pub website. It's very important to provide one when intending to publish it.
- `author`: Although not mandatory, it's important to provide contact information about the creator or creators of the library. Additionally, a library can have more than one author; in this case, the YAML list syntax can be used by setting the `authors` field instead (note the optional contact information):

  ```
  authors:
  - Alessandro Biessek <alessandrobiessek@gmail.com>
  - Alessandro Biessek
  ```

- `dependencies` and `dev_dependencies`: These refer to the real purpose of the `pubspec` file. A listing of third-party packages is required for the usage of the library and the development of the library, respectively.
- `environment`: Besides the third-party dependencies, there is one more, let's say, the *main* dependency of a package, which is the Dart SDK itself. In this field, you need to specify the target and the supported Dart SDK versions.

 The `environment` field is the SDK dependency; it's recommended that you specify the Dart SDK target version by using the `range` syntax, as the semantic range is not compatible with older versions (that is, < 1.8.3).

The typical `pubspec` structure has the fields that were specified earlier. For a complete explanation of the `pubspec` file and other purpose-specific fields, take a look at the Dart website: `https://www.dartlang.org/tools/pub/pubspec`.

You can use the # character to start a comment in `yaml`.

# Package dependencies – pub

Now that you understand the most important role of the `pubspec` file in the package when developing Dart applications, you can add third-party package dependencies to your project. There are important `pub` commands that you can work with when adding or updating package dependencies to your project. We also need to demonstrate how to properly specify the dependency version that we are required to use.

After you start a new Dart project, either manually or by using a generator tool such as Stagehand, the first thing you must do is run the following command:

**pub get**

For example, the following package contains only the following `pubspec` file:

Additionally, it contains the `pubspec` contents, as follows:

```
name: adding_dependencies
```

This is a minimal package description and it does not have any dependencies specified, not even the target Dart SDK version. However, let's execute the `pub get` command inside the `package` folder, as it will work in the same way:

**pub get**

We get the following successful output:

```
Resolving dependencies...
Got dependencies!
```

We will get a file structure like in the following screenshot:

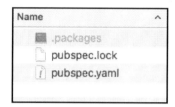

Notice the new files generated by the command inside the `.packages` folder; these files are important for the pub tool to work with the dependency packages:

- `.packages`: This maps the dependencies in the system's pub cache (previously mentioned in the *Stagehand – the Dart project generator* section). Instead of making copies in all of your packages, the pub tool simply stores the mapping between the package and its respective location in the system. After the package is mapped here, it will be available for you to import inside your Dart code. This file should not be included under the source code management system; this is because it's generated and managed by the pub tool.

- `pubspec.lock`: This is the auxiliary file to the pub tool that contains all of the dependency graphs of the package, that is, it lists all of the immediate dependencies and the transitive ones. It also contains the exact versions and other metadata information about all of the dependencies. It is recommended that you include this file in the source management system only if it is an application's package; this helps a `dev` team, for example, to work with the exact same dependency configuration. If you are using a library package, then it's typically not included, as it is expected to work with a large range of dependencies, that is, it should not be *locked* to specific versions.

 Remember, this is all made by the pub tool, so you should not touch these files.

# Specifying dependencies

Now that you know how the pub tool resolves packages inside the project, let's take a look at how to add dependencies to it.

Dependencies are specified in the `dependencies` field of the `pubspec` file. It is a YAML list field, so you can specify as many as needed in the field. Let's suppose that we need the `json_serializable` package in our project. We can specify it by simply adding to the list, as follows:

```
name: adding_dependencies

dependencies:
  json_serializable:
  # another packages below
```

The syntax to specify a dependency is as follows:

```
<package>:
  <constraints>
```

Here, you add its name (`<package>`) followed by the `<constraints>` fields: version and source. In this case, we did not specify any constraint, so it assumes any available version for the version constraint and default source (`pub.dartlang.org`).

> Note that the colon, `:`, after the package name is *not* optional; the dependency list expects every dependency to be a YAML map value. For more information, you can take a look at the YAML documentation at `https://docs.ansible.com/ansible/latest/reference_appendices/YAMLSyntax.html`.

## The version constraint

The version constraint can be a concrete version number, a range, or a minimum or maximum constraint. Let's explore how it looks in each situation:

- **Any/empty**: Like the previous example, we can use this without a version constraint, for example, `json_serializable:` or `json_serializable: any`.
- **Concrete version**: We can add the specific version number we want to work with, for example, `json_serializable: 2.0.1`.
- **Minimal bound**: Here, we can add a minimum acceptable version of the package we want in two ways: `json_serializable: '>1.0.0'`, where we accept any version later than the specified version (excluding the specified one), or `json_serializable: '>=1.0.0'`, where we accept any version above or equal to the specified version.

- **Maximal bound**: Like the previous minimum example but in the upper bound, we can add a maximum acceptable version of the package that we want in two ways: `json_serializable: '<2.0.1'`, where we accept any version below the specified one, or `json_serializable: '<=2.0.1'`, where we accept any version below or equal to the specified one.

- **Range**: By combining minimal and maximal bounds, we can specify an acceptable interval of versions: `json_serializable: '>1.0.0 <=2.0.1'`, `json_serializable: '>1.0.0 <2.0.1'`, `json_serializable: '>=1.0.0 <2.0.1'`, or `json_serializable: '>=1.0.0 <=2.0.1'`.

- **Semantic range**: This is similar to range but, by using the **caret** character, we can specify the range from a minimum acceptable version to the next breaking change. For example, `json_serializable: ^1.0.0` is the same as `json_serializable: '>=1.0.0 <2.0.0'`, and `json_serializable: ^0.1.0` is equal to `json_serializable: '>=0.1.0 <0.2.0'`.

 Semantic versioning helps the community usage of the libraries and it is widely adopted. To examine it in more detail, you can visit the pub tools page at `https://www.dartlang.org/tools/pub/versioning`.

## The source constraint

The pub tool does not look only in the `pub` repository for packages; if you have already used another package management system, you know that it may be useful, sometimes, to host your packages in other places than the public repository, such as company private packages or your personal usage ones. For the source part of the package specification, we have four alternatives to change where the pub tool should look for the package:

- **The hosted source**: This is the default `pub` repository or another alternative `http` server that implements the pub api. For example, consider the following code block:

```
dependencies:
  json_serializable:
    hosted:
      name: json_serializable
      url: http://pub-packages-private-server.com # changing server
```

As you can see, we only need to specify the hosted field if we are not using the `pub` repository—that is, the default source.

- **The path source**: Here, you can add a dependency to a package in your own system:

```
dependencies:
  json_serializable:
    path: /Users/biessek/json_serializable
```

Although you are not allowed to share a package with this kind of dependency, it may be useful in the development stages.

- **The Git source**: Here, you can specify a package from a `git` repository:

```
dependencies:
  json_serializable:
    git:
      url: git://github.com/dart-lang/json_serializable.git
      path: path/to/json_serializable # if the root of package is
                                       # not the root of the
                                       # repository
      ref: master  # to depend on specific commit, tag, branch
```

This can be useful in the development stages or if a published package source code is not yet present in the `pub` repository.

- **The SDK source**: An SDK may have its own packages that can be used as dependencies:

```
dependencies:
  flutter_localizations: # a dependency available in the flutter sdk
    sdk: flutter
```

Until now, this way of specifying source constraints is only used for Flutter SDK dependencies.

Package dependencies are a fundamental topic in Dart development; with these concepts in mind, you can add useful third-party dependencies to your projects and increase your productivity.

# Introducing async programming with Futures and Isolates

Dart is a single-threaded programming language, that is, all of the application code runs in the same thread. Put simply, this means that any code may block thread execution by performing long-time running operations such as I/O or `http` requests.

Although Dart is single-threaded, it can perform asynchronous operations through the use of **Futures**. Additionally, to represent the result of those asynchronous operations, Dart uses the `Future` object combined with the `async` and `await` keywords. Let's understand these important concepts to develop a responsive application.

## Dart Futures

The `Future<T>` object in Dart represents a value that will be provided sometime in the future. It can be used to mark a method, for example, with a future result; that is, a method returning a `Future<T>` object will not have the proper result value immediately but, instead, after some computation at a later point in time.

Consider the following code, where we have the `main` function that calls a long-running operation:

```
import 'dart:io';

void longRunningOperation() {
  for (int i - 0; i < 5; i++) {
    sleep(Duration(seconds: 1));
    print("index: $i");
  }
}

main() {
  print("start of long running operation");

  longRunningOperation();

  print("continuing main body");

  for (int i = 10; i < 15; i++) {
    sleep(Duration(seconds: 1));
    print("index from main: $i");
  }
```

```
    print("end of main");
}
```

If you execute the preceding code, you will notice that it stops the `main` function execution while the `longRunningOperation()` function is running. This is a synchronous execution of all of the code and it will likely not fit well in all use cases.

Now, let's say that the `longRunningOperation()` function is an asynchronous function and `main()` can continue executing without waiting for it to finish to proceed:

```dart
import 'dart:async';

Future longRunningOperation() async {
  for (int i = 0; i < 5; i++) {
    await Future.delayed(Duration(seconds: 1));
    print("index: $i");
  }
}

main() { ... } // main function is the same
```

We have made some changes to demonstrate how `Future` works properly:

- The `longRunningOperation()` function now has the `async` modifier to indicate that this will return a `Future` function and the `Future` function will be completed at the end of the function execution. Notice that the return type is also `Future`.
- We replaced the `sleep()` call with the `Future.delayed` call. This to demonstrate the use of the `await` keyword. The `await` keyword works with `async` functions. When calling a `Future` function, we may need the result of the `Future` function to continue execution. In this case, we want to proceed to the print only after the specified delay.

If you execute the preceding code, you may notice something strange; the output is as follows:

```
start of long running operation
continuing main body
index from main: 10
index from main: 11
index from main: 12
index from main: 13
index from main: 14
end of main
index: 0
```

```
index: 1
index: 2
index: 3
index: 4
```

It's not a concurrent code where one code executes after another like before; here, what changes is the order. In the preceding example, the change occurs when the `longRunningOperation()` function calls `await` in another `async` function. Here, the function is suspended and will be resumed only after a delay of 1 second. After the delay, however, the `main` function is already running again as it no longer `await`s for the long operation to complete, so the `longRunningOperation()` code will be executed only after the `main` function has finished.

One thing we can do is to make the `main()` function into an `async` function and `await` the execution of `longRunningOperation()`. In this way, the `main()` function will be suspended right when we call `await longRunningOperation()` and will only be resumed after its execution. This behaves like normal synchronous code, as follows:

```
main() async {
  print("start of long running operation");

  await longRunningOperation();

  print("continuing main body");

  for (int i = 10; i < 15; i++) {
    sleep(Duration(seconds: 1));
    print("index from main: $i");
  }

  print("end of main");
}
```

As you might have noticed, the preceding functions never run really asynchronously; this is because we `await` the execution of the `longRunningOperation()` method before executing the rest of its code. To make them run asynchronously, we should omit the `await` keyword, as follows:

```
main() async {
  print("start of long running operation");

  longRunningOperation();

  print("continuing main body");

  for (int i = 10; i < 15; i++) {
```

```
    sleep(Duration(seconds: 1));
    print("index from main: $i");
  }
  print("end of main");
}
```

This will make the `main()` method simply continue its execution, where we get the following output:

```
start of long running operation
continuing main body
index: 0
index from main: 10
index: 1
index from main: 11
index: 2
index from main: 12
index: 3
index from main: 13
index: 4
index from main: 14
end of main
```

Dart executes both `async` methods in the same thread. Both functions run asynchronously in this case, but this does not mean that they are executed in parallel.

> Dart executes one operation at a time; as long as one operation is executing, it cannot be interrupted by any other Dart code.

This execution is controlled by the Dart `Event` loop, which acts like a manager for Dart Futures and asynchronous code.

> You can refer to Dart's official documentation on the `Event` loop to understand how this works: `https://dart.dev/articles/archive/event-loop`.

To execute Dart code in parallel (that is, at the same time), we use Dart Isolates.

# Dart Isolates

So, you may have been wondering, how can you execute truly parallel code and improve performance and responsiveness? Dart Isolates are here for this. Every Dart application is composed at least of one `Isolate` instance, the `main Isolate` instance, where all of the application code runs. So, to create a parallel execution code, we must create a new `Isolate` instance that can run in parallel with `main Isolate`:

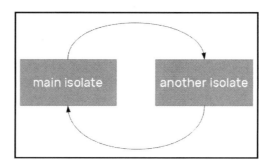

Isolates can be considered to be a sort of a thread, but they do not share anything between each other, as the name suggests. This means that they do not share memory, so we do not need to use locks and other thread synchronization techniques here.

To communicate between isolates, that is, to send and receive data between them, we need to exchange messages. Dart provides a way of accomplishing this.

Let's change the previous implementation to use an `Isolate` instance instead:

```
import 'dart:io';
import 'dart:isolate';

Future<void> longRunningOperation(String message) async {
  for (int i = 0; i < 5; i++) {
    await Future.delayed(Duration(seconds: 1));
    print("index: $i");
  }
}

main() {
  print("start of long running operation");

  Isolate.spawn(longRunningOperation, "Hello");

  print("continuing main body");

  for (int i = 10; i < 15; i++) {
```

```
        sleep(Duration(seconds: 1));
        print("index from main: $i");
    }

    print("end of main");
}
```

As you can see, the code displays small changes:

- The `longRunningOperation()` function becomes an `Isolate` instance, that is, it remains as a simple function.
- To dispatch the `Isolate` process to the execution, we use the `spawn()` method from the `Isolate` class. It takes two arguments—the function to be spawned and a parameter to be passed to the function.

Running the preceding code, you will note a different output, as follows:

```
start of long running operation
continuing main body
Hello from isolate
index from main: 10
index: 0
index from main: 11
index: 1
index from main: 12
index: 2
index from main: 13
index: 3
index from main: 14
end of main
```

Now both of these functions' code run independently after `Isolate` is spawned.

 When compiling to JavaScript, isolates get converted into web workers. You can read more about web workers in the W3Schools article at `https://www.w3schools.com/html/html5_webworkers.asp`.

# Introducing unit testing with Dart

In any language, we can write code that accomplishes some purpose; however, to write performant and bug-free code, we need to use every available resource we can.

Unit tests are one of the things that can help us to write modular, efficient, and bug-free code. The unit test is not the only way of testing code, of course, but it's a crucial part of testing small pieces of software in a manner that isolates it from other parts, helping us to focus on specific things.

Covering all of the application code with unit tests does not guarantee that it's 100% bug-free; however, it helps us to achieve mature code progressively, and this is one of the steps to ensuring a good development cycle, with stable releases from time to time.

Dart also provides some useful tools to work with tests; let's take a look at the starting point of unit testing Dart code: the Dart `test` package.

# The Dart test package

The Dart `test` package is not part of the SDK itself, so it has to be installed as a normal third-party dependency. You should already know how to do this.

 For reference, check the example, `4_unit_tests`, in this chapter's source code on GitHub. The test code is located inside the `test/` folder.

In this example (generated with the Stagehand tool), there is a development dependency; this is a dependency that is required only during development and not at runtime:

```
dev_dependencies:
  test: ^1.0.0
```

This enables us to use the `test` package's provided libraries to write unit tests.

# Writing unit tests

Now, let's suppose that we want to create a function that sums two numbers:

```
class Calculator {
  num sumTwoNumbers(num a, num b) {
    // TODO
  }
}
```

We can write a unit test to evaluate this method implementation by using the test package:

```dart
import 'package:test/test.dart';
import 'package:unit_tests/calculator.dart';

void main() {
  Calculator calculator;

  setUp(() {
    calculator = Calculator();
  });

  test('calculator sumTwoNumbers() sum the both numbers', () {
    expect(calculator.sumTwoNumbers(1, 2), 3);
  });
}
```

In the preceding example, we started by importing the test package main library that exposes functions, for example: setUp(), test(), and expect(). Each of the functions has specific roles, as follows:

- setUp() will execute the callback we pass to it before each of the tests in the test suite.
- test() is the test by itself; it receives a description and a callback with the test implementation.
- expect() is used to make the assertions about the test. In the preceding example, we are just asserting a sum of 1 + 2, which should result in the number 3.

To execute a test, we use the following command:

```
pub run test <test_file>
```

In the preceding example, the command would be (from the root of the project) as follows:

```
pub run test test/calculator_tests.dart
```

Before we effectively implement the sumTwoNumbers() method, the output of the test is as follows:

```
00:01 +0 -1: calculator sumTwoNumbers() sum the both numbers [E]
  Expected: <3>
    Actual: <null>

  package:test_api expect
```

```
        test\calculator_tests.dart 12:7 main.<fn>

  00:01 +0 -1: Some tests failed.
```

Additionally, after properly implementing the `sumTwoNumbers()` method, we will see the following:

```
  00:01 +1: All tests passed!
```

You can also create groups of tests, as you might be thinking that just one test case may not be sufficient to effectively test a unit of code. Let's suppose that we change our test suite to have a `group` of `sum tests`, as follows:

```dart
void main() {
  Calculator calculator;

  setUp(() {
    calculator = Calculator();
  });
  group("sum tests", () {
    test('calculator sumTwoNumbers() sum the both numbers', () {
      expect(calculator.sumTwoNumbers(1, 2), 3);
    });
    test('calculator sumTwoNumbers() sum null as it was 0', () {
      expect(calculator.sumTwoNumbers(1, null), 1);
    });
  });
}
```

Notice the output for the preceding test:

```
  00:01 +1 -1: sum tests calculator sumTwoNumbers() sum null as it was 0 [E]
  NoSuchMethodError: The method '_addFromInteger' was called on null.
  Receiver: null
  Tried calling: _addFromInteger(1)
  dart:core int.+
  package:unit_tests/src/calculator_base.dart 3:14 Calculator.sumTwoNumbers
  test\calculator_tests.dart 15:25 main.<fn>.<fn>

  00:01 +1 -1: Some tests failed.
```

There was one successful test (+1) and one failure (−1)—with the exception described right below the failing test description. With this in mind, we can change the `sumTwoNumbers()` implementation to accept a `null` value, as it was 0, and run the test again:

```
  00:01 +2: All tests passed!
```

As you can see, tests can help us to prevent logic errors from occurring in production; of course, we always might have some errors, but tests can help us to prevent as many as possible.

This was an introduction to unit testing with Dart. You can learn about all of the possibilities by reading the `test` package page on the pub website at `https://pub.dartlang.org/packages/test`.

# Summary

In this chapter, we have seen how the Dart language is structured in terms of the OOP paradigm. We have seen that the language proposes to provide all of the features to the developer when using the OOP paradigm, but also some particularities that are meant to extend developer possibilities, such as mixins for exploring multi-inheritance benefits and implicit interfaces that permit any class to be implemented by any other class, callable classes to add function behavior to simple objects, and top-level functions and variables that do not need to be bound to any class. It is very useful for utility functions that do not depend on context.

We explored how the Dart packages are structured and how to use the pub tool to add dependencies to the project and use third-party packages. We have checked the multiple ways to structure a library, and how it composes a Dart package. Additionally, we learned how to correctly describe a package in the `pubspec` file to create shareable packages. Finally, we examined `async` programming using futures and isolates. Also, we learned about unit testing Dart facilities to write better code.

In the next chapter, we will begin to understand and work with the Flutter framework. Additionally, you will keep going with the Dart knowledge that you have acquired so far.

# An Introduction to Flutter

## 3

In this chapter, you will learn the history of the Flutter framework, how and why it was created, and its evolution so far. You will learn how its community is contributing to it, and how and why it has grown quickly in the last few months. You will be introduced to the main features of Flutter, with short comparisons to other frameworks. Also, you will see how to make a basic Flutter project. To accomplish this, we will need a proper machine configured with Flutter and its various prerequisites.

 Follow the setup instructions of the Flutter framework environment here: `https://flutter.dev/docs/get-started/install`.

The following topics will be covered in this chapter:

- Comparisons with other mobile app development frameworks
- Flutter compilation
- Flutter rendering
- Introducing widgets
- Basic Flutter project structure

# Comparisons with other mobile app development frameworks

Although it's relatively new, Flutter has experienced a great deal of experimentation and evolution over the years. It was called Sky, at its first appearance at the *Dart Developer Summit 2015* presented by *Eric Seidel*. It was presented as the evolution of some previous Google experiments to create something better for mobile in terms of development and user experience, with the main goal of rendering with high performance. Presented as *Flutter* in 2016, and with its first alpha release in May 2017, it was already building for iOS and Android systems. Then it started to get mature and community adoption began to grow. It evolved from community feedback to its first stable release at the end of 2018.

There are many mobile development frameworks out there that seek a common goal: to build native mobile apps for Android and iOS with a single code base. Some of those frameworks are widely adopted by the community and provide similar solutions to the problems they purport to solve. Knowing this, we might ask the following:

- Why was Flutter created?
- Do we really need it?
- How it is better than rival frameworks?

Let's check out how Flutter works and answer some of these questions before we get our hands on it.

# The problems Flutter wants to solve

Since the beginning of the Flutter framework, it was intended to provide a better experience to the user through high-performance execution, but that's not the only promise of Flutter. The development experience was also focused on addressing some of the problems of multiple platform mobile development:

- **Long/more expensive development cycles**: To be able to cope with market demand, you must choose to build for a single platform, or create multiple teams. This has some consequences in terms of cost, multiple deadlines, and different capabilities of native frameworks.

- **Multiple languages to learn**: If a developer wants to develop for multiple platforms, they must learn how to do something in one OS and programming language, and later, the same thing on another OS and programming language. This certainly impacts in the developer's productive time.
- **Long build/compile time**: Some developers may already have experienced how build time may have an impact on productivity. In Android, for example, some developers experience multiple long build times after a few minutes of coding (this is evolving, and it's a lot better now, but it was already causing a lot of pain).
- **Existing cross-platform solutions side effects**: You adopt an existing cross-platform framework (that is, React Native, Xamarin, Ionic, Cordova) in an attempt to work around the preceding problems, but with that come some side effects, such as a performance impact, a design impact, or a user experience impact.

Now let's see how Flutter counters these problems.

# Differences between existing frameworks

There are a large number of high-quality and well-accepted frameworks and technologies. Some of them are as follows:

- Xamarin
- React Native
- Ionic
- Cordova

So, you might think it's hard for a new framework to find its place on an already full field, but it's not. Flutter has benefits that make space for itself, not necessarily by overcoming the other frameworks, but by already being at least on the same level as native frameworks:

- High performance
- Full control of the user interface
- Dart language
- Being backed by Google
- Open source framework
- Developer resources and tooling

Let's look at each of these in more detail.

# High performance

Right now, it is hard to say that Flutter's performance is always better than all of the other frameworks in practice, but it's safe to say that its aim is to be. For example, its rendering layer was developed with a high frame rate in mind. As we will see in the *Flutter rendering* section, some of the existing frameworks rely on JavaScript and HTML rendering, which might cause overheads in performance because everything is drawn in a webview (a visual component like a web browser). Some use **Original Equipment Manufacturer (OEM)** widgets but rely on a bridge to request the OS API to render the components, which creates a bottleneck in the application because it needs an extra step to render the **user interface (UI)**.

 See the *"Flutter Rendering "* section form more details of Flutter rendering approach compared to others.

Some points that make Flutter's performance great:

- **Flutter owns the pixels**: Flutter renders the application pixel by pixel (see next section), interacting directly with the **Skia** graphics engine.
- **No extra layers or additional OS API calls:** As Flutter owns the app rendering, it he does not need additional calls to use the OEM widgets, so no bottleneck.
- **Flutter is compiled to native code**: Flutter uses the Dart AOT compiler to produce native code. That means there's no overhead in setting up an environment to interpret Dart code on the fly, and it runs just like a native app, starting more quickly than frameworks that need some kind of interpreter.

# Full control of the UI

The Flutter framework chooses to do all the UI by itself rendering the visual components directly to the canvas, as we have seen previously, requiring nothing more than the canvas from the platform so it's not limited by rules and conventions. Most of the time, frameworks just reproduce what the platform offers in another way. For example, other webview-based cross-platform frameworks reproduce visual components using HTML elements with CSS styling. Other frameworks emulate the creation of the visual components and pass them to the device platform, which will render the OEM widgets like a natively developed app. We are not talking about performance here, so what else does Flutter offer by not using the OEM widgets and doing the job all by itself?

Let's see:

- **Ruling all the pixels on the device**: Frameworks limited by OEM widgets will reproduce at most what a native developed app would, as they use only the platform's available components. On the other hand, frameworks based on web technologies may reproduce more than platform-specific components, but may also be limited by the mobile web engine available on the device. By getting the control of the UI rendering, Flutter allows the developer to create the UI in their own way by exposing an extensible and rich Widgets API, which provides tools that can be used to create a unique UI with no drawbacks in performance and no limits in design.

- **Platform UI kits**: By not using OEM widgets, Flutter can break the platform design, but it does not. Flutter is equipped with packages that provide platform design widgets, the Material set in Android, and **Cupertino** in iOS.

> We will see more on platform UI Kits in `Chapter 4`, *Widgets: Building Layouts in Flutter*.

- **Achievable UI Design requirements**: Flutter provides a clean and robust API with the ability to reproduce layouts that are faithful to the design requirements. Unlike web-based frameworks that rely on CSS layout rules that can be large and complicated and even conflicting, Flutter simplifies this by adding semantic rules that can be used to make to complex but efficient and beautiful layouts.
- **Smoother look and feel**: In addition to native widget kits, Flutter seeks to provide a native platform experience where the application is running, so fonts, gestures, and interactions are implemented in a platform-specific way, bringing a natural feel the user, like a native application.

> We refer to visual components as widgets. This is also the way Flutter calls them. We will discuss more about that in the *Widgets introduction* section in this chapter.

Now let's dig deep into Dart.

# Dart

Since its inception, one of Flutter's main goals was to be a high-performance alternative to existing cross-platform frameworks. But not only that; to significantly improve the mobile developer's experience was one of the crucial points of the project.

With this in mind, Flutter needed a programming language that allowed it to accomplish these goals, and Dart seems to be the perfect match to the framework for the following reasons:

- **Dart AOT and JIT compilation**: Dart is flexible enough to provide different ways of running the code, so Flutter uses Dart AOT with performance in mind when compiling a *release* version of the application, and it uses JIT with sub-second compilation of code in development time, aiming for fast workflows and code changes.

 Dart Just in time compilation (JIT) and Ahead of time (AOT) refers to when the compilation phase takes place. In AOT, code is compiled before running. In JIT, code is compiled while running. (Check out the *Dart introduction* section in the first chapter).

- **High performance:** Due to Dart's support for AOT compilation, Flutter does not require a slow bridge between realms (for example, non-native to native), which makes Flutter apps also start up much more quickly. Also, Flutter uses a functional-style flow with short-lived objects, and this means a lot of short-lived allocations. Dart garbage collection works without locks, helping with fast allocation.

- **Easy learning:** Dart is a flexible, robust, modern, and advanced language. Although it's still evolving, the language has a well-defined object-oriented framework with familiar functionalities to dynamic and static languages, an active community, and well-structured documentation.

- **Declarative UI**: In Flutter, we use a **declarative** style to lay out widgets, what means that widgets are immutable from and are only lightweight "blueprints". To change the UI, a Widget triggers a rebuild on itself and its subtree. In the opposite **imperative** style (the most common), we can change specific component properties after they are created.

**Note**: Take a look at the official introduction to declarative UI from Flutter: `https://flutter.dev/docs/get-started/flutter-for/declarative`

- **Dart syntax to layout:** Different from many frameworks that have a separate syntax for layout, in Flutter, the layout is created writing Dart code, aiming for greater flexibility and ease to create a developer environment, with tools for debugging layout rendering performance, for example.

Dart and Flutter are developed by Google, and this is important, as we will see.

# Being backed by Google

Flutter is a brand new framework, and this means that it does not have a big section of the mobile development market yet, but this is changing, and the outlook for the next few years is highly positive.

Being backed by Google, the framework has all the tools it needs to succeed in the community, with support from the Google team, presence at big events such as Google IO, and investments into continuous improvement in the code base. From the launch of the third Beta version at Google IO 2018 to the first stable release launched during the *Flutter Live Event* at the end of 2018, its growth is evident:

- More than 200 million users of Flutter apps.
- More than 3,000 Flutter apps on the Play Store.
- More than 250,000 new developers.
- The 34th most popular software repository on GitHub—it was in the *Top 15* **at the beginning of 2019**.

## Fuchsia OS and Flutter

It's not a secret anymore that Google is working on its new Fuchsia OS as a replacement for the Android OS. One thing to pay attention to is that Fuchsia OS may be a universal Google system to run on more just than mobile phones, and this directly affects Flutter adoption. This is because Flutter will be the first method of developing mobile apps for the new Fuchsia OS, and, not only this, the UI of the system is being developed with it. With the system targeting more devices than just smartphones, as seems to be the case, Flutter will certainly have a lot of improvements.

The growth of the framework's adoption is directly related to the new Fuchsia OS. As it gets closer to launch, it is important for Google to have mobile apps targeting the new system. For example, Google has announced that Android apps will be compatible with the new OS, making the transition to and adoption of Flutter significantly easier.

# Open source framework

Having a big company such as Google behind it is fundamental to a framework such as Flutter (see React, for example, which is maintained by Facebook). In addition, community support becomes even more important as it becomes more popular.

By being open source, the community and Google can work together to:

- Help with bug fixes and documentation through code collaboration
- Create new educational content about the framework
- Support documentation and usage
- Make improvement decisions based on real feedback

Improving the developer experience is one of the main goals of the framework. Therefore, in addition to being close to the community, the framework provides great tools and resources for developers. Let's see them.

# Developer resources and tooling

The focus on developers in the Flutter framework goes from documentation and learning resources to providing tools to helping with productivity:

- **Documentation and learning resources**: Flutter websites are rich for developers coming from other platforms, including many examples and use cases, for example, the famous Google Codelabs (`https://codelabs.developers.google.com/?cat=Flutter`).

- **Command-line tools and IDE integration**: Dart tools that help with analyzing, running, and managing dependencies are also part of Flutter. Besides that, Flutter also has commands to help with debugging, deploying, inspecting layout rendering and integration with IDEs through Dart plugins. Here's a list of the various commands:

```
                          🏠 biessek — -bash — 80×31

Available commands:
  analyze                 Analyze the project's Dart code.
  attach                  Attach to a running application.
  bash-completion         Output command line shell completion setup scripts.
  build                   Flutter build commands.
  channel                 List or switch flutter channels.
  clean                   Delete the build/ directory.
  config                  Configure Flutter settings.
  create                  Create a new Flutter project.
  devices                 List all connected devices.
  doctor                  Show information about the installed tooling.
  drive                   Runs Flutter Driver tests for the current project.
  emulators               List, launch and create emulators.
  format                  Format one or more dart files.
  help                    Display help information for flutter.
  install                 Install a Flutter app on an attached device.
  logs                    Show log output for running Flutter apps.
  make-host-app-editable  Moves host apps from generated directories to
                          non-generated directories so that they can be edited
                          by developers.
  packages                Commands for managing Flutter packages.
  precache                Populates the Flutter tool's cache of binary
                          artifacts.
  run                     Run your Flutter app on an attached device.
  screenshot              Take a screenshot from a connected device.
  stop                    Stop your Flutter app on an attached device.
  test                    Run Flutter unit tests for the current project.
  trace                   Start and stop tracing for a running Flutter app.
  upgrade                 Upgrade your copy of Flutter.
```

- **Easy start**: Flutter comes with the **flutter doctor** tool, which is a command-line tool that guides the developer through the system setup by indicating what is needed in order to be ready to set up a Flutter environment. This is what it looks like:

```
● ● ●                    ⌂ biessek — -bash — 80×24
[Alessandros-iMac:~ biessek$ flutter doctor

    ┌──────────────────────────────────────────────────────────────────┐
    │ A new version of Flutter is available!                           │
    │                                                                  │
    │ To update to the latest version, run "flutter upgrade".          │
    └──────────────────────────────────────────────────────────────────┘


Doctor summary (to see all details, run flutter doctor -v):
[✓] Flutter (Channel beta, v0.11.3, on Mac OS X 10.13 17A365, locale en-BR)
[✓] Android toolchain - develop for Android devices (Android SDK 27.0.3)
[✓] iOS toolchain - develop for iOS devices (Xcode 9.2)
[✓] Android Studio (version 3.1)
[!] Connected device
    ! No devices available

! Doctor found issues in 1 category.
Alessandros-iMac:~ biessek$ █
```

The flutter doctor command also identifies connected devices and whether there are any upgrades available, as you can see.

- **Hot reload**: This is the feature that has been taking the focus in presentations about the framework. By combining the capabilities of the Dart language (such as JIT compilation) and the power of Flutter, it is possible for the developer to instantly see design changes made to code in the simulator or device. In Flutter, there is no specific tool for layout preview. Hot reload makes it unnecessary.

Now that we have learned about the benefits of Flutters, let's start looking at the software's compilations.

# Flutter compilation (Dart)

The way an application is built is fundamental to how it will perform on the target platform. This is an important step regarding performance. Even though you do not necessarily need to know this for every kind of application, knowing how the application is built helps you to understand and measure possible improvements.

As we've already pointed out, Flutter relies on the AOT compilation of Dart for release mode and the JIT compilation of Dart for development/debug mode. Dart is one of very few languages that's capable of being compiled to both AOT and JIT, and for Flutter this is great.

# Development compilation

During development, Flutter uses JIT compilation in development mode. This enables important development features such as hot reload, the feature mentioned in the preceding section. Due to the power of Dart's compiler, interactions between the code and the simulator/device are really fast, and debugging info helps developers step into the source code.

# Release compilation

In release mode, debugging information is not necessary, and the focus is performance. Flutter uses a technique that's common to game engines. By using AOT mode, Dart code is compiled to native code, and the app loads the Flutter library and delegates rendering, input, and event handling to it by using the Skia engine.

# Supported platforms

By now, Flutter supports ARM Android devices running at least on Jelly Bean 4.1.x version, and iOS devices from iPhone 4S or newer. Of course, Flutter apps can normally be run on simulators.

Google is intending to port the Flutter runtime to the web by using the Dart capability of compiling to JavaScript. Initially called **Hummingbird**, this project now is known as "Flutter for web".

We are not going to go into more detail on Flutter's compilation aspects as they are beyond the scope of this book. For more information, you can read https://flutter.dev/docs/resources/faq#how-does-flutter-run-my-code-on-android and https://flutter.dev/docs/resources/faq#how-does-flutter-run-my-code-on-ios.

# Flutter rendering

One of the main aspects that makes Flutter unique is the way that it draws the visual components to the screen. The big difference is how the application communicates with the platform's SDK, what it asks the SDK to do, and what it does by itself:

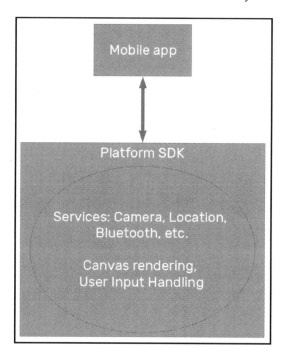

The platform SDK can be seen as the interface between applications and the operation system and services. Each system provides its own SDK with its own capabilities and is based on a programming language (that is, Kotlin/Java for the Android SDK and Swift/Objective C for the iOS SDK). We have looked at some rendering approaches used by different frameworks previously; let's take a more detailed look at them now.

# Web-based technologies

We have already seen frameworks that use webviews to reproduce a UI by combining HTML and CSS. In terms of platform usage, it would look like this:

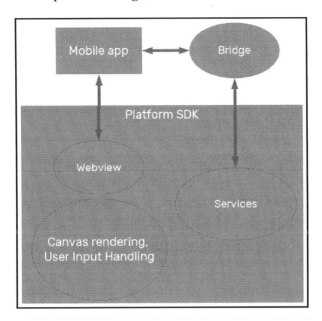

The application does not know how the rendering is done by the platform; the only thing it needs is the webview widget on which it will render the HTML and CSS code.

 Besides the rendering part, there is small point to notice, which is that to access system APIs, JavaScript code needs a bridge for calling native code, causing a small overhead in performance.

# Framework and OEM widgets

Another way of rendering widgets is by adding a layer above the platform widgets, but not changing the way the system renders visual components effectively:

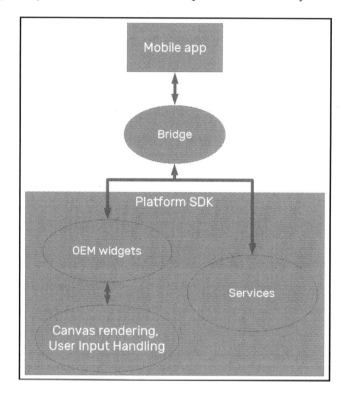

In this mode of rendering, the work is done by the SDK like a normal native app, but before it, the layout is defined by an additional step in the framework language. Every change in the UI causes communication between the application code and the native code that's responsible for calling the platform's SDK, working like an intermediary. Like the previous technique, it may cause a small overhead for the application, maybe a little bit bigger than the previous one, because rendering occurs often, and therefore so does the communication.

# Flutter – rendering by itself

Flutter chooses to do all the hard work by itself. The only thing it needs from the platform's SDK is access to **Services** APIs and a canvas to draw the UI on:

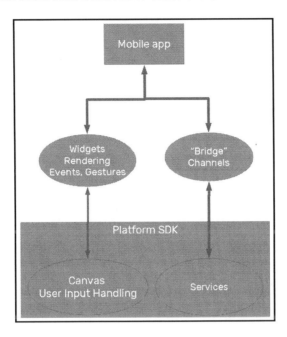

Flutter moves the widgets and rendering to the app, from where it gets the customization and extensibility. Through a canvas, it can draw anything and also access events to handle user inputs and gestures by itself. The bridge in Flutter is done by platform channels, which we will see in more detail in `Chapter 13`, *Improving User Experience*.

# Widgets introduction

Understanding Flutter widgets is essential if you want to work with it. You know Flutter takes control of rendering and does this with extensibility and customization in mind, intending to add power to the developer's hands. Let's see how Flutter applies the widgets idea in app development to create awesome UIs.

Widgets can be understood as the visual (but not only that) representation of parts of the application. Many widgets are put together to compose the UI of an application. Imagine it as a puzzle in which you define the pieces.

The intention of widgets is to provide a way for your application be modular, scalable, and expressive with less code and without imposing limitations. The main characteristics of the widgets UI in Flutter are composability and immutability.

# Composability

Flutter chooses composition over inheritance, with the goal of keeping each widget simple and with a well-defined purpose. Meeting one of the framework's goals, flexibility, Flutter allows the developer to make many combinations to achieve incredible results.

# Immutability

Flutter is based on the reactive style of programming, where the widget instances are short-lived and change their descriptions (whether visually or not) based on configuration changes, so it reacts to changes and propagates these changes to its composing widgets, and so on.

A Flutter widget may have a state associated with it, and when the associated state changes, it can be rebuilt to match the representation.

The terms *state* and *reactive* are well known in the React style of programming, disseminated by Facebook's famous React library.

# Everything is a widget

Flutter widgets are everywhere in an application. Maybe not everything is a widget, but almost everything is. Even the app is a widget in Flutter, and that's why this concept is so important. A widget represents a part of a UI, but it does not mean it's only something that is visible. It can be any of the following:

- A visual/structural element that is a basic structural element, such as the `Button` or `Text` widgets
- A layout specific element that may define the position, margins, or padding, such as the `Padding` widget
- A style element that may help to colorize and theme a visual/structural element, such as the `Theme` widget
- An interaction element that helps to respond to interactions in different ways, such as the `GestureDetector` widget

We will be checking out usage examples of these widgets in the following chapter.

Widgets are the basic building blocks of an interface. To build a UI properly, Flutter organizes the widgets in a widget tree.

## The widget tree

This is another important concept in Flutter layouts. It's where widgets come to life. The widget tree is the logical representation of all the UIs widgets. It is computed during *layout* (measurements and structural info) and used during *rendering* (frame to screen) and *hit testing* (touch interactions), and this is the things Flutter does best. By using a lot of optimization algorithms, it tries to manipulate the tree as little as possible, reducing the total amount of work spent on rendering, aiming for greater efficiency:

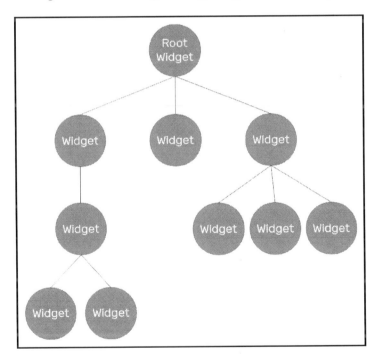

Widgets are represented in the tree as nodes. It may have a state associated with it; every change to its state results in rebuilding the widget and the child involved.

As you can see, the tree's child structure is not static, and it's defined by the widgets' description. The children relations in widgets are what makes the UI tree; it exists by composition, so it's common to see Flutter's built-in widgets exposing `child` or `children` properties, depending on the purpose of the widget.

The widget tree does not work alone in the framework. It has the help of the element tree; a tree that relates to the widget tree by representing the built widget on the screen, so every widget will have a corresponding element in the element tree after it is built.

The element tree has an important task in Flutter. It helps to map on-screen elements to the widget tree. Also, it determines how widget rebuilding is done in update scenarios. When a widget changes and needs to be rebuilt, this will cause an update on the corresponding element. The element stores the type of the corresponding widget and a reference to its children elements. In the case of repositioning, for example, a widget, the element will check the type of the corresponding new widget, and in a match it will update itself with the new widget description.

 The element tree can be seen as a prerender auxiliary tree to the widget tree. If you need more information on that, you can check the official docs: `https://docs.flutter.io/flutter/widgets/Element-class.html`.

# Hello Flutter

It's time to start getting our hands dirty with some code. With the Flutter development environment configured, we can start using Flutter commands. The typical way to start a Flutter project is to run the following command:

```
flutter create <output_directory>
```

Here, `output_directory` will be also the Flutter project name if you do not specify it as an argument.

By running the preceding command, the folder with the provided name will be generated with a sample Flutter project in it. We will analyze the project in few moments. First, it is good to know that there are some useful options to manipulate the resulting project from the `flutter create` command. The main ones are as follows:

- `--org`: This can be used to change the owner organization of the project. If you already know Android or iOS development, this is the reverse domain name, and is used to identify package names on Android and as a prefix in the iOS bundle identifier. The default value is `com.example`.
- `-s , --sample`: Most of the official examples for widget usage have a unique ID that you can use to quickly clone the example to your machine with this argument.

- Whenever you are exploring the Flutter docs website (`https://docs.flutter.dev`), you can take a sample ID from it and use it with this argument.

- `-i, --ios-language` and `-a, --android-language`: These are used to specify the language for the native part code of the project, and are only used if you plan to write native platform code. In `Chapter 13`, *Improving User Experience*, we will see how to add native code to the project.
- `--project-name`: Use this to change the project's name. It must be a valid Dart package identifier, as we have already seen on the `pubspec` format description page (`https://dart.dev/tools/pub/pubspec`):

  *"Package names should be all lowercase, with underscores to separate words, `just_like_this`. Use only basic Latin letters and Arabic digits: [a-z0-9_]. Also, make sure the name is a valid Dart identifier – that it doesn't start with digits and isn't a reserved word."*

- If you do not specify this parameter, it tries to use the same name as `output directory`. Note that this argument must be the last in the list of arguments provided.

Let's see a typical Flutter project structure created with the preceding command, `flutter create hello_world`:

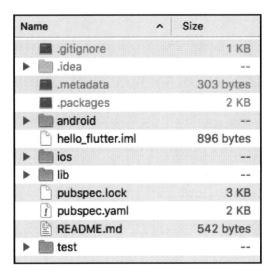

If you are thinking this looks similar to Dart packages, you might have a point. Flutter projects are a kind of Dart package, with some peculiarities, of course. Listing the basic structure elements, we get the following:

- `android/ios`: This contains the platform-specific codes. If you already know the Android project structure from Android Studio, there is no surprise here. The same goes for XCode iOS projects.

- `hello_flutter.iml`: This is a typical IntelliJ project file, which contains the `JAVA_MODULE` information used by the IDE.

- `lib` directory: This is the main folder of a Flutter application; the generated project should contains at least a `main.dart` file to start work on. We will be checking this file in detail in a few steps.

- `pubspec.yaml` and `pubspec.lock`: If you remember Chapter 2, *Intermediate Dart Programming*, this `pubspec.yaml` file is what defines a Dart package. That's what is happening here, and this is one of the main files of the project, where you list the application dependencies and in Flutter's case more than that. We will be looking at this in more details in Chapter 4, *Widgets: Building Layouts in Flutter*.

- README.md: This file typically has a description of the project, and it is very common in open source projects.
- test directory: This contains all the test-related files of the project. Here, we can add unit tests, like we have seen before, and also widget tests by using Flutter-specific packages.

In most of this book, we use command-line tools directly from the Terminal. Plus, for information purposes, the IDE used is Visual Studio Code. Remember, the IDEs use these tools behind the scenes to interact with the project.

# pubspec file

The pubspec file in Flutter is similar to a simple Dart package. Besides that, it contains an additional section for configurations specific to Flutter. Let's see the pubspec.yaml file's contents in details:

```
name: hello_flutter
description: A new Flutter project.
version: 1.0.0+1
```

The beginning of the file is simple. As we already know, the name property is defined when we execute the pub create command, followed by the default project description.

You can specify the description during the flutter create command by using the --description argument.

The version property follows the Dart package conventions: the version number, plus an optional build version number separated by +. In addition to that, Flutter allows you to override these values during the build. We will take a more detailed look at that in Chapter 12, *Testing, Debugging, and Deployment*, in the *App deployment* section.

Then we have the dependencies section of the pubspec file:

```
environment:
  sdk: ">=2.0.0-dev.68.0 <3.0.0"

dependencies:
  flutter:
    sdk: flutter
```

```
# The following adds the Cupertino Icons font to your application.
# Use with the CupertinoIcons class for iOS style icons.
cupertino_icons: ^0.1.2

dev_dependencies:
  flutter_test:
    sdk: flutter
```

Now, have a look at the explanation of the preceding code:

- We start with the `environment` property with the Dart SDK version constraints defined. You are OK to use the version provided by the tool because it's followed by the Flutter SDK updates as well.

 The Dart SDK comes embedded in the Flutter SDK, so you do not have to install them separately.

- Then we have the `dependencies` property, which starts with the main dependency of a Flutter application, the Flutter SDK itself, which contains many of Flutter's core packages.
- As an additional dependency, the generator adds the `cupertino_icons` package, which contains icon assets used by the built-in Flutter Cupertino widgets (there's more on that in the next chapter).
- The `dev_dependencies` property contains only the `flutter_test` package dependency provided by the Flutter SDK itself, and contains Flutter-specific extensions to the already-known Dart `test` package.

In the final block of the file, there's a dedicated `flutter` section:

```
flutter:

  uses-material-design: true

  # To add assets to your application, add an assets section, like this:
  # assets:
  #   - images/a_dot_burr.jpeg
  #   - images/a_dot_ham.jpeg
  # ...
  # To add custom fonts to your application, add a fonts section here,
  # fonts:
  #   - family: Schyler
  #     fonts:
  #       - asset: fonts/Schyler-Regular.ttf
```

```
#            - asset: fonts/Schyler-Italic.ttf
#              style: italic
#
```

This `flutter` section allows us to configure resources that are bundled in the application to be used during runtime, such as `images`, a `fonts`, and a JSON file, typically, any non-source code file that helps in the app's composition:

- `uses-material-design`: We will see the Material widgets provided by Flutter in the next chapter. In addition to them, we can use also Material Design icons (`https://material.io/tools/icons/?style=baseline`), which are in a custom font format. For this to work properly, we need to activate this property (set it to `true`) so the icons are included in the application.

- `assets`: This property is used to list the resource paths that will be bundled with the final application. Check the following code for more details on how to use it. The `assets` files can be organized in any way; what matters for Flutter is the path of the files. You specify the path of the file relative to the project's root. This is used later in Dart code when you need to refer to an asset file. Here's an example:

```
assets:
  - images/home_background.jpeg
```

To add an image to be used later, we add the path in the `assets` list, or if we want to add all files inside the directory, we just specify the directory path:

```
assets:
  - images/
```

This includes all files inside the directory. Note the / character at the end.

- `fonts`: This property allows us to add custom fonts to the application. There's more on that in Chapter 6, *Theming and Styling*, in the *Custom fonts* section.

 We will be checking how to load different assets in the course of the book whenever we need to. Also, you can read more on asset specification details on the Flutter docs website: `https://flutter.io/docs/development/ui/assets-and-images`.

# Running the generated project

The generated project uses the default Flutter template to create the project. This application has a counter to demonstrate the React style of programming in Flutter. We will be checking the details in the next chapter, when we talk about the different widgets that we can use to compose our application. In the `hello_flutter` example we created earlier using the `flutter create` command, `MyApp` is the root widget of the application.

## lib/main.dart file

The main file of the generated project is the entry point of the Flutter application:

```
void main() => runApp(MyApp());
```

The `main` function by itself is the Dart entry point of an application. What makes the Flutter application take the scene is the `runApp` function called by passing a widget as a parameter, which will be the root widget of the application (the application itself).

## Flutter run

To execute a Flutter application, we must have a connected device or simulator. The check is done by using the already-known `flutter doctor` and `flutter emulators` tools. The following command lets you know the existing Android and iOS emulators that can be used to run the project:

```
flutter emulators
```

You will get something similar to the following screenshot:

```
● ● ●                 hello_flutter — -bash — 80×24
[Alessandros-iMac:hello_flutter biessek$ flutter emulators
1 available emulator:

apple_ios_simulator • iOS Simulator • Apple

To run an emulator, run 'flutter emulators --launch <emulator id>'.
To create a new emulator, run 'flutter emulators --create [--name xyz]'.

You can find more information on managing emulators at the links below:
   https://developer.android.com/studio/run/managing-avds
   https://developer.android.com/studio/command-line/avdmanager
Alessandros-iMac:hello_flutter biessek$ ▊
```

You can check how to manage your Android emulators on `https://developer.android.com/studio/run/managing-avds`. For iOS device simulators, you should use the XCode Simulator developer tool. There's more information on the Apple documentation website (`https://developer.apple.com/library/archive/documentation/IDEs/Conceptual/iOS_Simulator_Guide/GettingStartedwithiOSSimulator/GettingStartedwithiOSSimulator.html`).

After asserting that we have a device connected that can run the app, we can use the following command:

```
flutter run
```

Refer to the following screenshot:

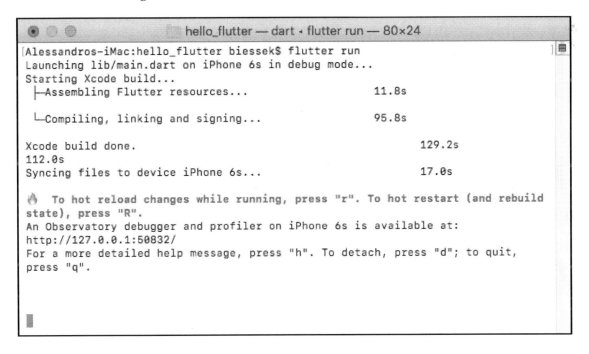

This command starts the debugger and makes the hot reload functionality available, as you can see. The first time the application is run might take a little longer than subsequent executions:

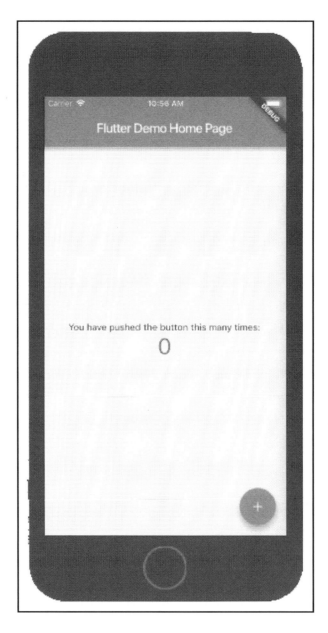

The application is up and running; you can see a debug mark in the top-right corner. That means it's not a release version running, as you already know; this is the development version of the app, with hot reload and debug facilities.

 The preceding example was run on an iPhone 6s simulator. The same result would be achieved by using an Android emulator, or an **Android virtual device (AVD)**.

# Summary

In this chapter, we finally started playing with the Flutter framework. First, we learned some important concepts about Flutter, mainly the concepts of widgets. We saw that widgets are the central part of the Flutter world, where the Flutter team continually works to improve existing widgets and add new ones. This is because the widget concept is everywhere, from rendering performance to the final result on screen.

We also saw how to start a Flutter application project with the framework tools, the basic project structure of files, and the peculiarities of the `pubspec` file. At the end, we saw how to run a project on an emulator.

 You can find the source code for this chapter on GitHub.

In the next chapter, we will delve deeper into types of widgets, such as stateful and stateless, and how and when they can be used. Also, we will learn about the built-in widgets and start a Flutter application project that we will follow for the rest of the book, in which we will cumulatively apply the knowledge acquired in each chapter.

# 2
# Section 2: The Flutter User Interface - Everything is a Widget

In this section, you will learn about the Flutter way of working with the UI, user data input, and the resources available to create rich UIs.

In this section, we will cover the following chapters:

- Chapter 4, *Widgets: Building Layouts in Flutter*
- Chapter 5, *Handling User Input and Gestures*
- Chapter 6, *Theming and Styling*
- Chapter 7, *Routing: Navigating between Screens*

# 4

# Widgets: Building Layouts in Flutter

In this chapter, you will learn about the central concepts of widgets, the differences between stateless and stateful widgets, the most common widgets in Flutter and how to add them to your application, and how to create complete interfaces from built-in widgets or custom widgets developed by yourself.

The following topics will be covered in this chapter:

- Stateful/stateless widgets
- Built-in widgets
- Understanding built-in layout widgets
- Creating custom widgets

## Stateful versus stateless widgets

From Chapter 3, *An Introduction to Flutter*, we have seen that widgets play an important role in Flutter application development. They are the pieces that form the UI; they are the code representation of what is visible to the user.

UIs are almost never static; they change frequently, as you know. Although immutable by definition, widgets are not meant to be final – after all, we are dealing with a UI, and a UI will certainly change during the life cycle of any application. That's why Flutter provides us with two types of widgets: stateless and stateful.

The big difference between these is in the way the widget is *built*. It's the developer's responsibility to choose which kind of widget to use in each situation to compose the UI in order to make the most of the power in the widget rendering layer of Flutter.

Flutter also has the concept of **inherited** widgets (the `InheritedWidget` type), which is also a kind of widget but is a little bit different from the other two types that we've mentioned. We will check it out after we've explored the `hello_flutter` example from `Chapter 3`, *An Introduction to Flutter*, in detail.

# Stateless widgets

A typical UI will be composed of many widgets, and some of them will never change their properties after being instantiated. They do not have a *state*; that is, they do not change by themselves through some internal action or behavior. Instead, they are changed by external events on parent widgets in the widgets tree. So, it's safe to say that stateless widgets give control of how they are built to some parent widget in the tree. The following is a representation of a stateless widget:

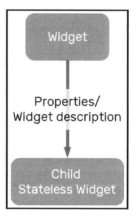

So, the child widget will receive its description from the parent widget and will not change it by itself. In terms of code, this means that stateless widgets have only `final` properties defined during construction, and that's the only thing that needs to be built on the device screen.

 We will be exploring the source code in detail in a moment, when we take the default generated Flutter project from the Flutter create tool used in the previous chapter.

# Stateful widgets

Unlike stateless widgets, which receive a description from their parents that persist during the widgets' lifetime, stateful widgets are meant to change their descriptions dynamically during their lifetimes. By definition, stateful widgets are also immutable, but they have a company `State` class that represents the current state of the widget. It is shown in the following diagram:

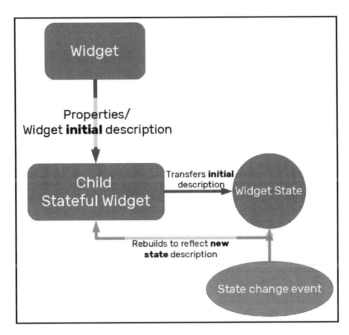

By holding the state of the widget in a separate `State` object, the framework may rebuild it whenever needed without losing its current associated state. The element in the elements tree holds a reference of the corresponding widget and also the `State` object associated with it. The `State` object will notify when the widget needs to be rebuilt and then cause an update in the elements tree, too.

# Stateful and stateless widgets in code

In the previous chapter, we generated a Flutter project by using the following command:

```
flutter create
```

That project was created with the default arguments from the default Flutter template, yielding a small application with a counter that shows the number of times the plus (+) button has been tapped:

The Flutter demo application from the preceding screenshot is useful for showing both widget types in practice.

# Stateless widget in code

Let's start by looking at stateless widgets in code. The very first stateless widget in the application is the application class itself:

```
class MyApp extends statelessWidget {
  @override
  Widget build(BuildContext context) {
    return MaterialApp(
      title: 'Flutter Demo',
      theme: ThemeData(
        primarySwatch: Colors.blue,
      ),
      home: MyHomePage(title: 'Flutter Demo Home Page'),
    );
  }
}
```

As you can see, the MyApp class extends statelessWidget and overrides the build(BuildContext) method. This method describes a UI part; that is, it builds the widgets subtree *below* it. In the preceding case, MyApp is the root of the widget tree and, therefore, it builds all the widgets down the tree. In this case, its direct child is MaterialApp. According to the documentation, this is defined as follows:

> *"A convenience widget that wraps a number of widgets that are commonly required for material design applications."*

BuildContext is an argument provided to the build method as a useful way to interact with the widget tree that allows to access important ancestral information that helps to describe the widget being built. Remember, the description depends only on this contextual information and the widget properties defined in the constructor.

 We will look at material design widgets in detail soon, when we explore the available built-in widgets, and also in Chapter 6, *Theming and Styling*.

In addition to other properties, MaterialApp contains the home property, which specifies the first widget displayed as the home page of the application. Here, home is the MyHomePage widget, which is the stateful widget of this example.

By using the `Navigator` class, `MaterialApp` allows you to define widgets to be displayed for specific routes with a logical history of navigation, by managing the back stack (we will be checking out routes and page navigation in `Chapter 7`, *Routing: Navigating between Screens*).

## Stateful widgets in code

`MyHomePage` is a stateful widget, and so it is defined with a `State` object, `_MyHomePageState`, which contains properties that affect how the widget looks:

```
class MyHomePage extends statefulWidget {
  MyHomePage({Key key, this.title}) : super(key: key);
  final String title;

  @override
  _MyHomePageState createState() => _MyHomePageState();
}
```

By extending `statefulWidget`, `MyHomePage` must return a valid `State` object in its `createState()` method. In our example, it returns an instance of `_MyHomePageState`.

Normally, stateful widgets define their corresponding `State` classes in the same file. Also, state is typically private to the widget library, as external clients do not need to interact with it directly.

The following `_MyHomePageState` class represents the `State` object of the `MyHomePage` widget:

```
class _MyHomePageState extends State<MyHomePage> {
  int _counter = 0;

  void _incrementCounter() {
    setState(() {
      _counter++;
    });
  }

  @override
  Widget build(BuildContext context) {
    return Scaffold(
      appBar: AppBar(
        title: Text(widget.title),
      ),
      body: Center(
```

```
        child: Column(
          mainAxisAlignment: MainAxisAlignment.center,
          children: <Widget>[
            Text(
              'You have pushed the button this many times:',
            ),
            Text(
              '$_counter',
              style: Theme.of(context).textTheme.display1,
            ),
          ],
        ),
      ),
      floatingActionButton: FloatingActionButton(
        onPressed: _incrementCounter,
        tooltip: 'Increment',
        child: Icon(Icons.add),
      ), // This trailing comma makes auto-formatting nicer.
    );
  }
}
```

A valid widget state is a class that extends the framework `State` class, which is defined in the documentation as follows:

> *"The logic and internal state for a statefulWidget."*

The state of the `MyHomePage` widget is defined by a single property, `_counter`. The `_counter` property retains the number of presses of the increment button at the bottom-right corner of the screen. This time, the `State` widget'sdescendant class is responsible for building the widget. It is composed of a `Text` widget that displays the `_counter` value.

 `Text` is a built-in widget used to display text on the screen. More on built-in widgets will be covered in the next section.

A stateful widget is meant to change its appearance during its lifetime – that is, what defines it will change – and so it needs to be rebuilt to reflect such changes. Here, the change occurs in the `_incementCounter()` method, which is called every time the increment button is tapped.

Notice the usage of the onPressed property of the FloatingActionButton widget. FloatingActionButton is the material design floating action button, and this property receives a function callback that will be executed on press:

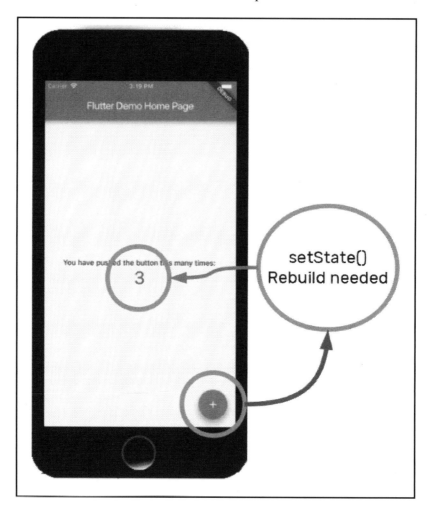

Flutter Demo Home Page (This is an image of Flutter Demo Home Page. The other (overlapped) information is not important here

How does the framework know when something in the widget changes and it needs to rebuild it? setState is the answer. This method receives a function as a parameter where you should update the widget's corresponding State (that is, the _incrementCounter method). By calling setState, the framework is notified that it needs to rebuild the widget. In the previous example, it is called to reflect the new value of the _counter property.

# Inherited widgets

Besides statelessWidget and statefulWidget, there is one more type of widget in the Flutter framework, InheritedWidget. Sometimes, one widget may need to have access to data up the tree, and in such a case, we would need to replicate the information down to the interested widget. This process is shown in the following diagram:

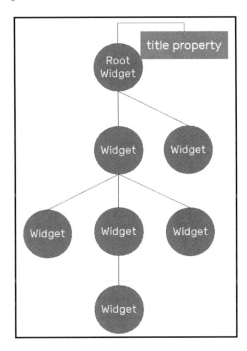

Let's suppose some of the widgets down the tree need to access the title property from the root widget. To do that, with statelessWidget or statefulWidget, we would need to replicate the property in the corresponding widgets and pass it down through the constructor. It can be annoying to replicate the property on all child widgets so that the value reaches the interested widget.

To address this problem, Flutter provides the `InheritedWidget` class, an auxiliary kind of widget that helps to propagate information down the tree as shown in the following diagram:

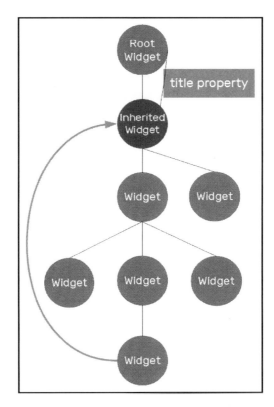

By adding a `InheritedWidget` to the tree, any widget below it can access the data it exposes by using the `inheritFromWidgetOfExactType(InheritedWidget)` method of `BuildContext` class that receives an `InheritedWidget` type as parameter and uses the tree to find the first ancestral widget of the requested type.

There are some very common appearances of the usage of `InheritedWidget` in Flutter. One of the most common uses is from the `Theme` class, which helps to describe colors for a whole application. We will look at it in `Chapter 5`, *Handling User Input and Gestures*.

# Widget key property

If you take a look at both constructors of `statelessWidget` and `statefulWidget` classes, you will notice a parameter named `key`. This is an important property for widgets in Flutter. It helps in the rendering from the widgets tree to the element tree. Besides the type and a reference to the corresponding widget, this element also holds the key that identifies the widget in the tree. The `key` property helps to preserve the state of a widget between rebuilds. The most common usage of `key` is when we are dealing with collections of widgets that have the same type; so, without keys, the element tree would not know which state corresponds to which widget, as they would all have the same type. For example, whenever a widget changes its position or level in the widgets tree, matching is done in the elements tree to see what needs to be updated in the screen to reflect the new widget structure. When a widget has a state, it needs the corresponding state to be moved around with it. In brief, that is what a key helps the framework to do. By holding the key value, the element in question will know the corresponding widget state that needs to be with it.

 We will be using keys in our app further on this book. If you need to find more details on how `key` affects the widget and the available types of keys now, please check out the official docs' introduction to keys: `https://flutter.io/docs/development/ui/widgets-intro#keys`.

# Built-in widgets

Flutter has a big focus on UI, and because of this, it contains a large catalog of widgets to allow the construction of customized interfaces according to your needs.

The available widgets of Flutter go from simple ones, such as the `Text` widget in the Flutter counter application example, to complex widgets that help to design dynamic UI with animations and multiple gesture handling.

# Basic widgets

The basic widgets in Flutter are a good starting point, not only for their ease of use, but also because they demonstrate the power and flexibility of the framework, even in simple cases.

We will not be studying all the available widgets because it would break this book's focus, so we will be listing only some of them for your knowledge and we will be using some of them in practice so that you can learn the basics to explore further.

# The Text widget

Text displays a string of text allowing styling:

```
Text(
  "This is a text",
)
```

The most common properties of the Text widget are as follows:

- style: A class that composes the styling of a text. It exposes properties that allow changing the text color, background, font family (allowing the usage of a custom font from assets; see Chapter 3, *An Introduction to Flutter*), line height, font size, and so on.
- textAlign: Controls the text horizontal alignment, giving options such as center aligned or justified, for example.
- maxLines: Allows specifying a maximum number of lines for the text that will be truncated if the limit is exceeded.
- overflow: Will define how the text will be truncated on overflows, giving options such as specifying a max-lines limit. It can be by adding an ellipsis at the end, for example.

To see all the available Text widget properties, please check the official Text widget docs page: https://docs.flutter.io/flutter/widgets/Text-class.html.

# The Image widget

Image displays an image from different sources and formats. From the docs, the supported image formats are JPEG, PNG, GIF, animated GIF, WebP, animated WebP, BMP, and WBMP:

```
Image(
  image: AssetImage(
    "assets/dart_logo.jpg"
  ),
)
```

The `Image` property from the widget specifies `ImageProvider`. The image to be shown can come from different sources. The `Image` class contains different constructors for different ways of loading images:

- `Image` (`https://api.flutter.dev/flutter/widgets/Image/Image.html`), for obtaining an image from `ImageProvider` (`https://api.flutter.dev/flutter/painting/ImageProvider-class.html`), like the previous example.

- `Image.asset` (`https://api.flutter.dev/flutter/widgets/Image/Image.asset.html`) creates `AssetImage`, which is for obtaining an image from `AssetBundle` (`https://api.flutter.dev/flutter/services/AssetBundle-class.html`) using the asset key. An example is as follows:

  ```
  Image.asset (
    'assets/dart_logo.jpg',
  )
  ```

- `Image.network` (`https://api.flutter.dev/flutter/widgets/Image/Image.network.html`) creates `NetworkImage` to obtain an image from a URL:

  ```
  Image.network (
    'https://picsum.photos/250?image=9',
  )
  ```

- `Image.file` (`https://api.flutter.dev/flutter/widgets/Image/Image.file.html`) creates `FileImage` to obtain an image from a file (`https://api.flutter.dev/flutter/dart-io/File-class.html`):

  ```
  Image.file (
    File(file_path)
  )
  ```

- `Image.memory` (`https://api.flutter.dev/flutter/widgets/Image/Image.memory.html`) creates `MemoryImage` to obtain an image from `Uint8List` (`https://api.flutter.dev/flutter/dart-typed_data/Uint8List-class.html`):

  ```
  Image.memory (
    Uint8List(image_bytes)
  )
  ```

Besides the `Image` property, there are some other commonly used properties:

- `height`/`width`: To specify the size constraints of an image
- `repeat`: To repeat the image to cover the available space
- `alignment`: To align the image in a specific position within its bounds
- `fit`: To specify how the image should be inscribed into the available space

To see all the available `Image` widget properties, please go to the official image widget docs page: `https://docs.flutter.io/flutter/widgets/Image-class.html`.

# Material Design and iOS Cupertino widgets

Many of the widgets in Flutter are descended in some way from a platform-specific guideline: **Material Design** or **iOS Cupertino**. This helps the developer to follow platform-specific guidelines in the easiest possible way.

If you do not know the Material Design or iOS Cupertino guidelines, then it's a good time to get to know them:

Material Design: `https://material.io/guidelines/material-design/introduction.html`.
iOS Cupertino: `https://developer.apple.com/design/human-interface-guidelines/ios/overview/themes/`.

Flutter, for example, does not have a `Button` widget; instead, it provides alternative button implementations for Google Material Design and iOS Cupertino guidelines.

We are not going to get deeper on each widget property or behavior, as these can be easily studied by running examples or visiting the docs. Also, you can check the Flutter Gallery app on Google Play (`https://play.google.com/store/apps/details?id=io.flutter.demo.gallery`) to find a short and cool demonstration of the available widgets.

## Buttons

On the Material Design side, Flutter implements the following button components:

- `RaisedButton`: A Material Design raised button. A raised button consists of a rectangular piece of material that hovers over the interface.
- `FloatingActionButton`: A floating action button is a circular icon button that hovers over content to promote a primary action in the application.
- `FlatButton`: A flat button is a section printed on a Material widget that reacts to touches by splashing/rippling with color.
- `IconButton`: An icon button is a picture printed on a Material widget that reacts to touches by splashing/rippling.
  Ink, from the Material Design guidelines website, can be explained as follows:

  > *"Component that provides a radial action in the form of a visual ripple expanding outward from the user's touch."*

- `DropDownButton`: Shows the currently selected item and an arrow that opens a menu for selecting another item.
- `PopUpMenuButton`: Displays a menu when pressed.

For iOS Cupertino style, Flutter provides the `CupertinoButton` class.

 Due to Material Design's guidelines, elevation, ink effects, and light effects, Material Design widgets are a bit more expensive than Cupertino widgets. Not to the point of worrying, but it's interesting to know.

## Scaffold

`Scaffold` implements the basic structure of a Material Design or iOS Cupertino visual layout. For Material Design, the `Scaffold` widget can contain multiple Material Design components:

- `body`: The primary content of the scaffold. Its displayed below `AppBar`, if any.
- `AppBar`: An app bar consists of a toolbar and potentially other widgets.
- `TabBar`: A Material Design widget that displays a horizontal row of tabs. This is generally used as part of `AppBar`.
- `TabBarView`: A page view that displays the widget that corresponds to the currently selected tab. Typically used in conjunction with `TabBar` and used as a `body` widget.

- `BottomNavigationBar`: Bottom navigation bars make it easy to explore and switch between top-level views in a single tap.
- `Drawer`: A Material Design panel that slides in horizontally from the edge of a scaffold to show navigation links in an application.

In iOS Cupertino, the structure is different with some specific transitions and behaviors. The available iOS Cupertino classes are `CupertinoPageScaffold` and `CupertinoTabScaffold`, which are composed typically with the following:

- `CupertinoNavigationBar`: A top navigation bar. It's typically used with `CupertinoPageScaffold`.
- `CupertinoTabBar`: A bottom tab bar that is typically used with `CupertinoTabScaffold`.

## Dialogs

Both Material Design and Cupertino dialogs are implemented by Flutter. On the Material Design side, they are `SimpleDialog` and `AlertDialog`; on the Cupertino side, they are `CupertinoDialog` and `CupertinoAlertDialog`.

## Text fields

Text fields are also implemented in both guidelines, by the `TextField` widget in Material Design and by the `CupertinoTextField` widget in iOS Cupertino. Both of them display the keyboard for user input. Some of their common properties are as follows:

- `autofocus`: Whether the `TextField` should be focused automatically (if nothing else is already focused)
- `enabled`: To set the field as editable or not
- `keyboardType`: To change the type of keyboard displayed to the user when editing

To see all the available `TextField` and `CupertinoTextField` widget properties, please go to the official widgets docs page: `https://docs.flutter.io/flutter/material/TextField-class.html` and `https://docs.flutter.io/flutter/cupertino/CupertinoTextField-class.html`.

## Selection widgets

The available control widgets for selection in Material Design are as follows:

- Checkbox allows the selection of multiple options in a list.
- Radio allows a single selection in a list of options.
- Switch allows the toggle (on/off) of a single option.
- Slider allows the selection of a value in a range by moving the slider thumb.

On the iOS Cupertino side, some of these widget functionalities do not exist; however, there are some alternatives available:

- CupertinoActionSheet: An iOS-style modal bottom action sheet to choose an option among many.
- CupertinoPicker: Also a picker control. It's used to select an item in a short list.
- CupertinoSegmentedControl: Behaves like a radio button, where the selection is a single item from an options list.
- CupertinoSlider: Similar to Slider in Material Design.
- CupertinoSwitch: This is also similar to Material Design's Switch.

## Date and time pickers

For Material Design, Flutter provides date and time pickers through showDatePicker and showTimePicker functions, which builds and displays the Material Design dialog for the corresponding actions. On the iOS Cupertino side, the CupertinoDatePicker and CupertinoTimerPicker widgets are provided, following the previous CupertinoPicker style.

## Other components

There are also design-specific components that are unique to each platform. Material Design, for example, has the concept of **Cards**, which are defined as follows in the documentation:

*"A sheet of Material used to represent some related information."*

On the other side of things, Cupertino-specific widgets may have unique transitions present in the iOS world.

For more details, feel free to check the Flutter widgets catalog on the `flutter.io` website: `https://flutter.io/docs/development/ui/widgets`.

# Understanding built-in layout widgets

Some widgets seem not to appear on screen to the user, but if they are in the widget tree, they will be there somehow, affecting how a child widget looks (such as how it is positioned or styled, for example).

To position a button in the bottom corner of the screen, for example, we could specify a positioning related to the screen, but as you may have noticed, buttons and other widgets do not have a `Position` property. So, you might be asking yourself, "*How are widgets organized on the screen?*" The answer is *widgets* again. That's right! Flutter provides widgets to compose the layout itself, with positioning, sizing, styling, and so on.

# Containers

Displaying a single widget onscreen is not a good way to organize a UI. We will usually lay out a list of widgets that are organized in a specific way; to do so, we use container widgets.

The most common containers in Flutter are the `Row` and `Column` widgets. They have a `children` property that expects a list of widgets to display in some direction (that is, a horizontal list for `Row`, or a vertical list for `Column`).

Another widely used widget is the `Stack` widget, which organizes children in layers, where one child can overlap another child partially or totally.

If you have developed some kind of mobile application before, you may have already used lists and grids. Flutter provides classes for both of them: namely, the `ListView` and `GridView` widgets. Also, other less typical but nonetheless important container widgets are available, such as `Table`, for example, which organizes children in a tabular layout.

# Styling and positioning

The task of positioning a child widget in a container, such as a `Stack` widget, for example, is done by using other widgets. Flutter provides widgets for very specific tasks. Centering a widget inside a container is done by wrapping it into a `Center` widget. Aligning a child widget relative to a parent can be done with the `Align` widget, where you specify the desired position through its `alignment` property. Another useful widget is `Padding`, which allows us to specify a space around the given child. The functionalities of these widgets are aggregated in the `Container` widget, which combines those common positioning and styling widgets to apply them to a child directly, making the code much cleaner and shorter.

# Other widgets (gestures, animations, and transformations)

Flutter provides widgets for anything related to UI. For example, gestures such as scrolling or touches will all be related to a widget that manages gestures. Animations and transformations, such as scaling and rotation, are also all managed by specific widgets. We will be checking out some of them in detail in the following chapters, when we develop parts of a small application.

We are not able to explore all the available widgets and all the possible combinations of them. We will start our journey by developing a small application in the following section, where we will explore some of the available widgets in all of the categories so that you can visualize how to use some of them. Most importantly, though, you will learn about the fundamentals of creating layouts in Flutter. Once that's done, learning about new and specific widgets will be an easy task.

 During the writing of this book, Flutter is evolving another great feature, **Platform View**, which allows us to utilize any native interfaces that are already available in iOS and Android. Read more in `Chapter 11`, *Platform Views and Map Integration*, in the *Displaying a map* section.

# Creating a UI with widgets (favor manager app)

Now that we know some of the available widgets from Flutter, it is time to start the small application that we will build during the course of the book.

The application we're going to develop will be a favor manager app. It will be a small network where a friend may ask a favor of another friend, and that friend may accept or refuse to do the favor. By accepting, the favor enters in the user's favors-to-do list. It's like a *to-do* app where tasks to do are proposed by the user's friends and only accepted or rejected by the user. In this app, we will explore many concepts that may help in application development.

In the following chapters, we will be adding functionalities to the application, gradually learning about all the different pieces that compose a Flutter app.

## The app screens

The *Friend Favors* app will consist of two screens. In both of them, we will be using Material Design components provided by Flutter. The first screen will be a list of favors, and the second one will be a form for asking a favor of a friend. For now, we will be using in-memory lists; that is, the information will not be stored anywhere other than the app.

## The app code

The app code is not fully functional yet. It's small enough to show up the layout. It builds a `MaterialApp` widget instance that sets the home screen to the favors list page, called `FavorsPage`:

```
class MyApp extends statelessWidget {
  // using mock values from mock_favors dart file for now
  @override
  Widget build(BuildContext context) {
    return MaterialApp(
      title: 'Flutter Demo',
      home: FavorsPage(
        pendingAnswerFavors: mockPendingFavors,
        completedFavors: mockCompletedFavors,
        refusedFavors: mockRefusedFavors,
        acceptedFavors: mockDoingFavors,
      ),
```

```
        );
      }
    }
```

`MaterialApp` is a widget that provides useful tools for the whole application. One of them is the `Theme` widget, which allows us to change our app styles and colors following the Material Design guidelines. Another useful tool is the `Navigator` widget, which manages a set of application widgets in a navigation stack-like way, where we can navigate to a screen by pushing it on the navigator or navigate back by popping it. We will be using both widgets in the app. `Navigator` is already applied here when we set the `home` property of the `MaterialApp` widget. `Navigator` works in a route-to-widget fashion; that is, there are a few ways to define specific routes pointing to specific widgets, and when we navigate to a route, it will be able of navigating to the corresponding widget. By setting the `home` property with some widget, we are saying the `Navigator` to use this widget as the `'/'` route (the initial route of the app).

 As you can see, the `FavorsPage` widget has some constructor parameters filled. Keep reading to see what they are.

In this first stage, we will be looking at the app layout initial structure, which will evolve to the end of the book with new styles and widgets. In the next chapter, you will be learning how to add some user input methods using taps and form fields. Later on, in `Chapter 6`, *Theming and Styling*, we will see how to customize the look of the app by using the material theme. So, let's start by taking a look at screen layouts.

# Favors app home screen

The first screen of the app is the home screen, which will consist of four tabs listing favors and their statuses:

- **Pending favors**: Favors requested by some friends that we have not answered yet
- **In-progress/doing favors**: The accepted favors; that is, the favors we are doing right now:

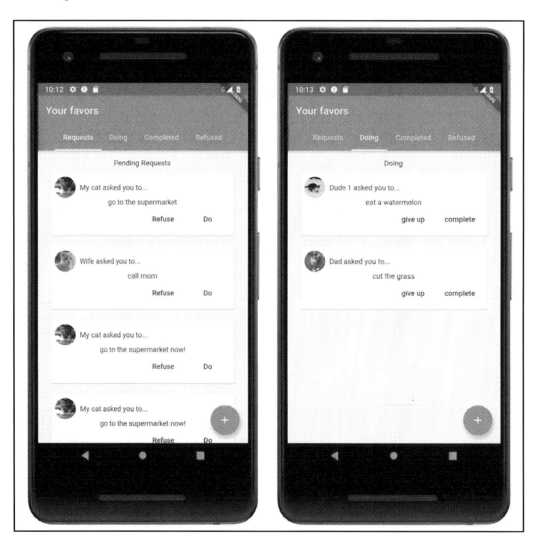

- **Completed favors**: The already-completed favors
- **Refused favors**: A list of favors that we refused to do (not accepted):

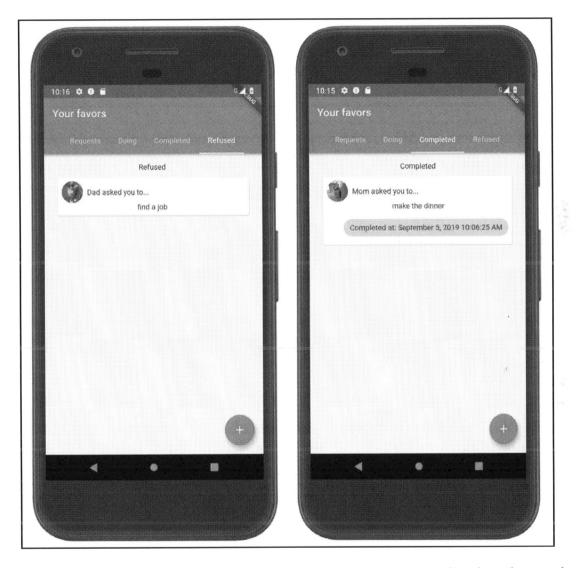

The list will contain all the favors of the app, separated by categories, as listed. At the top of the layout, we have a `TabBar` instance that will be used to change the tab to the desired list. Following that, on each tab, we have a list of `Card` items, which contain actions corresponding to its category.

We have created `Friend` and `Favor` classes to represent the app data. You can have a closer look at this in the chapter source code (the `hands_on_layouts` directory) for this book. Here they are, simple data classes, that do not contain any advanced business logic.

Also, the floating action button at the bottom end of the screen should redirect to the **Request a favor** screen, where the user will be able to ask a favor of some friend.

## The layout code

First of all, we will define our home page as a `statelessWidget` instance, as we now care only about layout and do not have any actions to be managed that would result in a state change. That is why the parent widget, `MyApp`, passes values to the defined list fields. Remember, when a widget is stateless, its description is defined by the parent widget during its creation. This is shown in the following code:

```
class FavorsPage extends statelessWidget {
    // using mock values from mock_favors dart file for now
    final List<Favor> pendingAnswerFavors;
    final List<Favor> acceptedFavors;
    final List<Favor> completedFavors;
    final List<Favor> refusedFavors;

    FavorsPage({
        Key key,
        this.pendingAnswerFavors,
        this.acceptedFavors,
        this.completedFfavors,
        this.refusedFavors,
    }) : super(key: key);

    @override
    Widget build(BuildContext context) {...} // for brevity
}
```

As shown in the preceding code, the widget is defined by the favors-specific lists. Also, notice the `key` parameter. Although it is not really needed here, we define it as it's recommended to do so as a good practice.

Let's take a look at the `build()` method to see what composes the widget:

```
@override
Widget build(BuildContext context) {
  return DefaultTabController(
    length: 4,
    child: Scaffold(
      appBar: AppBar(
        title: Text("Your favors"),
        bottom: TabBar(
          isScrollable: true,
          tabs: [
            _buildCategoryTab("Requests"),
            _buildCategoryTab("Doing"),
            _buildCategoryTab("Completed"),
            _buildCategoryTab("Refused"),
          ],
        ),
      ),
      body: TabBarView(
        children: [
          _favorsList("Pending Requests", pendingAnswerFavors),
          _favorsList("Doing", acceptedFavors),
          _favorsList("Completed", completedFavors),
          _favorsList("Refused", refusedFavors),
        ],
      ),
      floatingActionButton: FloatingActionButton(
        onPressed: () {},
        tooltip: 'Ask a favor',
        child: Icon(Icons.add),
      ),
    ),
  );
}
```

The first widget present in the `FavorsPage` widget subtree is the `DefaultTabController` widget, which handles the tab changing for us. After that, we have a `Scaffold` widget, which implements the basic structure of Material Design. Here, we are already using some of those elements, including the app bar and the floating action button. This widget is very useful for designing apps that follow the Material Design as it provides useful properties based on the guidelines:

- In `AppBar`, we have added a title with the help of a `Text` widget. In some cases, we may also add actions or a custom layout to it. Here, we added a `TabBar` instance right at the `bottom` of the app bar that will show the available tabs.
- In `FloatingActionButton`, we also have not changed too much; we only added an icon by using the `Icon` widget, which contains a Material Design icon provided by the framework.
- The `body` property of the `Scaffold` widget is where we design the layout itself. It is defined as follows: a `TabBarView` widget displays the corresponding widget for the selected tab in the `DefaultTabController` instance defined previously. Its `children` property is what requires attention; it matches the tabs of the tab bar and returns the corresponding widget of each tab.

The `Tab` bar items are created by the `_buildCategoryChip()` method, as follows:

```
class FavorsPage extends statelessWidget {
  //  ... fields, build method and others
  Widget _buildCategoryTab(String title) {
    return Tab(
      child: Text(title),
    );
  }
}
```

As you can see, the function creates a category tab item by simply building a `Tab` > `Text` subtree, where `title` is the item identifier.

In the same way, each favor list section is defined in its own method, _favorsList():

```
class FavorsPage extends statelessWidget {
  // ... fields, build method and others

  Widget _favorsList(String title, List<Favor> favors) {
    return Column(
      mainAxisSize: MainAxisSize.max,
      children: <Widget>[
        Padding(
          child: Text(title),
          padding: EdgeInsets.only(top: 16.0),
        ),
        Expanded(
          child: ListView.builder(
            physics: BouncingScrollPhysics(),
            itemCount: favors.length,
            itemBuilder: (BuildContext context, int index) {
              final favor = favors[index];
              return Card(
                key: ValueKey(favor.uuid),
                margin: EdgeInsets.symmetric(vertical: 10.0,
                horizontal: 25.0),
                child: Padding(
                  child: Column(
                    children: <Widget>[
                      _itemHeader(favor),
                      Text(favor.description),
                      _itemFooter(favor)
                    ],
                  ),
                  padding: EdgeInsets.all(8.0),
                ),
              );
            },
          ),
        ),
      ],
    );
  }
}
```

The favor section widget is represented by a Column widget that has two child widgets:

- A Text widget (with a Padding parent) containing the section title, as before
- A ListView instance that will contain each of the favor items

This list is built in a distinct way from the preceding ones. Here, we have used the `ListView.builder()` named constructor. This list constructor expects `itemCount` and `itemBuilder` instances, which we define using the list passed as an argument in the call to `_favorsList()`:

- `itemCount` is simply the size of the list.
- `itemBuilder` must be a function that returns the widget corresponding to the item in a specific position. This function receives `BuildContext`, like the `build()` method of the widget, and also an index position (here, we used the `index` argument to get the corresponding favor from the favors list).

This form of item building is optimal for big lists, lists that grow during the life cycle, or even infinite-scroll lists (which you might already have seen in some apps), because it builds items only if they are needed, preventing the waste of computational resources.

 Changing the favors list physics with (physics: `BouncingScrollPhysics()`) causes the list to have the scroll bouncing effect seen in iOS lists.

The `itemBuilder` function value builds a `Card` widget for every favor in the favors argument list by getting the corresponding item with `final favor = favors[index];`. The remaining part of the builder is as follows:

```
return Card(
    key: ValueKey(favor.uuid),
    margin: EdgeInsets.symmetric(vertical: 10.0, horizontal: 25.0),
    child: Padding(
      child: Column(
        children: <Widget>[
          _itemHeader(favor),
          Text(favor.description),
          _itemFooter(favor)
        ],
      ),
      padding: EdgeInsets.all(8.0),
    ),
);
```

When we talk about list items, we will always need a `key` to the widget, at least when we add tap event handling to it. This is because lists in Flutter may recycle many elements during scroll events, and by adding a key, we will assert that the specific widget has a specific state associated with it.

The new part here is the `margin` property of the `Card` widget, which adds a margin to the widget. In this case, we add `10.0` dip for the top and bottom, and `25.0` for the left and right. Its `body` child is split into three parts:

- First, there is the header, which shows the friend that has made the favor request, defined in the `_itemHeader()` function:

```
Row _itemHeader(Favor favor) {
  return Row(
    children: <Widget>[
      CircleAvatar(
        backgroundImage: NetworkImage(
          favor.friend.photoURL,
        ),
      ),
      Expanded(
        child: Padding(
            padding: EdgeInsets.only(left: 8.0),
            child: Text("${favor.friend.name} asked you to...
            ")),
      )
    ],
  );
}
```

The header is defined as a `Row > [CircleAvatar, Expanded]` subtree. It starts with a `Row` definition (works like the `Column` widget, but in the horizontal axis) that has a `CircleAvatar` instance, a circle image that represents a user. Here, we have used the `NetworkImage` provider; we simply pass a image URL to it and let it load for us. The remaining space of the `Row` widget is used by `Text` with some `Padding` on it that shows the friend name.

- Secondly, there is the content, which is just a `Text` widget with the favor description.
- Finally, there is the footer, which contains the available actions for the favor request depending on the favor category, defined in the `_itemFooter()` function:

```
Widget _itemFooter(Favor favor) {
  if (favor.isCompleted) {
    final format = DateFormat();
    return Container(
      margin: EdgeInsets.only(top: 8.0),
      alignment: Alignment.centerRight,
      child: Chip(
```

```
                      label: Text("Completed at:
           ${format.format(favor.completed)}"),
             ),
           );
         }
         if (favor.isRequested) {
           return Row(
             mainAxisAlignment: MainAxisAlignment.end,
             children: <Widget>[
               FlatButton(
                 child: Text("Refuse"),
                 onPressed: () {},
               ),
               FlatButton(
                 child: Text("Do"),
                 onPressed: () {},
               )
             ],
           );
         }
         if (favor.isDoing) {
           return Row(
             mainAxisAlignment: MainAxisAlignment.end,
             children: <Widget>[
               FlatButton(
                 child: Text("give up"),
                 onPressed: () {},
               ),
               FlatButton(
                 child: Text("complete"),
                 onPressed: () {},
               )
             ],
           );
         }

         return Container();
       }
```

The `_itemFooter()` function returns a widget depending on the favor status. The favor statuses are defined by `getters` in the `Favor` class:

- In the **request** phase (the favor has not been accepted or refused yet), we return a `Row` widget with two material `FlatButton` instances on it with the corresponding available actions, refuse or do. `FlatButton` is a Material Design button that does not have an elevation or background color on it.
- For the **doing** phase, we return a `Row` widget with rejected or complete actions as `FlatButtons`.
- For the **completed** status, we display the completed date and time formatted using the `DateFormat` class from Dart inside a `Chip` widget to differentiate from the rest of the text.
- In the **refused** status, we return a `Container` widget with no size constraints; this is an empty container (it does not take up space on a layout).

You can use the `EdgeInsets` helper class methods whenever you are defining padding or margin. It has useful methods for this. Check out the official documentation page: `https://api.flutter.dev/flutter/painting/EdgeInsets-class.html`.

As we have seen in the favor lists implementation, there are various widgets composing the layout. Notice however, that we are not handling any user action here; we will be checking in on all that in the next chapter. Let's take a look at the request favor screen.

Notice the `onPressed` property on `FlatButton`; it defines the action when the user taps on it. We will be looking at this in `Chapter 5`, *Handling User Input and Gestures*, so keep going!

# The request favor screen

The request favor screen will be the place where the user-app interaction occurs. For now, we will be looking only at the layout of this screen. As the book goes on, we will be joining the pieces to select the friend to ask the favor, and also save the favor to the Firebase remote database:

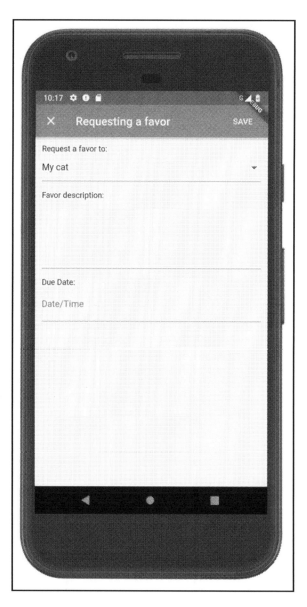

The request favor screen widget also contains a Material Design `Scaffold` widget with an app bar that contains actions this time. The body of the `Scaffold` widget contains fields that will have input information from the user for the creation of a favor request.

## The layout code

The `RequestFavorPage` widget is also stateless right now as we care only about its layout currently:

```
class RequestFavorPage extends statelessWidget {
  final List<Friend> friends;

  RequestFavorPage({Key key, this.friends}) : super(key: key);

  @override
  Widget build(BuildContext context) {...} // for brevety
}
```

As you can see, the only thing in the widget description is the friends list, which must be provided by the parent widget as this is a `statelessWidget` instance right now.

 To find out how to navigate between screens (that is, from the favors list to the **Request a favor** screen), jump to `Chapter 7`, *Routing: Navigating between Screens*, where we talk about routing and navigation.

The `build()` method of the widget begins as follows:

```
@override
Widget build(BuildContext context) {
  return Scaffold(
    appBar: AppBar(
      title: Text("Requesting a favor"),
      leading: CloseButton(),
      actions: <Widget>[
        FlatButton(
            child: Text("SAVE"), textColor: Colors.white, onPressed: ()
            {}),
      ],
    ),
    body: ... // continues below
  ...
```

`appBar` here contains two new properties:

- The `leading` property, which is a widget displayed *before* the title. In this case, we use a `CloseButton` widget that is a button integrated with the material `Navigator` widget (more on that in Chapter 7, *Routing: Navigating between Screens*).
- The `actions` property, which receives a list of widgets to display after the title; in this case, we display a `FlatButton` instance using which we will save the favor request.

The `body` of `Scaffold` defines the layout in a `Column` widget. It contains two new properties: the first is `mainAxisSize`, which defines the size in the vertical axis; here we use `MainAxisSize.min` so it only takes up as much space as is necessary. The second is `crossAxisAlignment`, which defines where to align the children in the horizontal axis. By default, `Column` aligns its children horizontally in the center. Using this property, we may change this behavior. There are three child widgets in `Column` that will take the user input:

- A `DropdownButtonFormField` widget that lists the `DropdownMenuItem` widget items in a popup when pressed:

```
...
DropdownButtonFormField(
  items: friends
      .map(
        (f) => DropdownMenuItem(
            child: Text(f.name),
          ),
      )
      .toList(),
),
...
```

Here, we use the `map()` method from the Dart `Iterable` type, where each element from the list (friends, in this case) is mapped to a new `DropdownMenuItem` widget. So, each element from the friends list will be displayed as a widget item in the drop-down list.

- A `TextFormField` widget that allows the input of text by typing on the keyboard:

```
TextFormField(
    maxLines: 5,
    inputFormatters: [LengthLimitingTextInputFormatter(200)],
),
```

The `TextFormField` widget allows text input. By adding `inputFormatters` to it, we can configure how it looks on the screen. Here we just limit the total length of the typed text to 200 characters by using the `LengthLimitingTextInputFormatter` class, which is provided by the `flutter/services` library.

> Check out all of the provided utilities from the `flutter/services` package at the package's webpage: https://api.flutter.dev/flutter/ services/services-library.html.

- A `DateTimePickerFormField` widget that allows the user to select a `DateTime` instance and maps it to a `DateTime` Dart type:

```
DateTimePickerFormField(
    inputType: InputType.both,
    format: DateFormat("EEEE, MMMM d, yyyy 'at' h:mma"),
    editable: false,
    decoration: InputDecoration(
        labelText: 'Date/Time', hasFloatingPlaceholder: false),
    onChanged: (dt) {},
),
```

The `DateTimePickerFormField` widget is not a built-in widget from Flutter. This is a third-party plugin from the `datetime_picker_formfield` library. Here, we define some properties to change how it appears:

- `inputType`: Whether to select date, time, or both.
- `format`: A `DateFormat` Dart type to define the string representation format of the value.
- `editable`: Whether the widget is to be manually editable by the user.
- `decoration`: Used to define a decoration for the input field in a Material Design way. Note that we have not defined it for other input fields.
- `onChanged`: Callback called with the new value selected by the user.

To find out about all the available options and how to use the `DateTimePickerFormField` widget, please visit `https://pub.dartlang.org/packages/datetime_picker_formfield`.

Besides the input fields, there are also some `Container` and `Text` widgets in the `Column` to help in the formatting and design of the screen. Take a look at the chapter source code for the full layout code.

# Creating custom widgets

When creating UIs with Flutter, we will always have to create some custom widgets; we cannot and do not want to escape from it. After all, the composition of widgets for building unique interfaces is what Flutter enables so well.

In the application, we have created some of the layout already, and the only custom widgets we have created are the `FavorsPage` and `RequestFavorPage` widgets.

You may have noted as well that due to the way of composing layouts in Flutter, the code may become huge and hard to maintain. To address this, we have created small methods that split the creation of the widget into parts to build up the full layout.

Splitting widgets into small methods is good for helping the code become smaller, but it's not as good for Flutter. In our case, we do not have a complex layout yet, so this is OK, but in the case of a complex layout where the widget tree can change many times, having widgets as built-in methods will not help the framework to optimize the rendering process.

To help the framework to optimize the rendering process, we should instead split our methods into small, purposeful widgets. So, the **Widget tree | Element tree** operations will be optimized. Remember, the type of widget helps the framework to know when a widget changes and needs to be rebuilt, impacting the whole rendering process. So, let's revisit our `FavorsPage` widget and convert the small widget methods into new custom small widgets.

The `_favorsList()` method (see the attached source code) can be refactored into a new `FavorsList` widget. Then, the `itemBuilder` property of the `FavorsList` widget can be refactored to return a `FavorCardItem` widget that returns the card item:

```
class FavorCardItem extends statelessWidget {
  final Favor favor;

  const FavorCardItem({Key key, this.favor}) : super(key: key);
```

```
@override
Widget build(BuildContext context) {
  return Card(
    key: ValueKey(favor.uuid),
    margin: EdgeInsets.symmetric(vertical: 10.0, horizontal: 25.0),
    child: Padding(
      child: Column(
        children: <Widget>[
          _itemHeader(favor),
          Text(favor.description),
          _itemFooter(favor)
        ],
      ),
      padding: EdgeInsets.all(8.0),
    ),
  );
}
Widget _itemHeader(Favor favor) { ... } // for brevity
Widget _itemFooter(Favor favor) { ... }// for brevity
}
```

The only thing that changes is the adding of a new class with the proper final fields that matter for the widget rendering; the build() method is almost the same as the previous _buildFavorsList() method.

Notice that the favor card item still contains the header and footer parts as methods, _itemHeader() and _itemActions() respectively. This way, they are small enough to not harm the rendering process. But remember, splitting them into widgets would not hurt, either.

With this technique of using the splitting widget, we will be giving the framework just enough information of our widgets, and they will behave like built-in widgets and be able to be optimized like built-in widgets.

 I recommend that you read this interesting blog post on widget performance: https://iirokrankka.com/2018/12/11/splitting-widgets-to-methods-performance-antipattern/.

# Summary

In this chapter, we have seen each of the available Flutter widget types and their differences. `stateless` widgets do not get rebuilt frequently by the framework; on the other hand, `stateful` widgets get rebuilt every time its associated `State` object changes (which could be when the `setState()` function is used, for example). We have also seen that Flutter comes with many widgets that can be combined to build unique UIs, and that also they do not need to be visual components on the user's screen; they can be layout, styling, and even data widgets, such as `InheritedWidget`. We have started the development of a small app that we will continue to develop in the next few chapters; we will be adding specific functions to it while we present new important concepts about Flutter.

In the next chapter, we will check out how to add user interaction to the app by adding responses to user taps and data input that later will be stored in Firebase.

# Handling User Input and Gestures

**5**

With the use of widgets, it is possible to create an interface that's rich in visual resources that also allows user interaction through gestures and data entry. In this chapter, you will get to learn about the widgets used to handle user gestures and receive and validate user input, along with how to create our own custom inputs.

The following topics will be covered in this chapter:

- Handling user gestures
- Understanding input widgets
- Learning input validation
- Creating custom inputs

## Handling user gestures

A mobile application would be nothing without some kind of interactivity. The Flutter framework allows the handling of user gestures in every possible way, from simple taps to drag and pan gestures. The screen events in Flutter's gesture system are separated into two layers, as follows:

- **Pointer layers**: These are the layers that have *pointer* events, which represent user interactions with details such as touch location and movement on the device screen.

- **Gestures**: Gestures in Flutter are interaction events at the highest level of definition, and you might already have seen some of them in action, such as taps, drags, and scale, for example. Also, they are the most typical way of implementing event handling.

# Pointers

Flutter starts event handling in a low-level layer (**pointer layers**), where you can, handle every pointer event and decide how to control it, such as with a drag or single tap.

The Flutter framework implements event dispatching on the widget tree by following a sequence of events:

- `PointerDownEvent` is where the interaction begins, with a pointer coming into contact with a certain location of the device screen. Here, the framework searches the widget tree for the widget that exists in the location of the pointer in the screen. This action is called a hit test.
- Every following event is dispatched to the innermost widget that matches the location, and then raised up the widget tree from the parent widgets to the root. This propagation of event actions cannot be interrupted. The event could be `PointerMoveEvent`, where the location of the pointer is changed. It could also be `PointerUpEvent` or `PointerCancelEvent`.
- An interaction might finish with `PointerUpEvent` or `PointerCancelEvent`. The former here is where the pointer stops being in contact with the screen, while the latter means that the application doesn't receive any more events about the pointer (the event is not complete).

Flutter provides the `Listener` class, which can be used to detect the pointer interaction events that we've previously discussed. You can wrap a widget tree with this widget to handle pointer events on its widget subtree.

Check out the `Listener` class documentation page at `https://api.flutter.dev/flutter/widgets/Listener-class.html`.

# Gestures

Although possible, it is not always practical to handle pointer events by ourselves using the `Listener` widget. Instead, the events can be handled on the second layer of the Flutter gesture system. The gestures are recognized from multiple pointer events, and even multiple individual pointers (multitouch). There are multiple kinds of gestures that can be handled:

- **Tap**: A single tap/touch on the device screen.
- **Double tap**: A double quick tap on the same location on the device screen.
- **Press and long press**: A press on the device screen, similar to tap, but contacting the screen for a long period of time before release.
- **Drag**: A press that starts with a pointer contacting the screen in some location, which is then moved and stops contacting at another location on the device screen.
- **Pan**: Similar to drag events. In Flutter, they are different in direction; pan gestures cover both horizontal and vertical drags.
- **Scale**: Two pointers used for a drag move to employ a scale gesture. This is also similar to a zoom gesture.

Like the `Listener` widget for pointer events, Flutter provides the `GestureDetector` widget, which contains callbacks for all of the preceding events. We should use them according to the effect we want to achieve.

# Tap

Let's see how to implement the tap event using the `GestureDetector` widget's `onTap` callback:

```
// part of tap_event_example.dart   (full source code in the attached files)

class _TapWidgetExampleState extends State<TapWidgetExample> {
  int _counter = 0;

  @override
  Widget build(BuildContext context) {
    return GestureDetector(
      onTap: () {
        setState(() {
          _counter++;
        });
      },
```

```
        child: Container(
          color: Colors.grey,
          child: Center(
            child: Text(
              "Tap count: $_counter",
              style: Theme.of(context).textTheme.display1,
            ),
          ),
        ),
      );
    }
  }
```

This is the state implementation of a widget that holds the example. It has a single counter to show how many taps were performed on the screen. In this example, the `onTap` property holds a callback that updates the widget state after a tap on the screen, by incrementing the `_counter` value.

 You can find the source code of `Chapter 5`, *Handling User Input and Gestures*, on GitHub.

## Double tap

The double tap callback is very similar in code:

```
// part of doubletap_event_example.dart (full source code in the attached
files)

GestureDetector(
  onDoubleTap: () {
    setState(() {
      _counter++;
    });
  },
  child: ... // for brevity
);
```

The only difference from the previous item is the property assigned, `onDoubleTap`, that will be called every time double taps are quickly performed at the same location on the screen.

# Press and hold

Again, the difference from the previous examples is minimal:

```dart
// part of press_and_hold_event_example.dart (full source code in the
attached files)

GestureDetector(
  onLongPress: () {
    setState(() {
      _counter++;
    });
  },
  child: ... // for brevity
);
```

The only difference from the previous item is the property assigned, `onLongPress`, which will be called every time a tap is performed and held for some time – a *long press* – before being released from the screen.

# Drag, pan, and scale

Drag, pan, and scale gestures are similar, and in Flutter we have to decide which one to use in each situation, as they cannot be used all together in the same `GestureDetector` widget.

Drag gestures are separated into *vertical* and *horizontal* gestures. Even the callbacks are separated in Flutter.

## Horizontal drag

Let's see how the **horizontal version** looks in code:

```dart
// part of drag_event_example.dart (full source code in the attached files)

GestureDetector(
  onHorizontalDragStart: (DragStartDetails details) {
    setState(() {
      _move = Offset.zero;
      _dragging = true;
    });
  },
  onHorizontalDragUpdate: (DragUpdateDetails details) {
    setState(() {
      _move += details.delta;
```

```
    });
  },
  onHorizontalDragEnd: (DragEndDetails details) {
    setState(() {
      _dragging = false;
      _dragCount++;
    });
  },
  child: ... // for brevity
)
```

This time, we need a bit more work than for tap events. In the example, we have three
properties present in the state:

- _dragging: Used to update the text viewed by the user while dragging.
- _dragCount: This accumulates the total number of drag events made from start
  to end.
- _move: That accumulates the offset of the dragging that is applied to the Text
  using the translate constructor of the Transform widget.

> We will be checking a bit more on Transform widgets on Chapter 14,
> *Widget Graphic Manipulations.*

As you can see, the drag callbacks receive parameters related to each event
– DragStartDetails, DragUpdateDetails, and DragEndDetails – that contains values
that may help on each stage of the dragging.

## Vertical drag

The **vertical version** of drag is almost the same as the horizontal version. The significant
differences are in the callback properties, which are
onVerticalDragStart, onVerticalDragUpdate, and onVerticalDragEnd.

> What changes for vertical and horizontal callbacks in terms of code is the
> delta property value of the DragUpdateDetails class. For horizontal, it
> will only have the horizontal part of the offset changed, and for vertical,
> the opposite is the case.

## Pan

The **pan version** is also very similar. The significant differences this time are in addition to the callback properties, which are now `onPanStart`, `onPanUpdate`, and `onPanEnd`. For pan drags, both axis offsets are evaluated; that is, both delta values in `DragUpdateDetails` are present, so the dragging has no limitation on direction.

 You can find the source code of the `gestures/lib/example_widgets/pan_example_event.dart` file on GitHub.

## Scale

The **scale version** is nothing more than panning on more than one pointer. Let's see what the scale version of panning looks like:

```
// part of scale_event_example.dart (full source code in the attached
files)

GestureDetector(
  onScaleStart: (ScaleStartDetails details) {
    setState(() {
      _scale = 1.0;
      _resizing = true;
    });
  },
  onScaleUpdate: (ScaleUpdateDetails details) {
    setState(() {
      _scale = details.scale;
    });
  },
  onScaleEnd: (ScaleEndDetails details) {
    setState(() {
      _resizing = false;
      _scaleCount++;
    });
  },
  child: ... // for brevity
)
```

The code here is very similar to the previous ones. We have three properties in the state:

- _resizing: This is used to update the text viewed by the user while resizing using the scale gesture.
- _scaleCount: This accumulates the total number of scale events made from start to end.
- _scale: This stores the scale value from the ScaleUpdateDetails parameter, and that later is applied to the Text widget using the scale constructor of the Transform widget.

As you can see, the scale callbacks look very similar to drag callbacks in that they also receive parameters related to each event – ScaleStartDetails, ScaleUpdateDetails, and ScaleEndDetails – which contain values that may help on each stage of the scale event.

# Gestures in material widgets

Material Design and iOS Cupertino widgets have many gestures abstracted to some property by using the GestureDetector widget internally in their code. For example, material widgets such as RaisedButton use the InkWell widget beside the tap event. It does the splash effect on the target widget. Also, the onPressed property of RaisedButton exposes the tap functionality that can be used to implement the action of the button. Consider the following example:

```
// part of main.dart file (attached "input" directory example)
RaisedButton(
    onPressed: () {
        print("Running validation");
        // ... validate
    },
    child: Text("validate"),
)
```

A Text child is displayed in the RaisedButton and its press is handled in the onPressed method, as stated previously.

# Input widgets

Having gestures managed is a good start point of interaction with the user, but it's obviously not enough. Getting user data is what adds content to many applications.

Flutter provides many input data widgets to help the developer to get different kinds of information from the user. We already have seen some of them in Chapter 4, *Widgets: Building Layouts in Flutter*, including TextField, and different kinds of Selector and Picker widgets.

Although we can manage all the data input by the user by ourselves (let's say, in a root widget that holds all the input fields), this can get cumbersome, because it could lead to us having many fields and so we would probably end up increasing code complexity. Splitting all the input widgets into small pieces helps, but does not resolve everything.

Flutter provides two widgets to help organize input in code, validate it, and provide feedback promptly to the user. These are the Form and FormField widgets.

# FormField and TextField

The FormField widget works as a base class to create our own form field, used to integrate Form widget. Its functions are as follows:

- To help the process of setting and retrieving the current input value
- To validate the current input value
- To provide feedback from validations

FormField can live without Form widgets, but this isn't not typical – only when we have, let's say, a single FormField onscreen.

Many built-in input widgets from Flutter come with a corresponding FormField widget implementation. For example, TextField widget has the TextFormField. The TextFormField widget helps with access to the TextField value and also adds Form related behaviors to it (such as, validation).

A TextField widget lets the user enter text with a keyboard. The TextField widget exposes the onChanged method, which can be used to listen for changes in its current value. Another way to listen for changes is by using a controller (see the *Using a controller* section).

## Using a controller

When used isolated from a `Form`, that is, by using the `TextField` widget, we need to use its `controller` property to access its value. This is done with the `TextEditingController` class:

```
final _controller = TextEditingController.fromValue(
  TextEditingValue(text: "Initial value"),
);
```

After instantiating the `TextEditingController`, we set it into the `controller` property of the `TextField` widget so that it "controls" the text widget:

```
TextField(
  controller: _controller,
);
```

As you can see, we can set an initial value for `TextField` as well.

`TextEditingController` is notified whenever the `TextField` widget has a new value. To listen to changes, we need to add a listener to our `_controller`:

```
_controller.addListener(_textFieldEvent);
```

`_textFieldEvent` must be a function that will be called every time the `TextField` widget changes.

 Check the full example in the attached chapter files.

## Accessing FormField state

If we are using the `TextFormField` widget, things get simpler:

```
final _key = GlobalKey<FormFieldState<String>>();
...
TextFormField(
  key: _key,
);
```

We can add a key to our `TextFormField` that later can be used to access the widget's current state through the `key.currentState` value, which will contain the updated value of the field.

The specialized type of `key` refers to the kind of data the input field works with. In the preceding example, this is `String`, because it is a `TextField` widget, so the `key` depends on the particular widget used.

The `FormFieldState<String>` class also provides other useful methods and properties to deal with `FormField`:

- `validate()` will call the widget's `validator` callback, which should check its current value and return an error message, or `null` if it's valid.
- `hasError` and `errorText` result from previous validations using the preceding function. In material widgets, for example, this adds some small text near to the field, providing proper feedback to the user about the error.
- `save()` will call the widget's `onSaved` callback. This is the action that happens when the input is done by the user (when it is being saved).
- `reset()` will put the field in its initial state, with the initial value (if any), clearing validation errors as well.

# Form

Having a `FormFieldWidget` helps us access and validate its information individually. But, to address the problem of having too many fields, we can use the `Form` widget. The `Form` widget groups the `FormFieldWidget` instances logically, allowing us to perform operations including accessing field information and validating it more straightforward.

The `Form` widget allows us to run the following methods on all descendant fields easily:

- `save()`: This will call all `FormField` instances' save method and will work as before. This is like a batch saving of all the fields.
- `validate()`: This will call all `FormField` instances' validate method, causing all the errors to appear all at once.
- `reset()`: This will call all `FormField` instances' reset method. This will bring the whole `Form` to its initial state.

# Accessing Form state

Providing access to the current form state-associated object is useful so that we can init its validation, save its contents, or reset it from anywhere in the widgets tree (that is, a button press). There are two ways of accessing the Form widget's associated State.

## Using a key

The Form widget is used with the companion of a key of the FormState type that contains helpers to manage all of the children of its FormField instances:

```
final _key = GlobalKey<FormFieldState<String>>();
...
Form(
  key: _key,
  child: Column(
    children: <Widget>[
      TextFormField(),
      TextFormField(),
    ],
  ),
);
```

Then, we can use the key to retrieve the Form associated state and call its validation with _key.currentState.validate(). Now, let's have a look at the second option.

## Using InheritedWidget

The Form widget comes with a helpful class to dispense with the need to add a key to it and still get its benefits.

Each Form widget in the tree has an associated InheritedWidget with it. Form and many other widgets expose this in a static method called of(), where we pass BuildContext, and it *looks up* the tree to find the corresponding State we are looking for. Knowing this, if we need to access the Form widget somewhere below it in the tree, we can use Form.of(), and we gain access to the same functions as we would have if we using the key property:

```
// part of input/main.dart example (full source code attached)
// build() in InputFormInheritedStateExamplesWidget class

Form(
  child: Column(
    mainAxisSize: MainAxisSize.min,
    children: <Widget>[
      TextFormField(
```

```
          validator: (String value) {
            return value.isEmpty ? "cannot be empty" : null;
          },
        ),
        TextFormField(),
        Builder(
          builder: (BuildContext context) => RaisedButton(
              onPressed: () {
                print("Running validation");
                final valid = Form.of(context).validate();
                print("valid: $valid");
              },
              child: Text("validate"),
            ),
        )
      ],
    ),
  );
  ...
```

Pay special attention to the `Builder` widget used to render `RaisedButton`. As we have
seen before, the inherited widget can be looked upon the tree. Consider the following usage
of `RaisedButton` directly in the `Column` widget, as follows:

```
Column(
children: [
//     ... other childs, removed for brevity
      TextFormField(),
    RaisedButton(
      onPressed: () {
        print("Running validation");
        final valid = Form.of(context).validate(); // this would not work
                                                    // (wrong context)
        print("valid: $valid");
      },
      child: Text("validate"),
    )
  ],
  ...
```

When we use `Form.of(context)`, we pass the current widget context. In the preceding
example, the context used in the `onPressed` callback will be
the `InputFormInheritedStateExamplesWidget` context, and so, looking up the tree will
not successfully find a `Form` widget. By using the `Builder` widget, we delegate its build to
a callback, this time using the correct context (the child one), and when it looks up the tree,
it will successfully find the `FormState` instance.

# Validating Input (Forms)

Handling multiple `FormField` widgets is OK when talking about few values, but when the quantity of data grows, organizing it onscreen, validating everything properly, and providing user feedback promptly can all become harder. That's why Flutter provides the `Form` widget.

# Validating user input

Validating user input is one of the main functions of the `Form` widget. In order to make the data input entered by the user consistent, it is fundamental to check it, as the user probably does not know all the allowed values.

The `Form` widget, combined with `FormField` instances, helps the developer to show an appropriate error message if some input values need to be corrected before saving the form data through its `save()` function.

We already have seen, in the previous `Form` examples, how to validate the `Form` field values:

1. Create a `Form` widget with a `FormField` on it.
2. Define the validation logic on each `FormField` validator property:

   ```
   TextFormField(
     validator: (String value) {
       return value.isEmpty ? "The value cannot be empty" : null;
     },
   )
   ```

3. Call `validate()` on `FormState` by using its `key`, or the `Form.of` method discussed previously. This will call each child `FormField` `validate()` method, and where the validation is successful, it will return `true`, and `false` otherwise.
4. `validate()` returns a `bool` so we can manipulate its result and do our logic based on it.

# Custom input and FormField

We have seen how the `Form` and `FormField` widgets help with input manipulation and validation. Also, we know that Flutter comes with a series of input widgets that are `FormField` variants, and so, contains helper functions to access and validate data, for example.

The extensibility and flexibility of Flutter is everywhere in the framework. So, creating custom fields is logically possible, where we can add our own input method, expose validation through `validator` callback, and also use the `save()` and `reset()` methods.

# Creating custom inputs

Creating a custom input in Flutter is as simple as creating a normal widget, with the additional methods described earlier. We normally do this by extending the `FormField<inputType>` widget, where `inputType` is the value type of the input widget.

So, the typical process is as follows:

1. Create a custom widget that extends `Stateful` widget (to keep track of the value) and accepts input from the user by encapsulating another input widget, or by customizing the whole process, such as by using gestures.
2. Create a widget that extends `FormField` that basically displays the input widget created in the previous step and also exposes its fields.

# Custom input widget example

Later, in Chapter 8, *Firebase Plugins*, we will see how to add authentication to our app. For now, we will be creating a custom widget that will be similar to the one used in that step. The authentication will be based on the Firebase auth services using the phone number, where the phone number provided receives a six-digits verification code of that must match the server value in order to successfully log in. For now, that's all the information we need to know for the creation of the custom input widget. This is what it's going to look like:

The widget will be a simple six-digit input widget, which will later become a FormField widget and expose the save(), reset(), and validate() methods.

Later, on the login screen, we will be using the Flutter community `code_input` plugin to replace this widget. More info can be found at https://pub.dartlang.org/packages/code_input.

# Creating an Input widget

We start by creating a normal custom widget. Here, we expose some properties. Bear in mind that in a real application, we would probably expose more than the properties exposed here, but it's enough for this example:

```
class VerificationCodeInput extends StatefulWidget {
  final BorderSide borderSide;
  final onChanged;
  final controller;

  ... // other parts removed for brevity
}
```

The only important property exposed here is `controller`. We will see the reason in a few moments. First, let's check the associated `State` class:

```
class _VerificationCodeInputState extends State<VerificationCodeInput> {
  @override
  Widget build(BuildContext context) {
    return TextField(
      controller: widget.controller,
      inputFormatters: [
        WhitelistingTextInputFormatter(RegExp("[0-9]")),
        LengthLimitingTextInputFormatter(6),
      ],
      textAlign: TextAlign.center,
      decoration: InputDecoration(
        border: OutlineInputBorder(
          borderSide: widget.borderSide,
        ),
      ),
      keyboardType: TextInputType.number,
      onChanged: widget.onChanged,
    );
  }
}
```

As you can see, the widget is simply a `TextField` with some predefined customization:

- `WhitelistingTextInputFormatter` allows us to specify a regex expression with the allowed characters for the input. By setting the keyboard type with `keyboardType: TextInputType.number` we can also limit the allowed characters to numbers.
- `LengthLimitingTextInputFormatter` specifies a maximum character limit for the input.
- Also, a border is added through the `OutlineInputBorder` class.

Take note of the important part of this code: `controller: widget.controller`. Here, we are setting the controller of the `TextField` widget to be our own controller so we can *take control* of its value.

## Turn the widget into a FormField widget

To turn the widget into a `FormField` widget, we start by creating a widget that extends the `FormField` class, which is a `StatefulWidget` with some `Form` facilities.

This time, let's start by checking out the new widget's associated `State` object. Let's do it by breaking it into parts:

```
// initial part of _VerificationCodeFormFieldState
final TextEditingController _controller = TextEditingController(text: "");

@override
void initState() {
  super.initState();
  _controller.addListener(_controllerChanged);
}
```

From the preceding code, you can check it has a single `_controller` field, which represents the controller used by the `FormField` widget. It must be in the `State` so it persists against layout changes. As you can see, it is initialized in the `initState()` function. This is called the first time the widget object is inserted on the widgets tree. Here, we add a listener to it, so we can know when the value is changed in the `_controllerChanged` listener.

The remainder of the widget is as follows:

```
void _controllerChanged() {
  didChange(_controller.text);
}

@override
void reset() {
  super.reset();
  _controller.text = "";
}

@override
void dispose() {
  _controller?.removeListener(_controllerChanged);
  super.dispose();
}
```

There are also other important methods that we must override to make it work properly:

- With initState(), we can find its opposite equivalent in the dispose() method. Here, we stop to listen for changes in the controller.
- The reset() method is overridden, so we can set the _controller.text to empty, making the input field clear again.
- The _controllerChanged() listener notifies the super FormFieldState state via its didChange() method so it can update its state (via setState()) and notify any Form widget that contains it about the change.

Now let's examine the FormField widget code to see how it works:

```
class VerificationCodeFormField extends FormField<String> {
  final TextEditingController controller;

  VerificationCodeFormField({
    Key key,
    FormFieldSetter<String> onSaved,
    this.controller,
    FormFieldValidator<String> validator,
  }) : super(
          key: key,
          validator: validator,
          builder: (FormFieldState<String> field) {
            _VerificationCodeFormFieldState state = field;
            return VerificationCodeInput(
              controller: state.controller,
            );
```

```
        },
      );

  @override
  FormFieldState<String> createState() =>
_VerificationCodeFormFieldState();
}
```

The new part here is in the constructor. The `FormField` widget contains the builder callback that should build its associated input widget. It passes the current state of the object so we can build the widget and retain the current info. As you can see, we use this to pass the controller constructed in the state, so it persists even when the field is rebuilt.

That's how we maintain the widget and `State` synchronized, and also integrate with the `Form` class.

 You can check the full source code of this custom `FormField` widget in the `verification_code_input_widget.dart` file of the input examples project.

# Putting it all together

Now that we know how to use gesture events and input widgets to add user interaction to our app screens, it's time to increment our app with these functions. Let's revisit our screens to add some gestures and input validations to them.

## Favors screen

The first screen of the app lists different favors and their statuses. Besides the listing, the only actions the user can do are as follows:

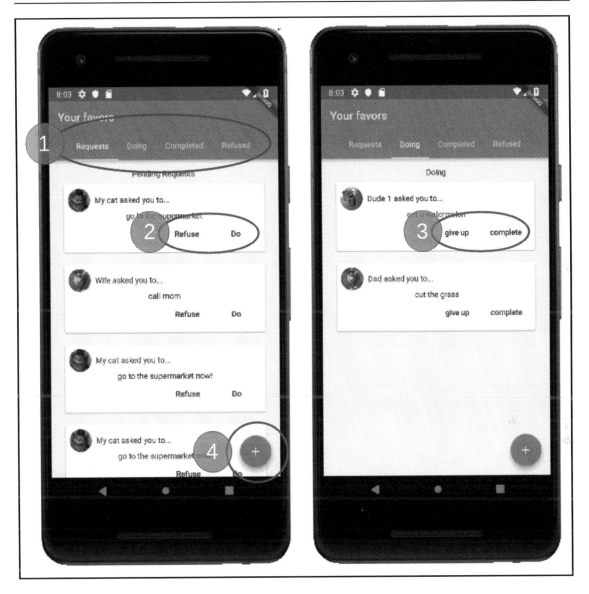

Favors screen (This is an image of the favors screen. The other (blurred out and overlapped) information is not important here.

1. Focus on the selected favor category section. This is already done for us by the `DefaultTabController` widget (there is a `ListView` widget that will handle swipe/scroll gestures internally).

2. **Refuse** or **Do** the requested favors. For example, a favor was requested by a friend, and the user may accept or reject it. So, *tapping* on one of the buttons makes the favor change its status to **Refused** or **Doing**.

3. Similarly to the preceding case, but this time, an accepted favor request is pending completion, and these buttons allow the user to give up or complete a favor; that is, tapping on them makes the favor status change to **Refused** and **Completed**, respectively.

4. Last, we have the **Request a favor** button, which basically opens a second app screen on tap to allow us to request a favor from some of our friends.

As you can see from the preceding gestures, we will be dealing with tap, scroll, and swipe gestures. All of them can be done with the `GestureDetector` directly, but, as we are using `Button` and `ListView` widgets, this changes a little bit. Remember, Flutter's built-in widgets are also composed of a lot of other built-in widgets, so we will be dealing with `GestureDetector` indirectly.

In practice, we will be handling taps by ourselves, as the other gestures are handled by the widgets that we have used: scrolling with `ListView`, and swipes and taps with `TabBar` and `TabView`.

## Tap gestures on the favor tab

As we pointed previously, the `DefaultTabController` changes the currently visible tab widget when the user taps on the tab bar or swipes to the left or right on the view. By using this widget, we do not need to specify a controller in the `TabBar` and `TabView` descendants.

For more details about the `TabController` widget, check out the documentation page at `https://docs.flutter.io/flutter/material/TabController-class.html`.

# Tap gestures on FavorCards

From the `FavorCardItem` widget's `favor` property, we can manipulate its status by changing its `accepted` and `completed` field values. However, it will not remove the item from the current list and add it to the new target list. To do that, we would need access the current list, remove the favor item from there, and add it into the new list, depending on the button pressed.

We could use our global favors list directly in the card item's `onPressed` method, but this would imply distributing business logic through the widgets, which seems fine now, but can get messy easily.

So, where should we handle this action effectively? We could handle all of these actions in the `FavorsPage` widget, which contains all of the favors lists. But wait – `FavorsPage` is a `StatelessWidget`, the favors lists are loaded into its constructor method, and as it's stateless, they will be loaded on every rebuild of the widget, losing our changes to it.

## Making FavorsPage a StatefulWidget

The first step to make our app interactive is to change `FavorsPage` to be a `StatefulWidget`:

```
class FavorsPage extends StatefulWidget {
  FavorsPage({
    Key key,
  }) : super(key: key);

  @override
  State<StatefulWidget> createState() => FavorsPageState();
}
```

The first thing we change is the ancestor of `FavorsPage`, and now its only job is to return a `FavorsPageState` instance in the `createState()` method:

```
class FavorsPageState extends State<FavorsPage> {
  // using mock values from mock_favors dart file for now
  List<Favor> pendingAnswerFavors;
  List<Favor> acceptedFavors;
  List<Favor> completedFavors;
  List<Favor> refusedFavors;

  @override
  void initState() {
    super.initState();
```

```
        pendingAnswerFavors = List();
        acceptedFavors = List();
        completedFavors = List();
        refusedFavors = List();

        loadFavors();
    }

    void loadFavors() {
      pendingAnswerFavors.addAll(mockPendingFavors);
      acceptedFavors.addAll(mockDoingFavors);
      completedFavors.addAll(mockCompletedFavors);
      refusedFavors.addAll(mockRefusedFavors);
    }

    @override
    Widget build(BuildContext context) { ... } // hidden for brevety
  }
```

Now the `State` object holds the information that needs to be persisted between rebuilds, and this object will be the location of all the actions for the favors. Although not optimal, it will at least be centralized in one single place. I would say we need some kind of architecture to do this properly: MVP, MVVM, BloC, and Redux are some examples. However, to keep things simple, we will use the approach we've taken here.

 You can check the official state management guide as an initial step for app architecture, along with some architecture alternatives, available at `https://flutter.dev/docs/development/data-and-backend/state-mgmt` and `https://medium.com/flutter-community/flutter-app-architecture-101-vanilla-scoped-model-bloc-7eff7b2baf7e`.

So, let's start by handling the pending request actions. They were defined as **Refuse** or **Do**. To handle them, we need to pass a handler to the `onPressed` property of our already defined `FlatButton` widgets in the `FavorCardItem`.

From the button's `onPressed` method, we need to somehow access `FavorsPageState` to perform those actions. This can be done with the `ancestorStateOfType()` method from the `BuildContext` class, which looks up the tree for a `State` object of the given type:

```
// part of FavorsPageState class
static FavorsPageState of(BuildContext context) {
  return context.ancestorStateOfType(TypeMatcher<FavorsPageState>());
}
```

A common pattern to provide this function is by adding a static method on the given type, called `of`, that will make the call to the framework function. This is done to provide a shorthand way to access the state with less code.

## Refuse action handling

This is how the **Refuse** button looks after using the aforementioned functionality:

```
// part of hands_on_input/lib/main.dart FavorCardItem class
// _itemFooter method
  FlatButton(
    child: Text("Refuse"),
    onPressed: () {
      FavorsPageState.of(context).refuseToDo(favor);
      // we have changed _itemFooter to get the context so we
      // can it to fetch the favors page state
    },
  )
```

By calling `FavorsPageState.of(context)`, we get access to the current state of the `FavorsPageState` type associated with the context.

To apply the change, we call the `refuseToDo(favor)` method from the `FavorsPageState` class that is implemented as follows:

```
void refuseToDo(Favor favor) {
  setState(() {
    pendingAnswerFavors.remove(favor);

    refusedFavors.add(favor.copyWith(
      accepted: false
    ));
  });
}
```

As you can note, the setState() method is used here to notify the framework to rebuild the interested widgets. Inside of its callback, we remove the favor from the pending list and add a modified version of it to the refused list. The modified version is obtained by making a copy of the original favor and changing its accepted property. This is how the copyWith method from the Favor class looks in the code:

```
Favor copyWith({
    String uuid,
    String description,
    DateTime dueDate,
    bool accepted,
    DateTime completed,
    Friend friend,
}) {
    return Favor(
      uuid: uuid ?? this.uuid,
      description: description ?? this.description,
      dueDate: dueDate ?? this.dueDate,
      accepted: accepted ?? this.accepted,
      completed: completed ?? this.completed,
      friend: friend ?? this.friend,
    );
}
```

Note that it uses the null-aware (??) operator to create a new Favor instance with the original values (if set), or the ones received as arguments.

 The copyWith() method is very common in the Flutter world, so try to get used to it. It is present in many of the Flutter framework's widgets and classes. It's not mandatory, but it's a good pattern.

## Do action handling

This is how the "Do" button looks after using the preceding technique:

```
FlatButton(
  child: Text("Do"),
  onPressed: () {
    FavorsPageState.of(context).acceptToDo(favor);
  },
)
```

And the corresponding `acceptToDo(favor)` method is done as follows:

```
void acceptToDo(Favor favor) {
  setState(() {
    pendingAnswerFavors.remove(favor);

    acceptedFavors.add(favor.copyWith(accepted: true));
  });
}
```

As you can see, it is almost the same as the `refuseToDo()` method; the only differences are in the target list and accepted status.

 The **Give up** and **Complete** actions are also very similar to the previous ones. Please check out the attached source files to see how they look.

## Tap on Request a favor button

When the user taps on the floating action button with the plus sign at the bottom of the page, they should see the `RequestFavorPage` widget on the screen:

```
Navigator.of(context).push(
  MaterialPageRoute(
    builder: (context) => RequestFavorPage(
      friends: mockFriends,
    ),
  ),
);
```

We do this by using the `Navigator` widget, which shows up a new widget on the screen. For now, you can see the gesture was handled like another button. Check out Chapter 7, *Routing: Navigating Between Screens*, for more details on how this widget works.

# The Requesting a favor screen

The **Requesting a favor** screen has a few gestures of its own to handle:

This is how the process works:

1. The *close* button is already handled by the `CloseButton` widget, along with the `Navigator` widget (this is handled internally for us).
2. The **SAVE** button will validate the input information from the user, and send the favor request to a friend.

# The close button

The `CloseButton` widget is integrated with `Navigator`. It pops the last pushed widget from it, returning to the previous one. We do not have to implement a gesture on it. By using the `Navigator` to push the widget on the screen, we can use the close button to remove it.

# The SAVE button

The **SAVE** button will be responsible for validating and saving new favor requests. Saving will be covered in `Chapter 8`, *Firebase Plugins*, when we talk about Firebase integration.

The `RequestFavorPage` widget needs to be converted to a `StatefulWidget` as well, as we will need to hold information and manipulate the new favor requests with actions. This will be the place where we will store the favor later on Firebase.

 Again, we use this to centralize all the favors-related actions, that are few in our app. Application architecture such as MVP, MVVM, or BloC could be the solution for a real application.

### Validating input using the Form widget

We must add the `Form` widget to our layout to be capable of validating all the fields at once during saving. This is done by simply wrapping our form field widgets with a `Form` widget. We also set the `key` property of our `Form` with a `GlobalKey` instance (`_formKey` in the `State` object of the following code) so that we can use it later in the `save()` method:

```
class RequestFavorPageState extends State<RequestFavorPage> {
  final _formKey = GlobalKey<FormState>();

  @override
  Widget build(BuildContext context) {
```

```
      // returns the widget subtree wrapped in a Form. hidden for brevety.
    }
  }
```

The `save()` method looks similar to previous ones:

```
FlatButton(
  child: Text("SAVE"),
  textColor: Colors.white,
  onPressed: () {
    RequestFavorPageState.of(context).save(); // we could call save()
                                              // method directly as we
                                              // are in the same class.
                                              // Intentionally left for
                                              // exemplification.
  },
)
```

It looks up the tree for the corresponding state and asks it to save. The `save()` method does the hard work:

```
void save() {
  if (_formKey.currentState.validate()) {
    // store the favor request on firebase
    Navigator.pop(context);
  }
}
```

OK, right now, it does nothing much; it only calls the validation for the corresponding form that walk through all the form fields and validates them, as you already know.

Check the chapter's attached source code files to check the validation code for the form fields.

# Summary

In this chapter, we have seen how gesture handling works in the Flutter framework, along with the methods for handling gestures, such as tap, double tap, pan, and zoom, for example. We have seen some widgets that use `GestureDetector` by itself to handle gestures. We also have seen how to use the `Form` and `FormField` widgets to properly handle user data input.

Last, we have grabbed our project and made some additions to the event handling of the actions on favors, which helped us to make the app more interactive.

In the next chapter, we will be learning how to add some color to our widgets, use themes, and get into more practical applications of Material Design and Cupertino widgets by making our favors app more attractive.

# 6
# Theming and Styling

Creating UIs with built-in themes and styles make an application look professional and easy to use. In addition, the framework allows the creation of customized and unique themes and styles. In order to do that, you will learn how to customize an app's look by adding custom fonts, using themes, and exploring the famous platform standards, iOS Cupertino and Google Material Design. Additionally, you will see how to use media queries for dynamic styling.

Every app must have its own identity. Our Favors app for example, needs to have its own colors and styles. Knowing how to apply styles, colors, custom fonts is fundamental to achieve this in any app.

The following topics will be covered in this chapter:

- Theme widgets
- Material Design
- iOS Cupertino
- Using custom fonts
- Dynamic styling with MediaQuery and LayoutBuilder

## Theme widgets

Developing an application goes beyond good features. It is also about the user experience that the app offers.

The composability of Flutter widgets helps in this part of development. By defining single responsibility for each widget type, we can choose to define themes and styling that apply to a single widget, to all widgets in a subtree, or to the entire application.

By using the Theme widget, we can customize the whole look and feel of an application with custom colors for text, error messages, highlights, and also custom fonts. Flutter also uses this widget in its own widgets. MaterialApp is a great example of how the framework internal widgets are composed: it uses the Theme widget internally to customize the look of the Material Design-based widgets such as AppBars and Buttons. Let's check out how to use Theme widgets in practice to apply different styles to other Flutter widgets.

# Theme widget

In Flutter, everything is a widget, and we can construct the user interface by adding widgets using the child and children properties of each widget. The Theme widget behaves like any other, it defines properties and can have a child.

The Theme widget also works with the InheritedWidget technique, so every descending widget can access it by using Theme.of(context), which internally makes a call to the helper inheritFromWidgetOfExactType method from the BuildContext class. That's how Material Design widgets use the Theme widget to style themselves:

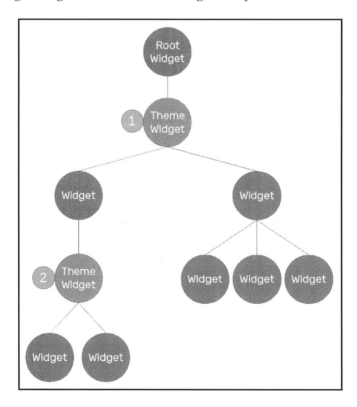

So, the theme data is applied to descending widgets but can be overridden in local parts of the widget tree. In the preceding diagram, the theme with the number *2* will override the theme with the number *1* defined at the very beginning of the tree. The number *2* subtree will have different theme from the rest of the tree.

Also, with this structure it is possible to create a complete new theme for some widgets, or to inherit from a base theme and change only some properties to affect the subtree.

 When you're styling widgets with iOS Cupertino, there is also the CupertinoTheme and CupertinoThemeData equivalents to Theme and ThemeData respectively, which are present in the Material Design widget suite.

The ThemeData class helps the Theme widget on the styling task. Let's see it in details.

# ThemeData

The Theme widget contains a property called data, which accepts a ThemeData value that holds all the information about the styling, theme brightness, colors, font, and so on.

 During the writing of this book, alternatives to iOS Cupertino guidelines are being developed and are not present in the stable channel of Flutter. (The code in this book uses the stable channel.)

By using ThemeData class properties, you will be able to customize all of the application-related styles, such as colors, typography, and specific components. You can choose to follow Material Design guidelines from Google that targets app design for mobile, web and desktop devices or iOS Cupertino that are specific to the Apple's platform.

When theming, you can choose to follow Material Design guidelines from Google that targets app design for mobile, web and desktop devices or iOS Cupertino that are specific to the Apple's platform. Both design guidelines have singularities due the target platforms and researches about it. The choice of whether to follow the Material Design, iOS Cupertino guidelines or none of them is yours, Flutter has Theme based widgets designed for both, so you can apply the guidelines accurately or to design in your own unique way.

 We will be exploring Material Design and iOS Cupertino guidelines further through the next sections.

Coloring is an important subject in widgets theming. Give enough contrast to texts over backgrounds, or to emphasize some UI piece for example, require the correct usage of colors. **Brightness** is one of the key properties of ThemeData class that helps on manipulating colors, let's see.

## Brightness

One important property of a theme is brightness. Defining this property is as important as defining theme colors, as its name suggests, it exposes the brightness of the application's theme. With this property, the frameworks can determine text, buttons, highlight colors to make enough contrast between background and foreground content.

This is what the ThemeData class docs(https://api.flutter.dev/flutter/material/ThemeData-class.html) say about it:

> *"The brightness of the overall theme of the application. Used by widgets such as buttons to determine what color to pick when not using the primary or accent color."*

It helps to contrast between text, buttons, and the background of materials (with Material Design widgets). The ThemeData class has a fallback() constructor that returns a light theme through the Brightness.light value. You can use its dark() and light() constructors to try it out yourselves.

When choosing the primary and accent colors, it's important to experiment with the corresponding primaryColorBrightness and accentColorBrightness. Flutter estimates the brightness based on some calculations of the luminosity of the colors, but it's always good to experiment and check.

 Many other ThemeData properties relate to styling directly, that's why we are not exploring those further. Feel free to check all the properties available in the ThemeData class at https://docs.flutter.io/flutter/material/ThemeData-class.html.

Now, let's dive into some theming.

# Theming in practice

Styling widgets in Flutter can be done in a few ways, and everything related to styles is based on a `Theme` widget. It is time to check out how this works. Let's say, for example, that we have a simple app, as follows:

```
class MyAppDefaultTheme extends StatelessWidget {
  @override
  Widget build(BuildContext context) {
    return Container(
      color: Colors.red,
      child: Center(
        child: Text(
          "Simple Text",
          textDirection: TextDirection.ltr,
        ),
      ),
    );
  }
}
```

As you can see, we are just using a `Container` widget as our root widget without a `Theme` widget. So, we can assume we do not have any styles applied to its descendant widgets. Also, the `textDirection` property is new at this point. When using the `MaterialApp` widget in our layout, it provides a default `textDirection` value for us implicitly. More on that in the next section.

We can, for example, use the `Theme` widget to change the style of a `Text` widget. The `ThemeData` class contains the `textTheme` property, which contains the `Text` style configuration following the Material Design guidelines:

```
Text(
  "Simple Text",
  textDirection: TextDirection.ltr,
  style: Theme.of(context).textTheme.display1,
),
```

The `style` property of the `Text` widget accepts a `TextStyle` value that we can get from the `Theme` widget. However, as you may remember, we have not specified a `Theme` widget in our app tree. In the preceding example, this works because, the `Theme.of` method returns a `ThemeData` widget fallback when one isn't defined. If you execute the code, you will see that the `Text` widget is displayed with a larger font size than the default, this because we're using the `display1` style from Material Design.

We can also customize the styling; here's an example:

```
class MyAppCustomTheme extends StatelessWidget {
  @override
  Widget build(BuildContext context) {
    return Container(
      color: Colors.blue,
      child: Center(
        child: Theme(
          data: Theme.of(context).copyWith(
            textTheme: Theme.of(context).textTheme.copyWith(
              display1: TextStyle(
                color: Colors.yellow,
              ),
            ),
          ),
          child: Text(
            "Simple Text",
            textDirection: TextDirection.ltr,
            style: Theme.of(context).textTheme.display1,
          ),
        ),
      ),
    );
  }
}
```

In this case, we add a `Theme` widget right before the `Text` widget and customize it by using its `copyWith` method:

- We make a copy of the default `Theme` widget from the app, and change only its `textTheme` property. The `copyWith` function is not mandatory, however, it is seen very often when developing Flutter apps, so get used to it!
- Like before, this time we make a copy of `textTheme` from the base theme and only change its `display1` property to a new `Text` style object.

We expect to see a yellow text, but that's not what we see, right? This is because we are using the `context` parameter from the root tree level, which will look up the tree and will not find a `Theme` instance, returning the fallback, as we saw in our first example. To make this work, we can use the `Builder` widget, which will delegate the `Text` widget building:

```
Builder(
  builder: (context) => Text(
      "Simple Text",
      textDirection: TextDirection.ltr,
      style: Theme.of(context).textTheme.display1,
    ),
)
```

This works because the `Builder` widget delegates the build to occur in a lower level of the tree, passing its `context` instance to the lower level, which will find the correct `Theme` instance when looks up the tree. So, when we run the preceding code, the `Text` widget is displayed with the correct `display1` style, which is almost the same as the default text style, only its color is different, now yellow.

 The previous examples were defined in different app classes. You can find the source code of `themes/lib/main.dart` on GitHub and try it out for yourself by commenting out the previous `runApp` function and uncommenting the one that you want to test.

As theming refers to app styling, we always need to care about the underlying platform the app is being executed, let's see how the `Platform` class can help on this.

# Platform class

When developing mobile apps for multiple platforms, we may need to make different designs for different targets. To do that, we can use the `Platform` class, which helps us get information about the environment, mainly the target operating system, through its getters:

- `isAndroid`
- `isFuchsia`
- `isIOS`
- `isLinux`
- `isMacOS`
- `isWindows`

With these getters, we can make our whole widget tree have specific implementations for each platform. Here's an example:

```
// part of theme/lib/main.dart example

class PlatformSpecificWidgets extends StatelessWidget {
  @override
  Widget build(BuildContext context) {
    return Platform.isAndroid
        ? MaterialApp(
            theme: ThemeData(primaryColor: Colors.grey),
          )
        : CupertinoApp(
            theme: CupertinoThemeData(primaryColor:
            CupertinoColors.lightBackgroundGray),
          );
  }
}
```

As you can see, based on the *target platform*, we switch our app widget (and theme as well) to `MaterialApp` and `ThemeData` (for Android) or `CupertinoApp` and `CupertinoThemeData` for any other target platform.

 Check out the documentation website, `https://docs.flutter.io/flutter/dart-io/Platform-class.html`, to learn more about this important class.

We have seen how to use `Theme` widget and helper classes, like `ThemeData` and `Platform` class to apply styles to our widgets. Material Design and iOS Cupertino guidelines are present in the basis of many widgets in Flutter. Let's see its fundamentals to be able to follow these specifications efficiently.

# Material Design

Material Design is the Google design guidelines to help developers to build high-quality digital experiences. Present in Flutter and is still evolving along with the platform with the addition of new widgets that follow Material Design component specifications.

The importance of Material Design styles for the Flutter platform is evident. There is already a section of the Material Design guidelines website dedicated to it (`https://material.io/develop/flutter/`).

The main Material Design widgets in Flutter are `MaterialApp` and `Scaffold`. Both help developers to design an app following the Material Design guidelines without too much work.

 If you want to know what Material Design is in detail, please check out https://material.io/.

The first basic widget for applying Material guidelines in Flutter apps is the `MaterialApp` widget. Let's see how it works in details.

# MaterialApp widget

The `Theme` widget is not the only way to theme an application. The `MaterialApp` widget is the other only widget that also accepts a `ThemeData` value through its `theme` property. Along with `theme`, `MaterialApp` adds helper properties for localization, for example, and also navigation between screens, which we will check out in Chapter 7, *Routing: Navigating Between Screens*.

By adding a `MaterialApp` widget as the root widget of the app, you are stating your intention to follow Material Design guidelines, and that is the purpose of it, right?

Now that it knows that you will be following Material Design guidelines, the framework will be slightly different in relation to the default theme. In the following code, we do not specify a style for our text:

```
class MaterialAppDefaultTheme extends StatelessWidget {
  @override
  Widget build(BuildContext context) {
    return MaterialApp(
      home: Container(
        color: Colors.white,
        child: Center(
          child: Text(
            "Simple Text",
            // textDirection: TextDirection.ltr, don't need
            // now thanks to materialapp
          ),
        ),
      ),
    );
  }
}
```

In this code, we have stated our intention to follow Material Design guidelines by adding `MaterialApp` widget as our root widget, it will produce a fallback to a not very attractive `DefaultTextStyle` style to advise that the developer that they are not using Material Design effectively in the `Text` widgets. The result of the previous code is as follows:

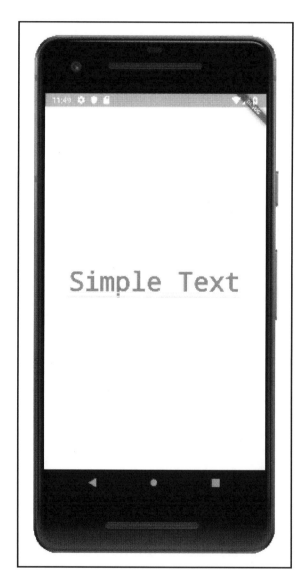

In other words, we should always wrap Text widgets inside some Material Design based widget to apply the typography styles proposed by the guidelines properly.
The Material widget is the simplest example; it has a DefaultTextStyle property and other typical Material Design properties, such as elevation for the shadow effect from the guidelines.

Note that we also did not provide a textDirection property of the Text widget this time. One of the functions of MaterialApp is to allow us to apply **internationalization** to our app, and textDirection is based on the ambient Locale.

> We will be looking at how to work with localization in Chapter 13, *Improving the User Experience*.

By using MaterialApp widget, we have seen how to init the following Material Design guidelines. Another important widget to help on this task is the Scaffold widget. Let's see how to use it in the next section.

# Scaffold widget

We saw in Chapter 4, *Widgets: Building Layouts in Flutter*, that the Scaffold widget has properties that help to construct the layout with a Material Design look. Its purpose is as important as the MaterialApp widget; it helps the developer to follow the Material Design guidelines by simply adding the corresponding widgets to its properties. Our Favors app main screen follows some Material Design aspects.

Let's see:

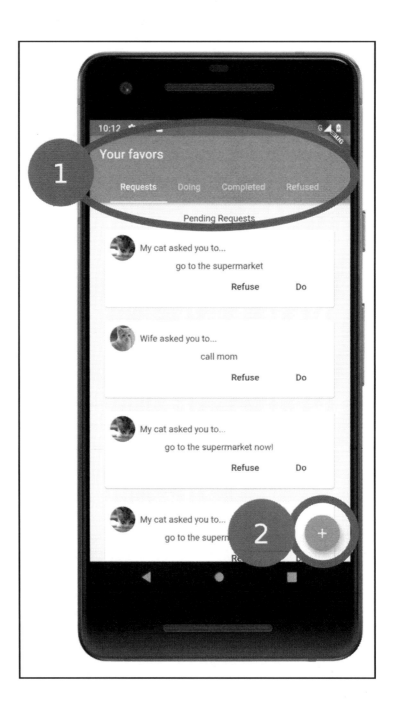

Here, we have used some Material Design components and also the `Scaffold` widget. Some of the pieces used are as follows:

- The *app bar* shown at the top of the app typically contains a title and user context actions such as filters or settings. In this example, through the `appbar` property of the `Scaffold` widget, we show an AppBar widget that has a title and a `TabBar` to display tabs.
- The *floating action button* is one of the most famous Material Design components; it's a floating round button typically displayed in the bottom-right corner of the screen. In this example, it contains the main action of the app, **Request a favor**, following the Material Design guidelines.

Now that we have seen how the default theme looks like in some widgets. Let's see how to build our own custom theme with colors of our choice.

# Custom theme

Our Favors app has not used any properties of `Theme` or `ThemeData` until now. It's time to customize the style of the app to make it more attractive. This is what it's going to look like after we refactor its styles:

Your favors page (This is an image of Your favors page. The other (blurred out) information is not important here)

We will start by creating a custom `lightTheme` definition. We have few ways to color of our app: we can set custom colors to each of the color properties in the `ThemeData` class (it has properties for each of the Material Design available widgets, such as cards or buttons). The key is to experiment with the color properties and the guidelines.

 Remember, you can always overwrite the app's `Theme` definition in the widget tree (with a different card color, for example) by wrapping it in another `Theme` widget.

Now, let's define `ThemeData`:

```
final lightTheme = ThemeData(
  primarySwatch: Colors.lightGreen,
  primaryColor: Colors.lightGreen.shade600,// not necessary when
                                           // primarySwatch is defined
                                           // as above
  accentColor: Colors.orangeAccent.shade400,
  primaryColorBrightness: Brightness.dark,
  cardColor: Colors.lightGreen.shade100,
);
```

We have defined a new `ThemeData` widget that is light bright by default, and we have modified its `primarySwatch` property. We have used a color based on the Material palette, where we can define some colors and the whole scheme will be derived from this swatch. Although the default theme is light (light background/dark texts), we have set `primaryColorBrightness` to `Brightness.dark` so that text that appears on top of a background is white by default.

Also, notice that we have defined the theme in a new Dart file to help with code organization. So, we need to import it in order to use it in our application:

```
return MaterialApp(
  theme: lightTheme,
  home: FavorsPage(),
);
```

As you may expect, the app uses the imported `lightTheme` through its `theme` property.

 For the color scheme definition of the application, we have used the color tool from Material Design website. Take a look at `https://material.io/tools/color/` for more information. Another tip: if you are using macOS for development, the Material Theme Editor can help you make your own theme. Check it out at `https://material.io/tools/theme-editor/`.

Changing the colors is not enough to change the look of the app. Another thing we can do is to change the text styles and use Material Design styles. As we have seen before, this is done by using the `style` property of `Text` widgets. So, after making some changes, our favors cards could emphasize some parts of the text.

In the list headers, for example, we have added a style to make it bigger:

```
final titleStyle = Theme.of(context).textTheme.title;
```

We get the `titleStyle` style from the application theme and apply it direct to the `Text` widget:

```
Text(
  title,
  style: titleStyle,
)
```

The same is done for other `Text` widgets in the app. As you could see in our Favors app example, modify our widgets styles is easy by using `Theme` widget and helper classes. You can check out the source code of this chapter on GitHub for more details, and we encourage you to experiment with some values for practice.

Now that you know the basics of Material Design, let's introduce iOS Cupertino to have some comparative info.

# iOS Cupertino

The aim of making an application look native is important on Flutter. With this in mind, a lot of effort is made to bring the Cupertino side of the framework to the same level of coverage as the Material Design side. During the writing of this book, many Cupertino widgets have been added to the framework.

The idea is that their behavior is faithful to native apps, so this is not an easy task. The community has an important role in this task by using the components and giving feedback.

Like Material Design widgets, `CupertinoApp`, `CupertinoPageScaffold`, and `CupertinoTabScaffold` are the main Cupertino widgets of available in Flutter.

 We're not entering in `CupertinoPageScaffold` and `CupertinoTabScaffold` widgets in details here. You can check these and all the available Cupertino widgets in details `https://flutter.io/docs/development/ui/widgets/cupertino`.

The iOS Cupertino alternative to `MaterialApp` widget is `CupertinoApp` widget, let's see its key properties and how it compares to `MaterialApp` widget.

# CupertinoApp

`CupertinoApp` behaves the same way for Cupertino as `MaterialApp` does for Material Design. It adds striking features and facilities for the developer to follow the design patterns of Cupertino. For example, it makes the app use, by default, a bouncing scroll that's typical in iOS, a custom font that's different from Android, and more.

Along with `theme`, `CupertinoApp` adds helper properties for localization, for example, and also navigation between screens, which we will explore in Chapter 7, *Routing: Navigating Between Screens.*

This works the same way as Material Design. We can choose to use `CupertinoApp` or not. So, we still be able to use the `CupertinoTheme` and `CupertinoThemeData` widgets, the same way as we would do for Material Design. What changes from one to another in practice are its available properties.

 As this is very similar to the previous section; we are not going to go into detail here. You can experiment with the themes and take a look at the attached `cupertino_theme` folder for small examples of how to use it.

Although it's not recommended, we can always mix everything in code, making some parts follow Material Design and some follow Cupertino. We can create two app classes, one for Material Design and one for Cupertino. We can even create a generic app class that changes the widget layout based on the platform (the `Platform` class).

Let's experiment some of the iOS Cupertino widgets in our Favors app.

# Cupertino in practice

Our Favors app is designed to use Material Design components, but we can choose to make it look more native in iOS by using Cupertino widgets. This can be done with a combination of conditions during the build of our widgets using the `Platform` class.

We can, for example, design a Cupertino alternative for the first favors screen:

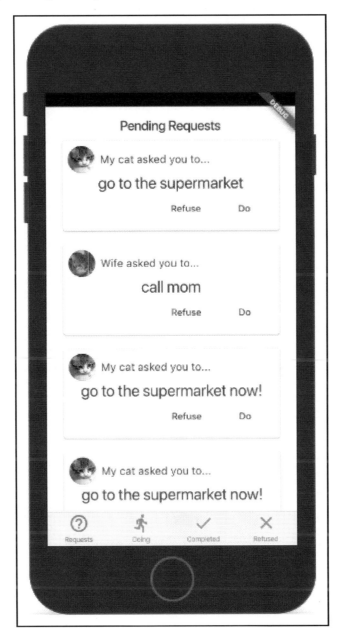

As you can see, in the iOS Cupertino variant, we have the navigation bar at the bottom of the screen instead. OK, this does not look very good, but the important thing is the idea of making custom layouts based on the target platform. Flutter gives you the tools; you must use them properly.

 You can find the source code of `hands_on_cupertino_theme` example on GitHub to see all the conditions and changes made to use Cupertino widgets. The theme part is omitted as it works in very similar way to Material Design.

We need to make a check on target platform and build different widgets depending on it. This can be quite complicated, so an alternative is to develop separated widget classes for each platform and to not mix up all the code, which helps with organization.

In our example, we have only made the first screen in order to illustrate how the tree can be conditioned based on the platform. The Favors app will have the same style on both platforms. Now, let's see how to use custom fonts to give a brand focus on applications.

# Using custom fonts

Material Design and Cupertino provide good fonts for application design, but sometimes it's useful to change the default font to one that's more brand/product focused.

As the font is specified in `Theme` widget, we can add it to the root application theme, and then it's applied to the whole application. If you prefer to specify the font per widget, this is also possible. The first step to use a custom font in Flutter applications is to import font files into the project.

## Importing fonts to the Flutter project

This time, we will be using our Favors app directly to show the example. We will be importing and using a custom font as the default font for the whole application.

To do that, we can put the font files in a project sub-directory and later, declare these font files in the `pubspec.yaml` file. In this example, we will be using the Ubuntu fonts found on the Google Fonts website.

Check out the different fonts available at https://fonts.google.com/.

The first step is adding the files to the project directory. It is common practice to put font files in a fonts/ or assets/ sub-directory of the Flutter project. Here, we will be using a fonts/ directory:

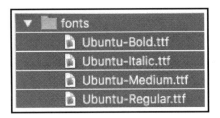

After that, we need to declare the font assets in the pubspec.yaml file so the framework will know where to find the desired font during text styling:

```
// pubspec.yaml file - the full source code can be found in hands_on_fonts
example folder
// .. hidden for brevity
flutter:
  uses-material-design: true
  fonts:
    - family: Ubuntu
      fonts:
        - asset: fonts/Ubuntu-Regular.ttf
        - asset: fonts/Ubuntu-Italic.ttf
          style: italic
        - asset: fonts/Ubuntu-Medium.ttf
          weight: 500
        - asset: fonts/Ubuntu-Bold.ttf
          weight: 700
```

As you can see, we have defined the font in a few sections:

- The `family` field names the font in the framework context. It does not need to match the font filenames. It will be used to refer to it in code, so be consistent.
- After that, we have a `fonts` field followed by a list of `asset` fields of the imported font. All of the specified assets will be included in the application asset bundle. We need to specify each `asset` with details corresponding to its style:
    - `weight`: This determines the weight of the font in the asset. It corresponds to the `FontWeight` enum values applied during layout, so specify it properly.
    - `style`: This determines whether the asset file corresponds to a normal font outline or an *italic* variant. These values correspond to the `FontStyle` enum.

Check out the documentation for how to specify the `weight` and `style` properties correctly and the typical values of each type: `https://api.flutter.dev/flutter/dart-ui/FontWeight-class.html` and `https://api.flutter.dev/flutter/dart-ui/FontStyle-class.html`.

After importing the font into the project, let's apply the font to our `Text` widgets.

# Overriding the default font in the app

The next step is to make the font active in the application. We can do that in the root theme inside a `MaterialApp` and `CupertinoApp` widget, or, if we prefer, we can add a font directly to a `Text` widget through its style property:

```
final lightTheme = ThemeData(
    fontFamily: "Ubuntu",
    primarySwatch: Colors.lightGreen,
    primaryColor: Colors.lightGreen.shade600,
    accentColor: Colors.orangeAccent.shade400,
    primaryColorBrightness: Brightness.dark,
    cardColor: Colors.lightGreen.shade100,
);
```

Our app now uses the Ubuntu font family by default in all widgets that contain text. Remember, this behavior can be overridden in small sections of the app, if you prefer, by using `Theme` widgets or changing the style property of `Text` widgets directly.

If you try to use a bold variant weight of a custom font family that is not declared in the `pubspec.yaml` file, the framework will use the more generic files for the font and will attempt to extrapolate outlines for the requested weight and style.

As you could see, applying a custom font to the whole application by simply importing the desired font and declaring it in the project. Another important aspect in theming and styling is to adapt layouts for different devices. `MediaQuery` and `LayoutBuilder` widgets can help on this task, let's see.

# Dynamic styling with MediaQuery and LayoutBuilder

Adapting a layout to a platform may help us to cater to a bigger audience. But another thing to realize is the massive number of different devices, which poses other challenges to developer.

Developing to support multiple screen sizes is a challenge that will be always present in the life of a developer, so we need mechanisms to adapt to this in the best way. Flutter, again, gives us the tools that we need to know about the ecosystem the app is running so that we can act on it.

To help with this task, the main classes Flutter provides are `LayoutBuilder` and `MediaQuery`.

# LayoutBuilder

The `LayoutBuilder` widget provides a builder property of the `LayoutWidgetBuilder` type. Although it's similar to the `Builder` widget, `LayoutWidgetBuilder` comes with additional info about the parent widget size inside a `BoxConstraints` value.

With this information, the `build` method can be changed according to the available space. So, in different devices there will be a different amount of space available in the root widget of the tree, which may limit its children's sizes as well. By using this widget, we can choose whether or not to show some parts of the layout.

This widget is dependent on the parent widget's size, so it gets rebuilt every time the size changes. This can occur in different ways on mobile devices. The simplest example is when the app orientation changes, that is, when the user rotates the phone.

Let's check out how to respond to a size change on the screen. In this example, we will change the way two widgets are displayed based on the available space. So, the widgets are displayed one on top of the other when there is not sufficient room for them (we evaluate this using the BoxContraints instance given by the LayoutBuilder widget), or side-by-side when there is more space available (such as in the landscape position):

```
class MyApp extends StatelessWidget {
  @override
  Widget build(BuildContext context) {
    return MaterialApp(
      home: LayoutBuilder(
        builder: (BuildContext context, BoxConstraints constraints) {
          // build the layout based on constraints values
        }
      )
    )
  }
}
```

As you can see, we have added a LayoutBuilder widget, and we can build the layout based on the given constraints:

```
if (constraints.maxWidth <= 500) {
    return Column(
        mainAxisSize: MainAxisSize.max,
        children: <Widget>[
            Expanded(
                child: Container(
                    color: Colors.green,
                    child: Center(child: Text("1")),
                ),
            ),
            Expanded(
                child: Container(
                    color: Colors.blue,
                    child: Center(child: Text("2")),
                ),
            ),
        ],
    );
}
```

Conditionally, we display a Column widget when the available width is less than 500. And when we have enough room we change the returned widget:

```
return Row(
    mainAxisSize: MainAxisSize.max,
```

```
    children: <Widget>[
        Expanded(
            child: Container(
                color: Colors.yellow,
                child: Center(child: Text("1")),
            ),
        ),
        Expanded(
            child: Container(
                color: Colors.purple,
                child: Center(child: Text("2")),
            ),
        ),
    ],
);
```

In this case we return a Row widget, as we have sufficient space (greater than 500).

This is how it looks in different orientations:

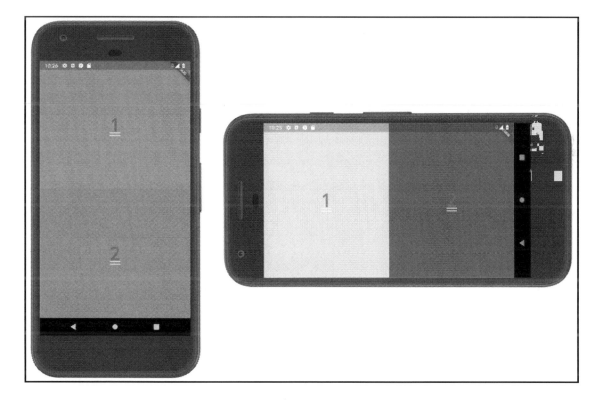

As you can see, we make changes to the layout based not solely on orientation, but on the available width. Another way to respond to changes in available size is by using the `MediaQuery` class. Now, let'see how the `MediaQuery` alternative works.

# MediaQuery

`MediQuery` is an `InheritedWidget` descendant that contains information about the size of the whole screen, and not only the parent widget. As an `InheritedWidget` widget, this also provides the previously introduced `MediaQuery.of` method, which looks up the tree for a `MediaQuery` instance.

Its use is conditioned by the presence of an instance in the context. This can be easily done by adding a `WidgetsApp` instance as our root widget. `WidgetsApp` is not platform-specific, like `MaterialApp` or `CupertinoApp`, which use this class in their internal implementation.

Let's see how to use `MediaQuery` class to make a responsive layout.

# MediaQuery example

Our Favors app is not responsive in terms of screen size so far. It displays a vertical list of cards that fills the available space on the screen. For typical smartphones, it looks good, but this is how it looks on devices with a bigger screen:

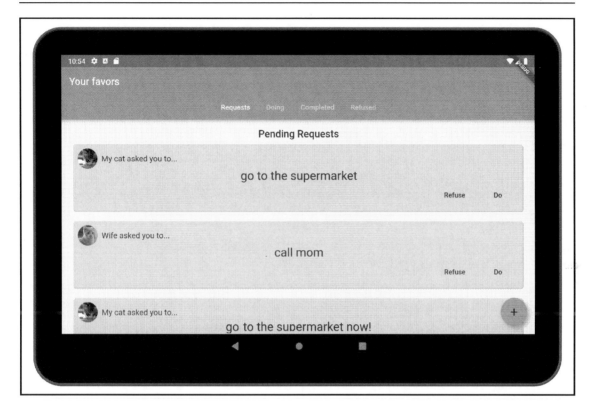

As you can see, each card fills each row, and they are a lot larger than necessary. We can change this according to the screen size and make the list display more items if there is more space than we need to display a card.

By using the MediaQuery class, we have made a calculation to change the number of cards displayed per row:

```
// part of hands_on_mediaquery/lib/main.dart file

class FavorsList extends StatelessWidget {
  // ... hidden for brevity
  @override
  Widget build(BuildContext context) {
    return Column(
      mainAxisSize: MainAxisSize.max,
      children: <Widget>[
        Padding(
          child: Text(
            title,
            style: titleStyle,
```

```
        ),
        padding: EdgeInsets.only(top: 16.0),
      ),
      Expanded(
        child: _builldCardsList(context),
      ),
    ],
  );
}
```

In the preceding code, by wrapping the favors list into an Expanded widget, all the available space of the Column widget is occupied, and we let the logic of resizing with MediaQuery to the _buildCardsList() method as follows:

```
const kFavorCardMaxWidth = 450.0; // a maximum card width

class FavorsList extends StatelessWidget {
  // ... hidden for brevity

  Widget _builldCardsList(BuildContext context) {
    final screenWidth = MediaQuery.of(context).size.width;
    final cardsPerRow = max(screenWidth ~/ kFavorCardMaxWidth, 1);
    // max() function from dart:math package
    if (screenWidth > 400) {
      return GridView.builder(
        physics: BouncingScrollPhysics(),
        itemCount: favors.length,
        scrollDirection: Axis.vertical,
        itemBuilder: (BuildContext context, int index) {
          final favor = favors[index];
          return FavorCardItem(favor: favor);
        },
        gridDelegate: SliverGridDelegateWithFixedCrossAxisCount(
          childAspectRatio: 2.8,
          crossAxisCount: cardsPerRow,
        ),
      );
    }
    return ListView.builder(
      physics: BouncingScrollPhysics(),
      itemCount: favors.length,
      itemBuilder: (BuildContext context, int index) {
        final favor = favors[index];
        return FavorCardItem(favor: favor);
      },
    );
  }
}
```

For the resizing to work properly, we have made some changes to `FavorCardItem` to make the layout more adaptable to the layout changes. You can find the source code of `hands_on_mediaquery` example on GitHub.

In the preceding code, you can see that we can divide the available screen width(taken from `MediaQuery.of(context).size.width`) by the desired maximum width of a card(`kFavorCardMaxWidth`) and store it into the `cardsPerRow` variable. Later, we use it to check if there is room for one more card in a row. Then, if there's room, we list the cards using a `GridView` widget displaying `cardsPerRow` columns. If there's no room for more than a single card, we display a `ListView` widget as before. This is the result:

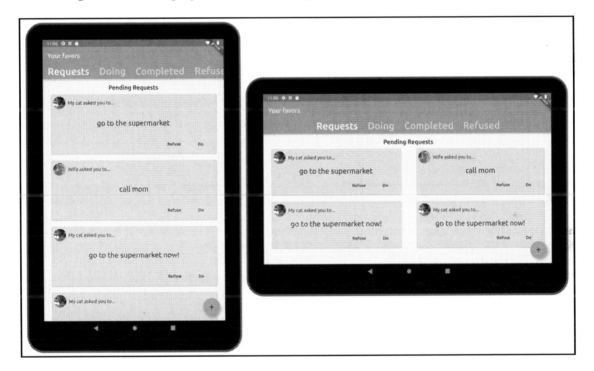

There are some other Flutter widgets available for this task, so maybe a better approach would be to use a container other than a list to display the cards in a more flexible way. Other classes may help on layout adjustments. Let's see some of them in the next section.

# Additional responsive classes

There are other few widgets that help with the task of creating responsive layouts:

- CustomMultiChildLayout gives you the freedom to choose how a set of child widgets are laid out on the screen using a delegate class: MultiChildLayoutDelegate.
- FittedBox changes its child size and position according to a specific fit. Have a look at https://docs.flutter.io/flutter/painting/BoxFit-class.html to see the available values.
- AspectRatio attempts to force the size of its child according to a specific aspect ratio.

By using all these available classes, we can make our Flutter layouts adaptative. We are able to style our widgets and make the whole app customized.

# Summary

Customizing apps in terms of styles is fundamental to create a unique experience for the user and achieve the app goals. Knowing the Flutter framework classes that help on this task is crucial to the development of any app, including our Favors app throughout the book.

In this chapter, we have seen some ways to change the style of our applications. By using the Theme and ThemeData widgets we can specify styles that will change all the widgets below them in the tree. Also, by using the available app classes, MaterialApp and CupertinoApp, we can change the style of the whole application in a simple way.

We have seen how to add a custom font family to our application so that we can change the default look of our texts and labels. Lastly, we have seen that is possible to change how our app looks in different sizes or orientations by using the MediaQuery and LayoutBuilder classes, or even specifically for the target platform by using the Platform class.

In the next chapter, we will learn how navigation between screens works in Flutter, and how to use the Navigator property to change what is visible to the user.

# 7
# Routing: Navigating between Screens

Mobile apps are typically organized on multiple screens. In Flutter, the route corresponding to a screen is managed by the `Navigator` widget of the application. The `Navigator` widget manages the navigation stack, pushing a new route or pop to the previous one. In this chapter, you will learn how to use the `Navigator` widget to manage your app routes and how to add transition animations between screens.

The following topics will be covered in this chapter:

- Understanding the Navigator widget
- Understanding routes
- Learning about transitions
- Exploring Hero animations

## Understanding the Navigator widget

Mobile applications will often contain more than one screen. If you are an Android or iOS developer, you probably know about `Activity` or `ViewController` classes that represent screens on those platforms respectively.

An important class in navigation between screens in Flutter is the `Navigator` widget that is responsible for managing screen changes with a logical history idea.

A new screen in Flutter is just a new widget that is placed in front of another. This is managed by the concept of `Routes`, which defines possible navigation in the app. As you may already have guessed, the `Route` class is a helper for Flutter to work on the navigation workflow.

The main players in the navigation layer are as follows:

- `Navigator`: The `Route` manager
- `Overlay`: Navigator uses this to specify appearances of the routes
- `Route`: A navigation endpoint

# Navigator

The `Navigator` widget is the main player in the task of moving from one screen to another. Most of the time, we will be switching screens and passing data between them, which is another important task for the `Navigator` widget.

Navigation in Flutter is made in a *stack* structure. The stack structure is suitable for this task because its concept is very similar to a screen's behavior:

- We have one element at the *top of the stack*. In `Navigator`, the top-most element on the stack is the currently visible screen of the app.
- The last element inserted is the first to be removed from the stack (commonly refereed as **last in first out (LIFO)**). The last screen visible is the first that is removed.
- Like stack, the `Navigator` widget's main methods are `push()` and `pop()`.

# Overlay

In its implementation, `Navigator` uses the `Overlay` widget. The following is from the documentation:

> *"Overlays let independent child widgets appear on top of other widgets by inserting them into the overlay's Stack."*

The overlay lets each of these widgets manage their participation in the overlay using `OverlayEntry` objects.

We'll go through a few steps to check that the most common way to use a `Navigator` and its `Overlay` is with the app widgets, `WidgetsApp`, `MaterialApp`, and `CupertinoApp`, which provide multiple ways to manage navigation through the `Navigator` widget.

# Navigation stack/history

As you already may have noticed, the `push()` method adds a new screen to the top of the *navigation stack*. `Pop()`, in turn, removes it from the navigation stack.

So, in summary, the navigation stack is the stack of screens that entered the scene thanks to the `Navigator` widget's `push()` method.

> The navigation stack is also known as **navigation history**.

# Route

The navigation stack elements are `Routes`, and there are multiple ways to define them in Flutter.

When we want to navigate to a new screen, we define a new `Route` widget to it, in addition to some parameters defined as a `RouteSettings` instance.

## RouteSettings

This is a simple class that contains information about the route relevant to the `Navigator` widget. The main properties it contains are as follows:

- `name`: Identifies the route uniquely. We will explore it in detail in the next section.
- `arguments`: With this, we can pass anything to the destination route.

> You can check more details about this class in documents: `https://docs.flutter.io/flutter/widgets/RouteSettings-class.html`.

# MaterialPageRoute and CupertinoPageRoute

The Route class is a high-level abstraction through the navigation feature. However, we will not use it directly, as we have seen that a screen is a route in Flutter. Different platforms may require screen changes to behave differently. In Flutter, there are alternative implementations in a platform-adaptive way. This job is done with MaterialPageRoute and CupertinoPageRoute, which adapt to Android and iOS respectively. So, we must decide when developing an application whether to use the Material Design or iOS Cupertino transitions, or both, depending on the context.

# Putting it all together

It is time to check out how to use the Navigator widget in practice. Let's create a basic flow to navigate to a second screen and back. It will look something like this:

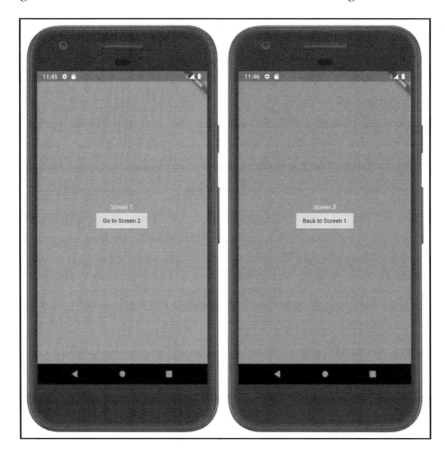

The basic way to use a `Navigator` widget is like any other—by adding it to the widget tree:

```
class NavigatorDirectlyApp extends StatelessWidget {
  @override
  Widget build(BuildContext context) {
    return Directionality(
      child: Navigator(
        onGenerateRoute: (RouteSettings settings) {
          return MaterialPageRoute(
              builder: (BuildContext context) => _screen1(context));
        },
      ),
      textDirection: TextDirection.ltr,
    );
  }
  _screen1(BuildContext context) {...} // hidden for brevity
  _screen2(BuildContext context) {...} // hidden for brevity
}
```

The `Directionality` widget was added here so that we could show `Text` widgets. Remember, `WidgetsApp` and variations manage this and more for us.

The `Navigator` widget contains an `onGenerateRoute` property, a callback that is responsible for creating a `Route` widget based on a `RouteSettings` object passed as an argument.

In the preceding example, you can see that we did not use the `settings` argument; instead, we returned a default route. The most common approach would check the settings' `name` property, which works as the identifier of the route. The framework uses the `'/'` name as the initial route by default and will make an initial call to the callback, passing this as an argument. So, the preceding example uses the `_screen1` returned widget as the initial route.

Check the *Named routes* section later in this chapter for more details and examples of route names.

The result from the `onGenerateRoute` callback is a `Route` object. We have used the `MaterialPageRoute` type here. In its most basic implementation, we should pass an `onGenerateRoute` callback to it too. It should return a widget to be displayed as the `Route`. You might be asking: *why not use a child property to add the child widget directly?* Its creation depends on the context in which it is built, as the `Navigator` widget may create this `Route` widget in different contexts.

But if you check the following code, you will see that we can navigate from one screen to another by clicking the corresponding button. We can see this in the `_screen1` method, for example:

```
Widget _screen1(BuildContext context) {
  return Container(
    color: Colors.green,
    child: Column(
      mainAxisSize: MainAxisSize.max,
      mainAxisAlignment: MainAxisAlignment.center,
      children: <Widget>[
        Text("Screen 1"),
        RaisedButton(
          child: Text("Go to Screen 2"),
          onPressed: () {
            Navigator.of(context).push(
              MaterialPageRoute(
                builder: (BuildContext context) {
                  return _screen2(context);
                },
              ),
            );
          },
        )
      ],
    ),
  );
}
```

Here, you can check that the `Navigator` widget is accessed by using its `Navigator.of` static method. You will be familiar with this by now and, as you might be guessing, this is the way we access the corresponding `Navigator` ancestor from a specific context, and yes, we can have many `Navigator` widgets in a tree. That is great, as we can have different pieces of independent navigation in subsections of an application.

Back to the example, let's have a look at the `RaisedButton` widget's `onPressed` callback, where we push a new `Route` into the navigation. From here, the value we pass to the `push` method is similar to the one returned from the `onGenerateRoute` callback in the previously added `Navigator`.

To summarize, our top `Navigator` widget uses the `onGenerateRoute` callback just to initialize the navigation by providing the initial `Route`. Later on, screen buttons were added to push a new `Route` to the navigation, using the `push()` method from the `Navigator` widget:

```
// button on screen 2 to navigate back
onPressed: () {
  Navigator.of(context).pop();
},
// _NavigatorDirectlyAppState
```

The `_screen2` widget is almost equal to `_screen1`; the only difference is that it pops itself from the navigation and goes back to the `_screen1` widget.

There is a problem with the preceding example, though. If we press the back button on Android, for example, while on **Screen 2**, we should go back to **Screen 1** as a result, but that is not the case. As we have added the `Navigator` widget by ourselves, the system is not aware of it: we need to manage it by ourselves as well.

To manage the back button, we need to use `WidgetsBindingObserver`, which can be used to react to lifecycle messages related to a `Flutter` application. As you can see in the source codes on GitHub (in the `navigation` directory), we first converted our app to `Stateful` and added `WidgetsBindingObserver` as a mixin to our `State` class. We also started the observer in `initState()` with `WidgetsBinding.instance.addObserver(this);` and stopped the observer with `WidgetsBinding.instance.removeObserver(this);` on `dispose()`. With this setup, we can override the `didPopRoute()` method from `WidgetsBindingObserver` and manage what happens when the system tells the app to pop a route. The `didPopRoute()` method is described as follows in the documentation:

> *"[It is] called when the system tells the app to pop the current route. For example, on Android, this is called when the user presses the back button."*

Inside the `didPopRoute()` method, we need to pop a Route from our `Navigator` widget. However, we cannot access `Navigator` through its static `of` method, as we do not have the context below this here. We can alternatively add a key to `Navigator` and access its state here:

```
// navigation_directly.dart
class _NavigatorDirectlyAppState extends State<NavigatorDirectlyApp> {
  final _navigatorKey = GlobalKey<NavigatorState>();
  // ... other fields and methods

  // part of build method
  Navigator(
    key: _navigatorKey,
    ...
  )
}
```

And we can add the `didPopRoute()` method as well:

```
@override
Future<bool> didPopRoute() {
  return Future.value(_navigatorKey.currentState.pop());
}
```

Here, we have used the `pop()` method from the `Navigator` state to pop the top-most route from the navigation. As this method expects a `true` return if the observer was managed from the pop route notification, we return it from the `Navigator` pop values as well, so that when there are no more `Routes` from it to pop, the default behavior still happens (it quits the app).

## The WidgetsApp way

As we have seen before, this is not the most practical way to use `Navigator` in our applications: we have many things to manage that could be avoided.

The typical way to use it is through the app widgets. They offer some properties and methods to include navigation in the application:

- `builder`: The `builder` property allows us to add an alternative path to the Navigator, which is added by the `WidgetsApp`.
- `home`: Lets us specify the widget equivalent to the first route in the app (normally `'/'`).

- initialRoute: Allows us to change the initial route of the app (defaults to '/').
- navigatorKey and navigatorObserver: Allows us to specify corresponding values to the built Navigator widget.
- onGenerateRoute: Creates widgets based on the name of the route settings, such as the one used in the previous example. It is the callback to create Routes from a RouteSettings argument.
- onUnknownRoute: Specifies a callback to generate a Route for when there is a failure in a Route building process (for example, a path not found).
- pageRouteBuilder: Similar to onGenerateRoute, but specialized on the PageRoute type.
- routes: Accepts a Map<String, WidgetBuilder>, where we can add a list of routes of our app with its corresponding building blocks.

Writing the previous example is easier as we can skip all the Navigator-specific implementations, like back button observer, or navigator key:

```
class NavigatorWidgetsApp extends StatefulWidget {
  @override
  _NavigatorWidgetsAppState createState() => _NavigatorWidgetsAppState();
}

class _NavigatorWidgetsAppState extends State<NavigatorWidgetsApp> {
  @override
  Widget build(BuildContext context) {
    return WidgetsApp(
      color: Colors.blue,
      home: Builder(
        builder: (context) => _screen1(context),
      ),
      pageRouteBuilder: <Void>(RouteSettings settings, WidgetBuilder
      builder) {
        return MaterialPageRoute(builder: builder, settings: settings);
      },
    );
  }
  _screen1(BuildContext context) {...} // hidden for brevity
  _screen2(BuildContext context) {...} // hidden for brevity
}
```

As you can see, the preceding implementation is much simpler than the first one; we just specify the `home` and `pageRouteBuilder` property from the app, and the rest works automatically:

- In `home`, we set the initial route of the navigation. We add it in a builder to delegate its creation for a low level in the tree, so when it looks up to find a `Navigator`, it will work.
- In `pageRouteBuilder`, we set which kind of `PageRoute` object should be built when navigating between routes.

We can make it even better by using named routes. See the next section. Also, check the `WidgetsApp` documentation for details on how to use these properties combined, at: `https://docs.flutter.io/flutter/widgets/WidgetsApp-class.html`. The same applies for `MaterialApp` and `CupertinoApp`.

The full source code of these examples can be found in the navigation project in the chapter examples directory.

# Named routes

The route name is an important piece of navigation. It is the identification of the route with its manager, the `Navigator` widget.

We can define a series of routes with names associated with each of them. It provides a level of abstraction to the meaning of a route and a screen. By the way, they can be used in a path structure; in other words, they can be seen as subroutes.

Have a look at the `home` property of the `WidgetsApp`. It implicitly sets the home route widget for the `Navigator` widget. It is referred to as the `'/'` path.

# Moving to named routes

Our previous example using the `WidgetsApp` widget is very simple, but we can turn it into a more organized way of doing things. By using named routes, we can do the following:

- Organize the screens in a clear way
- Centralize the creation of screens
- Pass parameters to screens

Let's check it out:

```
// navigation_widgetsapp_named_routes.dart
class _NavigatorNamedRoutesWidgetsAppState extends
State<NavigatorNamedRoutesWidgetsApp> {
  @override
  Widget build(BuildContext context) {
    return WidgetsApp(
      color: Colors.blue,
      routes: {
        '/': (context) => _screen1(context),
        '/2': (context) => _screen2(context),
      },
      pageRouteBuilder: <Void>(RouteSettings settings, WidgetBuilder
      builder) {
        return MaterialPageRoute(builder: builder, settings: settings);
      },
    );
  }
}
```

From the preceding example, you can see that we used the `routes` property to set a routing table for the `Navigator` to know what to build for each path.

We can still use the `home` property if we want to, as shown in the following example:

```
WidgetsApp(
  home: Builder(
    builder: (context) => _screen1(context),
  ),
  routes: {
    '/2': (context) => _screen2(context),
  },
  ...
)
```

Notice that when doing that, we should not add the `'/'` route to the `routes` map.

Another benefit of using named routes is in pushing new routes. We can use the `pushNamed` method when we want to navigate to **Screen 2** from **Screen 1**:

```
Navigator.of(context).pushNamed('/2');
```

This way, we do not need to create the `Route` object in every call; it will use our previously defined builder in the routes map of `routesWidgetsApp`.

# Arguments

The `pushNamed` method also accepts arguments, to pass to the new `Route`:

```
Navigator.of(context).pushNamed('/2', arguments: "Hello from screen 1");
```

In this case, we need to use `onGenerateRoute` from `WidgetsApp` so that we have access to these arguments through the `RouteSettings` object:

```
// navigation_widgetsapp_named_routes_arguments.dart
class _NavigatorNamedRoutesArgumentsAppState
    extends State<NavigatorNamedRoutesArgumentsApp> {
  @override
  Widget build(BuildContext context) {
    return WidgetsApp(
      color: Colors.blue,
      onGenerateRoute: (settings) {
        if(settings.name == '/') {
          return MaterialPageRoute(
            builder: (context) => _screen1(context)
          );
        } else if(settings.name == '/2') {
          return MaterialPageRoute(
            builder: (context) => _screen2(context, settings.arguments)
          );
        }
      },
    );
  }
  ...
}
```

After that, we use the argument normally found in in the `_screen2` builder, to display an additional message.

When using the `Routes` creation on demand, it looks easier to pass arguments, as you will build the widget at the time you need and can customize the creation by passing arguments as you need.

# Retrieving results from Route

When a route is pushed to the navigation, we may want to expect something back from it—for example, when we ask for something from the user in a new route, we can take the value returned via the `pop()` method's result parameter.

The `push` method and its variants return a `Future`. The `Future` resolves when the route is popped and the value of `Future` is the `pop()` method's result parameter.

We have seen that we can pass arguments to a new `Route`. As the inverse path is also possible, instead of sending a message to the second screen, we can take a message when it pops back.

In **Screen 2**, we just make sure to return something when doing the pop from `Navigator`:

```
// part of navigation_widgetsapp_navigation_result.dart
class _NavigatorResultAppState
    extends State<NavigatorResultApp> {

  Widget _screen2(BuildContext context) {
    // ... hidden for brevety
    RaisedButton(
      child: Text("Back to Screen 1"),
      onPressed: () {
        Navigator.of(context).pop("Good bye from screen 2");
      },
    ),
    ...
}
```

The second argument in the pop method is the result from the route.

In the caller screen, we need to take the result back:

```
// part of navigation_widgetsapp_navigation_result.dart
class _NavigatorResultAppState
    extends State<NavigatorResultApp> {

  Widget _screen1(BuildContext context) {
    // ... hidden for brevety
```

```
RaisedButton(
  child: Text("Go to Screen 2"),
  onPressed: () async {
    final message = await Navigator.of(context).pushNamed('/2') ??
    "Came from back button";
    setState(() {
      _message = message;
    });
  },
),
...
    }
}
```

 Please check out the source code of this chapter on GitHub for the full example.

The result of push is a Future we need to take using the await keyword. Here, we just set it to a new _message variable that is displayed in a text.

 If you do not remember how to work with Future, take a look back at Chapter 2, *Intermediate Dart Programming*, in the *Futures and async* section.

# Screen transitions

Changing screens needs to be smooth from a user experience perspective. We have seen that Navigator widgets work on an Overlay to manage Routes. The transition between routes is also managed at this level.

As we have seen, MaterialPageRoute and CupertinoPageRoute are classes that add a modal route to the overlay with a platform-adaptive transition between the old and new Route.

On Android, for example, the entrance transition for the page slides the page upward and fades it in. The exit transition does the same in reverse. On iOS, the page slides in from the right and exits in reverse. Flutter also lets us customize this behavior by adding our own transitions between screens.

# PageRouteBuilder

PageRouteBuilder is the definition of a Route creation. The documentation provides the following definition:

*"A utility class for defining one-off page routes in terms of callbacks."*

If you remember, WidgetsApp contains a pageRouteBuilder property where we define which PageRoute should be used by our app, and where the transitions are normally defined.

PageRouteBuilder contains multiple callbacks and properties to help in the PageRoute definition. Here are some examples:

- transitionsBuilder: The builder callback for the transition, where we build the transition from previous to new route
- transitionDuration: The duration for the transition
- barrierColor and barrierDismissible: This defines partially covered routes of model and not full-screen

Check the full docs for more details on the PageRouteBuilder class: https://docs.flutter.io/flutter/widgets/PageRouteBuilder-class.html.

## Custom transitions in practice

We can create a custom transition and apply it globally in our application using pageRouteBuilder:

```
// part of navigation_transition.dart
class _NavigatorTransitionAppState extends State<NavigatorTransitionApp> {
  @override
  Widget build(BuildContext context) {
    return WidgetsApp(
      color: Colors.blue,
      routes: {
        '/': (context) => _screen1(context),
        '/2': (context) => _screen2(context),
      },
      pageRouteBuilder: <Void>(RouteSettings settings, WidgetBuilder
      builder) {
        return PageRouteBuilder(
```

```
transitionsBuilder:
  (BuildContext context, animation, secondaryAnimation, widget) {
  return new SlideTransition(
    position: new Tween<Offset>(
      begin: const Offset(-1.0, 0.0),
      end: Offset.zero,
    ).animate(animation),
    child: widget,
  );
},
pageBuilder: (BuildContext context, _, __) => builder(context),
  );
},
  );
}
...
}
```

By doing this, we change the default transition from a `MaterialPageRoute` class to our custom slide transition. We do this as follows:

- Our `pageRouteBuilder` now returns a `PageRouteBuilder` instance.
- We implement its `pageBuilder` callback to return our widgets normally, by calling the builder callback.
- We implement its `transitionBuilder` callback to return a new widget, typically an `AnimatedWidget` instance or similar. Here, we return a `SlideTransition` widget that encapsulates the animation logic for us: a transition from left to right, until it becomes fully visible.

 We have not checked out animations in details yet. Jump to `Chapter 15`, *Animations*, to find out more about it.

Another way of implementing custom transitions is by on-demand creation of the `Route` object. In this case, a good approach would be to extend the `PageRouteBuilder` class and create a reusable transition.

# Hero animations

The name *Hero* may look strange at first, but everyone that has used a mobile application has already seen this kind of animation. If you develop for mobile platforms, perhaps you have already heard of, or worked with, *shared elements*, that is, elements that persist between screens. This is the definition of a Hero.

Flutter contains ways to facilitate the creation of this kind of movement. That's why we can see how the Hero animations work even before we get deeper into the subject of animations itself.

The most important player this time is the `Hero` widget. Typically, it is just a single piece of the UI for which it makes sense to fly from one `Route` to another.

## The Hero widget

In Flutter, a Hero is a widget that flies between screens. Here is an example:

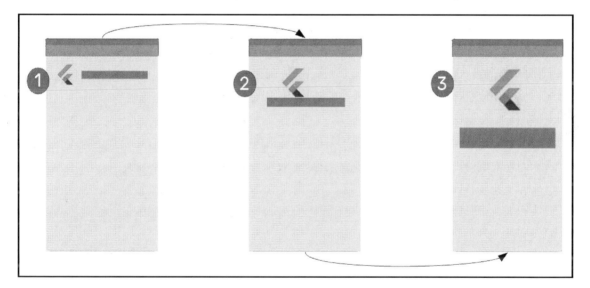

The Hero, in reality, is not the same object from screen to screen. However, from the user perspective, it is. The idea is to make a widget that lives between screens and just changes its appearance in some way. As in the preceding screenshot, the element scales up and moves at the same time the new screen appears. This is what we learn from the three images in the preceding screenshot:

1. This is when we tap on a list item. For example, the transition starts while the detailed screen is shown.
2. A cut-scene from the transition process. Here, the Hero widget will be changes its position and size until it matches the final result (**3**).
3. The final screen, with the Hero from *step 1*, with a new size.

The Flutter documentation contains great explanations and examples about the Hero animation. Don't hesitate to check it out, at: `https://flutter.dev/docs/development/ui/animations/hero-animations`.

# Implementing Hero transitions

We are going to change our Favors app to have a Hero animation between the **Your favors** list screen and the **Requesting favor** screen, so that when we tap on the Request a favor floating button  to request a favor, there will be a smooth transition between it and the next page. The same effect works when going back from **Requesting favor** to the **Your favors** screen:

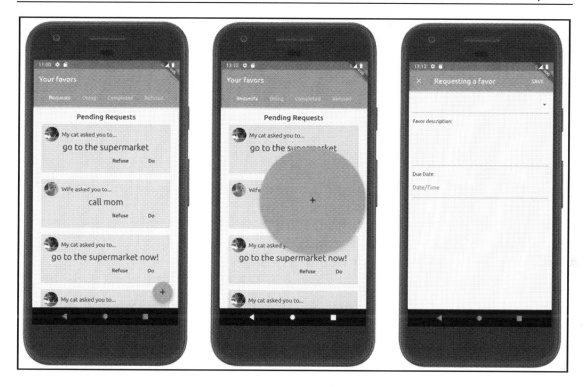

Your favors (This is an image of Your favors. The other (overlapped) information is not important here)

We start the change by adding a `Hero` widget to our tree. It should wrap the widgets involved in the animation:

```
class FavorsPageState extends State<FavorsPage> {
  // ...
  @override
  Widget build(BuildContext context) {
    // ...
    floatingActionButton: FloatingActionButton(
      heroTag: "request_favor",
      child: FloatingActionButton(
        onPressed: () {
          Navigator.of(context).push(
            MaterialPageRoute(
              builder: (context) => RequestFavorPage(
                friends: mockFriends,
              ),
            ),
          );
        },
```

```
      tooltip: 'Ask a favor',
      child: Icon(Icons.add),
    ),
  ),
 ...
 }
```

The most important thing to notice here is simplicity. Our
`FloatingActionButton` contains a `heroTag` tag property that makes it behave like a
`Hero` widget, which means that it can animate a transition to another screen. For the second
screen, we just need to repeat the process:

```
// part of RequestFavorPageState build method
  @override
  Widget build(BuildContext context) {
    return Hero(
      tag: "request_favor",
      child: Scaffold(
        // rest of scaffold
      ),
    );
  }
...
```

 Check out the `hands_on_hero` file on GitHub.

Pay attention to the `tag` property: this is where the magic occurs. The following is from the
Flutter website:

> *"It's essential that both hero widgets are created with the same tag, typically an object that
> represents the underlying data."*

Also, it's recommended that the Hero widgets have virtually identical widget trees, or even
better, be the same widget, for the best animation results.

In our previous example, we were animating our `FloatingActionButton` to the whole
**Requesting favor** screen widget. That makes a cool effect from the button to the new
screen. However, it does not show the best capability from the Hero animation – sharing
elements between screens. Also, the `FloatingActionButton` widget and the target
`Scaffold` widget does not have anything in common in its widgets subtree, which causes
our effect to not be the best one possible, according to the documentation.

Let's stick to another example. Suppose we have a details screen for our favors, and when the user taps on a `FavorCardItem`, it shows the corresponding favor in full screen, animating this transition with a Hero widget. This is what the effect will looks like:

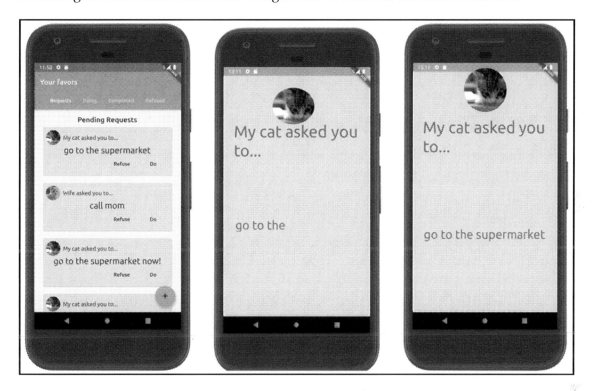

 I know it may not look cool in the screenshots, but take a look at the attached code to see the potential of the `Hero` widget.

To have the avatar and the text animating to the new screen during the transition, we need to create two Heroes, one for the image and one for the description. This is what we have changed in the `FavorCardItem` widget:

```
class FavorCardItem extends StatelessWidget {
...
  @override
  Widget build(BuildContext context) {
  ...
      _itemHeader(context, favor),
      Hero(
```

```
                tag: "description_${favor.uuid}",
                child: Text(
                    favor.description,
                    style: bodyStyle,
                ),
            ),
          _itemFooter(context, favor)
      ...
        }
     ...
     }
```

In the same way, we have modified the _itemHeader method to have a Hero widget wrapping our avatar:

```
Widget _itemHeader(BuildContext context, Favor favor) {
...
     Hero(
        tag: "avatar_${favor.uuid}",
        child: CircleAvatar(
          backgroundImage: NetworkImage(
            favor.friend.photoURL,
          ),
        ),
     ),
  ...
  }
```

Pay attention to the tag property of Hero. We have specified it by using the favor's uuid value to make the Hero uniquely identifiable in the context.

To launch the **Favor details** screen, we need a small change in our FavorsList widget:

```
class FavorsList extends StatelessWidget {
...
  @override
  Widget build(BuildContext context) {
  ...
    Expanded(
        child: ListView.builder(
          physics: BouncingScrollPhysics(),
          itemCount: favors.length,
          itemBuilder: (BuildContext context, int index) {
            final favor = favors[index];
            return InkWell(
              onTap: () {
                Navigator.push(
                  context,
```

```
                     PageRouteBuilder(
                       // transitionDuration: Duration(seconds: 3),
                       // uncomment to see it transition slower
                       pageBuilder: (_, __, ___) =>
                         FavorDetailsPage(favor: favor),
                       ),
                   );
                 },
                 child: FavorCardItem(favor: favor),
             );
           },
         ),
       ),
     ...
   }
   ...
 }
```

We have wrapped our `FavorCardItem` into an `InkWell` widget to handle taps on it. When the user taps on it, a new `Route` will be pushed to the `Navigator` to display the `FavorDetailsPage` widget.

 We have used `PageRouteBuilder` this time, instead of `MaterialPageRoute`, as we do not want Material effects in this transition. Check the `PageRouteBuilder` documentation for details, at: https://api.flutter.dev/flutter/widgets/PageRouteBuilder-class.html.

The last part to take a look at is the `FavorDetailsPage` widget. Here, we create the final look of the favor details screen, and by wrapping the favor avatar and description into `Hero` widgets, we have an awesome transition. This is how its `build()` method looks:

```
// part of hands_on_hero/lib/main.dart
class _FavorDetailsPageState extends State<FavorDetailsPage> {
  @override
  Widget build(BuildContext context) {
    final bodyStyle = Theme.of(context).textTheme.display1;
    return Scaffold(
      body: Card(
        child: Padding(
          padding: EdgeInsets.symmetric(vertical: 10.0, horizontal: 25.0),
          child: Column(
            mainAxisSize: MainAxisSize.min,
            crossAxisAlignment: CrossAxisAlignment.stretch,
            children: <Widget>[
              _itemHeader(context, widget.favor),
```

```
              Container(height: 16.0),
              Expanded(
                child: Center(
                  child: Hero(
                    tag: "description_${widget.favor.uuid}",
                    child: Text(
                      widget.favor.description,
                      style: bodyStyle,
                    ),
                  ),
                ),
              ),
            ],
          ),
        ),
      ),
    );
  }
}
```

And, in the same way, the `_itemHeader()` is defined as follows:

```
Widget _itemHeader(BuildContext context, Favor favor) {
  final headerStyle = Theme.of(context).textTheme.display2;

  return Column(
    mainAxisSize: MainAxisSize.min,
    crossAxisAlignment: CrossAxisAlignment.center,
    children: <Widget>[
      Hero(
        tag: "avatar_${favor.uuid}",
        child: CircleAvatar(
          radius: 60,
          backgroundImage: NetworkImage(
            favor.friend.photoURL,
          ),
        ),
      ),
      Container(height: 16.0),
      Text(
        "${favor.friend.name} asked you to... ",
        style: headerStyle,
      ),
    ],
  );
}
```

As you can see, it looks similar to the `FavorCardItem` widget, aiming to have minimal differences in the tree to get a better transition result. Also, note that the main thing to be concerned about is the `tag` property of `Hero`, which must match the origin tag for the effect to work.

> Please check out the attached source code of this chapter for the full example.

`Navigator` still has its importance here, as do the push or pop actions that trigger the Hero animation (by signaling that the route is changing).

Besides the `tag` property, `Hero` contains other properties to enable the customization of the flight:

- `transitionOnUserGestures`: To enable/disable the `Hero` animation on user gestures such as back on Android
- `createRectTween` and `flightShuttleBuilder`: Callbacks to change the transition appearance
- `placeholderBuilder`: A callback to return a widget that can be shown in the source Hero's place during the transition

> In `Chapter 15`, *Animations*, as we develop our understanding of animations, you will be able to work with these properties like a natural.

Hero animations are easy to implement in Flutter, as you can see, and even a default animation provided by the framework can be enough to create a good effect on some pieces of layout.

> Check the documentation on the `Hero` widget: `https://docs.flutter.io/flutter/widgets/Hero-class.html`, and try it out.

# Summary

In this chapter, we have seen how to add navigation between our screens. First, we got to know the `Navigator` widget, the main player when it comes to navigation in Flutter. We have seen how it composes the navigation stack or history by using the `Overlay` class.

We have also seen another important piece of navigation, `Route`, and how to define it for use in our applications. We checked out different approaches to implement the navigation, with the most typical way being with the `WidgetsApp` widget.

Finally, we have seen how to customize transitions between screens to change the default platform-specific moves from Material and iOS Cuperitno apps, and also, how to use Hero animations to share elements between transitions to create cool effects.

In the next chapter, we will be taking our favors application to a higher level by integrating it with Firebase services.

# Section 3: Developing Fully Featured Apps

**3**

To develop a professional app, the developer needs to add features that encompass a number of advanced and custom mechanisms, using plugins to extend the framework to as needed.

The following chapters are included in this section:

# 8
# Firebase Plugins

Developers commonly create modular codes that can be used in multiple apps. That's not different in the Flutter world; the community is very involved in the success of the framework and a lot of great plugins are available to developers. In this chapter, you will get to know and learn how to use the interesting Firebase plugins, such as Auth, Cloud Firestore, and ML Kit, to create a fully featured app without a complex backend.

The following topics will be covered in this chapter:

- Configuring Firebase project
- Firebase authentication
- Cloud Firestore
- Firebase Storage
- Firebase AdMob
- Firebase ML Kit

## Firebase overview

Firebase is a Google product that provides multiple technologies for multiple platforms. If you are a mobile or web developer, you will be familiar with this amazing platform.

Among its offered technologies, the important ones are as follows:

- **Hosting**: Enables the deployment of single-page applications, progressive web applications, or static sites.
- **Real-time database**: A NoSQL (non-relational database) database on the cloud. With this, we can store and synchronize data in real time.
- **Cloud Firestore**: A powered NoSQL database, with a focus on big and scalable applications that provide advanced query support compared to the real-time database.
- **Cloud functions**: Functions triggered by many Firebase products, such as previous ones, and also by the user (using the SDK). We can develop scripts to react to changes in database, user authentication, and more.
- **Performance monitoring**: Collect and analyze information about the applications from the user perspective.
- **Authentication**: Facilitates the development of the authentication layer of an application, improving user experience, and security. It enables the usage of multiple authentication providers, such as email/password, phone authentication, and also, Google, Facebook, and other login systems.
- **Firebase Cloud Messaging**: Cloud messaging to exchange messages between applications and server, available on Android, iOS, and web.
- **AdMob:** Displays ads to monetize applications.
- **Machine learning kit**: Tools to implant advanced **machine learning (ML)** resources in any application.

Flutter contains a variety of plugins to work with Firebase. We will be using some of them in the next sections to integrate our application with these awesome services.

# Setting up Firebase

We will be adding some of the Firebase technologies to our previously developed Favors app, such as Firebase authentication and Cloud Firestore. The steps, however, are always the same for any Flutter application.

The first step to connect an application to Firebase is creating a Firebase app project.

We do this on the **Firebase console** tool (`https://console.firebase.google.com/`). This tool allows us to manage all of our Firebase projects, enable/disable specific technologies, and monitor usage:

1. This is the initial screen of the Firebase console where you can see the recent projects and also add a new project:

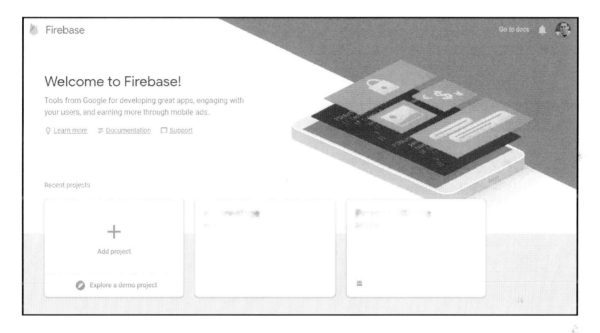

2. The process of initiating a Firebase project is simple and easy to follow, as shown in the following screenshot:

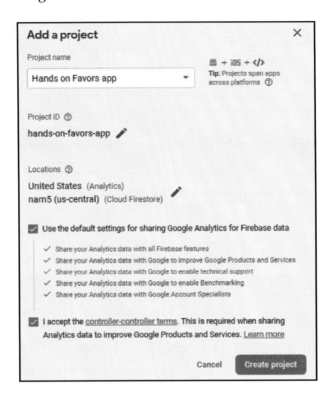

3. The project will generate within a few seconds like so:

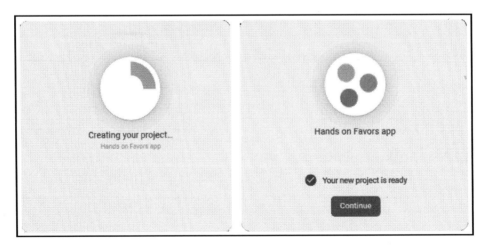

4. After the project is created, you will be redirected to the project screen, as shown here:

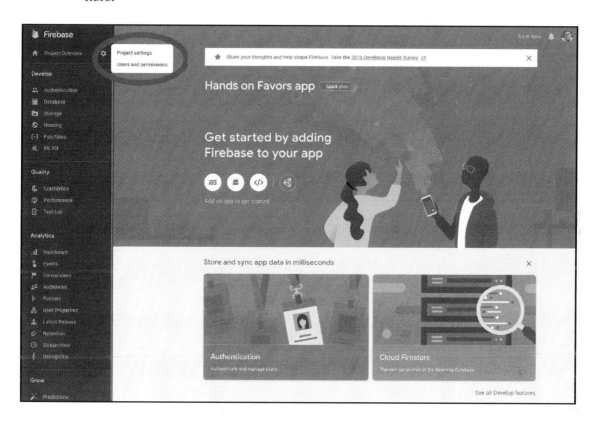

5.  The following screen shows all the options regarding the project and also the setup shortcut to project settings:

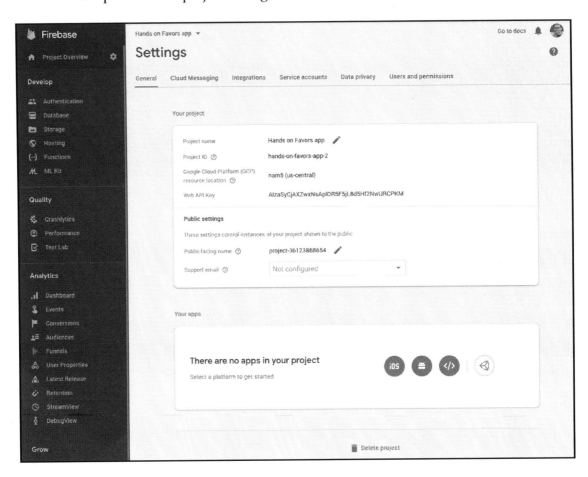

Here, we configure our project apps, as we can have multiple applications per project (that is, one for each mobile platform) and also check the project credentials used to set up the SDK on Flutter.

# Connecting the Flutter app to Firebase

As we have seen before, it is possible to configure multiple applications from multiple platforms to connect with a Firebase project. In the Firebase project page, we have the option to add apps for iOS, Android, and web.

We need to configure two applications in Firebase—one for iOS and one for Android, as though we were developing mobile-native applications. So, if you already have done this setup before for any application, the following section might look simple.

## Configuring an Android app

We can configure an Android app through the Android configuration assistant shortcut in the general project page seen previously:

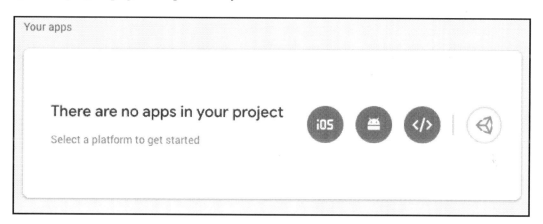

That brings the configuration page to the Android app shown in the following screenshot:

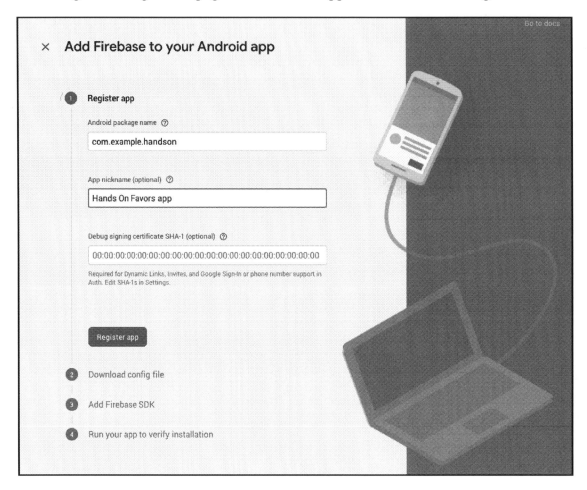

Here, the important setting is the package name that is checked in the Firebase SDK. The signing certificate is also important for auth; we will cover that shortly.

You can find the package name of your Android app in the `android/app/build.gradle` file, through the `applicationId` property.

After the registration, a `google-services.json` file is generated and should be added to our application project. In Android, it should be located in the `android/app` directory.

The final step is to add the Firebase SDK to the Gradle files. In Android, Gradle can be seen as the `pubspec` Flutter equivalent. One of its responsibilities is to manage the app dependencies:

1. First, we add the `google-services` dependency to `classpath` in the `android/build.gradle` file like so:

```
buildscript {
    repositories {
        google() // add this if not present
        ...
    }

    dependencies {
        ...
        classpath 'com.google.gms:google-services:3.2.1' // add
                                                          // this
                                                          // line
    }
}
```

2. After that, in `android/app/build.gradle`, we need to activate the plugin and add a dependency on `'androidx.annotation'` lib, as shown in the following code:

```
// part of android/app/build.gradle
...
dependencies {
    implementation 'androidx.annotation:annotation:1.0.2'
    ...
}

// firebase
// Add the following line to the bottom of the file:
apply plugin: 'com.google.gms.google-services'
```

The `androix.annotation` library is not directly related to Firebase. We should add it, though, as some libraries need it internally, such as, the ones from Firebase.

3. Finally, by running the following command, we will be all set up in the Android environment:

```
flutter packages get
```

# Configuring iOS app

For the iOS version, the process looks very similar. Starting with the configuration in the Firebase console, where we set the package name like we did for Android.

After that, we can download the generated `GoogleService-Info.plist` (iOS equivalent to `google-services.json`) file and add it to the project iOS `ios/Runner` directory. It's important to do this in Xcode by opening the iOS project on it and dragging the file into Xcode so that it gets registered for inclusion during builds.

 The step of adding the `GoogleService-Info.plist` file is changing, depending on Flutter plugins' versions. Check out the most appropriate way here: `https://firebase.google.com/docs/flutter/setup`.

Unlike Android, there is no need to add specific iOS dependencies for Firebase. The next step is to work in the Flutter context.

# FlutterFire

Flutter applications rely on a set of Flutter plugins to access Firebase services. `FlutterFire` contains specific implementations for target iOS and Android platforms.

 Check out the FlutterFire plugins page for more info about recent versions of Firebase plugins: `https://firebaseopensource.com/projects/flutter/plugins/`.

### Adding the FlutterFire dependency to the Flutter project

We should add the core plugin to our project as the initial fundamental dependency as shown in the following code:

```
# part of pubspec.yaml
dependencies:
  ...
  firebase_core: 0.2.5 # Firebase Core
```

Besides that, we should add any Firebase dependencies as needed. Furthermore, we should add `firebase_auth` to work with phone authentication:

```
# part of pubspec.yaml
dependencies:
  ...
  firebase_core: 0.3.4 # Firebase Core
```

**Note on Android**:
As we are using the latest versions of the Firebase plugins that are based on AndroidX versions of dependencies, our app project was migrated to AndroidX. Due to AndroidX compatibility issues, I recommend you to check out more here: `https://flutter.dev/docs/development/packages-and-plugins/androidx-compatibility`.

Running the `flutter packages get` command finishes the setup process, meaning and now we are able to start working with the plugins.

If you find it easier, you can follow the official Firebase documentation steps for Firebase initialization in Flutter: `https://firebase.google.com/docs/flutter/setup`.

# Firebase authentication

As we have seen before, Firebase contains a collection of useful technologies and we need to configure each one that we might need for our project. Let's configure the authentication layer of our app. The authentication layer is fundamental for our app; if you remember, the user favor requests are made to friends, and for this to happen, we need the user to be capable of sending the request to a specific user. We do this identification by using the user's phone number as its identity. We need to do that in the following steps:

1. Add the Firebase `auth` plugin to the project
2. As pointed out before, we simply need to add the `firebase_auth` plugin dependency to our `pubspec`, as shown in the following code:

   ```
   # part of pubspec.yaml
   dependencies:
     ...
     firebase_core: 0.3.4 # Firebase Core
     firebase_auth: 0.8.4+5 # Firebase Auth  // add this
   ```

3. Enable phone authentication for our Firebase project in the Firebase console
4. Create the `auth` screen
5. Check whether the user is logged in, and if they are not, redirect to the login page

# Enabling Authentication services in Firebase

To enable **Authentication** services in Firebase, we need to visit the **Authentication** section in the Firebase console as shown in the following screenshot:

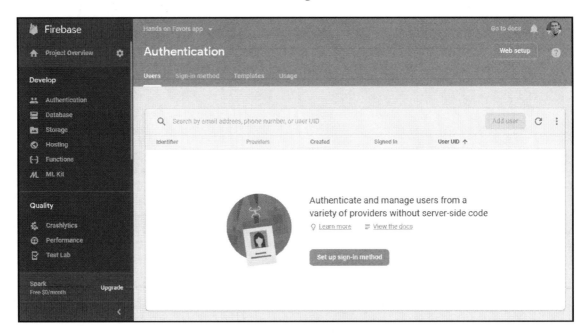

After enabling it, we can add a test phone number during development so we do not affect resource usage for other users, as shown here:

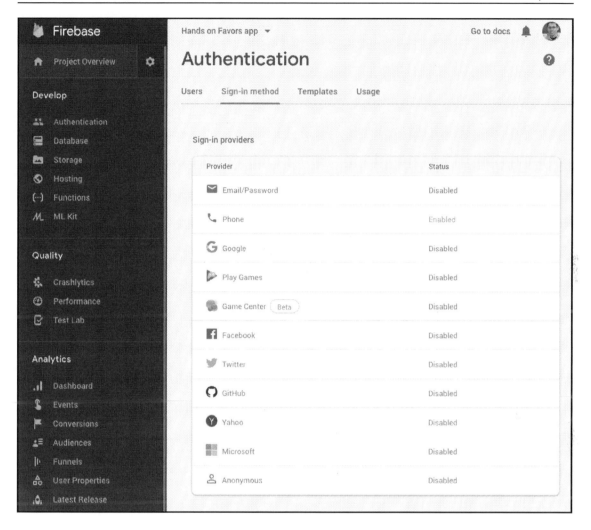

It is important for you to set up a test phone number and verification code. During development, your Android app is signed with a **Debug** certificate. This way, in the login screen, when you are prompted to enter the phone number, it will only work with the previously listed phone numbers. Also, instead of receiving the verification code, you simply type the one registered there.

After this setup, we can start to work on Flutter code.

For authentication with real numbers and receiving a verification code, you must sign your app in release mode. More on release mode later on in Chapter 12, *Testing, Debugging, and Deployment.*

# Authentication screen

In this screen, we are not going to talk about layout details. The only new widget here is the Stepper widget, from Material Design. The general idea is the user enters their phone number, receives a validation code, and after confirming it, gets logged in. We also have used our custom input from Chapter 5, *Handling User Input and Gestures*:

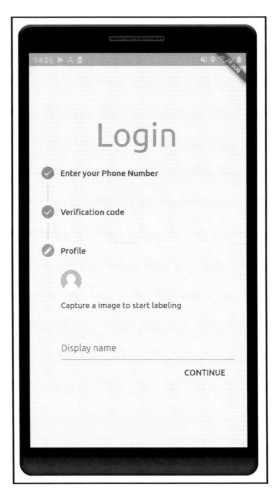

As you can see, the layout is simple and the `Stepper` widget helps on the login workflow, going step by step through the following:

1. User fills in their phone number
2. User fills in the verification code (received by SMS)
3. User fills in the display name and profile image

 You can check out more about this widget on its `material.io` page: `https://material.io/archive/guidelines/components/steppers.html`.

# Logging in with Firebase

You can check the fullscreen code in the attached `hands_on_firebase` project. The main functions here are `_sendVerificationCode()` and `_executeLogin()` from `LoginPageState`.

If you check the attached source code, you will notice that we have added the following two `<Step>`s to our `Stepper` widget:

1. **Send verification code**: In this first step, the user fills in their phone number to retrieve a verification code.
2. **Enter the retrieved 6-digit verification code**: To confirm the user's identity. After that, the user gets logged in.

Besides the `Stepper` widget properties, let's concentrate on its `onStepContinue` field, which is as shown here:

```
// part of LoginPageState build method. The Stepper callback:
onStepContinue: () {
    if (_currentStep == 0) {
        _sendVerificationCode();
    } else if (_currentStep == 1) {
        _executeLogin();
    } else {
        _saveProfile();
    }
},
```

This field expects a callback that is called when the user presses the **Continue** button of each step. As we retain the currently active step in the `_currentStep` field, we know which action to perform. So, let's see how each action is performed.

 We have customized the look of step actions; check the `_stepControlsBuilder` method on the `LoginPageState` class to see it in detail. Also, check out the documentation of this `Stepper` property: `https://docs.flutter.io/flutter/material/Stepper/controlsBuilder.html`.

## Sending verification code

The first stage of phone authentication is when the server (Firebase, in our case) sends a verification code through SMS to the phone number the user entered.

This is done by using the Firebase SDK method called `verifyPhoneNumber`, which requests the server to *start* a phone authentication as shown here:

```
// _sendVerificationCode method (LoginPageState) login_page.dart

void _sendVerificationCode() async {
  final PhoneCodeSent codeSent = (String verId, [int forceCodeResend]) {
    _verificationId = verId;
    _goToVerificationStep();
  };

  final PhoneVerificationCompleted verificationSuccess = (FirebaseUser user) {
    _loggedIn();
  };

  final PhoneVerificationFailed verificationFail = (AuthException exception) {
    goBackToFirstStep();
  };

  final PhoneCodeAutoRetrievalTimeout autoRetrievalTimeout = (String verId) {
    this._verificationId = verId;
  };

  await FirebaseAuth.instance.verifyPhoneNumber(
    phoneNumber: _phoneNumber,
    codeSent: codeSent,
    verificationCompleted: verificationSuccess,
```

```
    verificationFailed: verificationFail,
    codeAutoRetrievalTimeout: autoRetrievalTimeout,
    timeout: Duration(seconds: 0),
  );
}
```

The verifyPhoneNumber method executes asynchronously (another with async and returns Future), so the await keyword is needed before the call.

The following are some important things to notice in the previous code:

- FirebaseAuth.instance reflects the single instance of the Firebase auth SDK that makes the bridge between Flutter and native Firebase auth libraries
- There are multiple callbacks to implement and properties to set on the authentication API call; namely these:
    - phoneNumber: The phone number to send the verification code to
    - codeSent: Called when the code is sent to phoneNumber
    - verificationCompleted: Called when the code is auto-retrieved by the Firebase auth SDK
    - verificationFailed: Called when some error occurs during phone number verification
    - timeout: Maximum time for the library to wait for an auto-retrieval, 0 means disabled
    - codeAutoRetrievalTimeout: Called when the timeout specified is reached meaning auto-retrieval did not work properly (unless it is set to 0)
- When the codeSent callback is invoked, it will make the Stepper widget move to the second step, where the user should input their verification code

It is fundamental for you to inspect the FlutterFire site and also the documentation of the firebase_auth plugin for an understanding of the preceding properties: https://pub.dartlang.org/packages/firebase_auth.

Also, we have auto-retrieval disabled as it is not fully working at the time of writing this book; you can change the callbacks to test for yourself.

# Verifying the SMS code

The second step is to verify the user has retrieved the correct code, and by doing so, should log in to the application. This is done in the `signInWithCredential` method as shown here:

```
// _executeLogin method (LoginPageState) login_page.dart

void _executeLogin() async {
  setState(() {
    _showProgress = true;
  });

  await FirebaseAuth.instance.signInWithCredential(
      PhoneAuthProvider.getCredential(
          verificationId: _verificationId, smsCode: _smsCode,
  ));

  FirebaseAuth.instance.currentUser().then((user) {
    if (user != null) {
      goToProfileStep();
    }
  });
}
```

As you can see, this is a simple call to the `signInWithCredential` method from the Firebase `auth` plugin that expects the following two arguments:

- `verificationId`: This is the identifier of the whole login process. Take a look at the previous callbacks where we receive this and store it for later use here. This identifies the login so that we do not need to send all the information (phone number, in this case) again.
- `smsCode`: The code the user entered for validation; if both are valid, the login will succeed.

 If you perform some tests, you will notice the app is not showing messages to the user to notify them of login errors (such as for an incorrect verification code). In a real-world app, this is not the ideal behavior. Take a look at the callbacks and try to improve the behavior.

# Updating the profile and login status

The Firebase user object contains more than phone numbers, it contains a set of information for another method of login, such as email, for example, and also contains properties that help to define the user's profile, such as a display name and photo URL. Here, in the last step of the login process, we can save the user profile with its `displayName` so that other users can identify easily. This is done in the `_saveProfile()` method as shown here:

```
// part of LoginPageState class
void _saveProfile() async {
    setState(() {
      _showProgress = true;
    });

    final user = await FirebaseAuth.instance.currentUser();

    final updateInfo = UserUpdateInfo();
    updateInfo.displayName = _displayName;

    await user.updateProfile(updateInfo);

    // ... the last part is explained below
  }
```

The `currentUser()` method is useful for any action related to the logged in user. In this case, we get it and update the requested info (the display name, for now). `UserUpdateInfo` is a helper class to store the update data; in the next section, we will be using one more property of it to store the user profile picture URL.

As we know the user is logged in, we can redirect to the Favors page using the well-known `Navigator` class as follows:

```
// final part of _saveProfile() LoginPage
Navigator.of(context).pushReplacement(
    MaterialPageRoute(
        builder: (context) => FavorsPage(),
    ),
);
```

This screen is the initial screen of our app. However, we should not ask the user to fill all the information every time. Before anything, we must check whether the user is already logged in, and if they are, simply redirect as we did before. We can do that by using the `FirebaseAuth.instance.currentUser()` method again. A great place to check this is the `initState()` method of the `LoginPageState` class:

```
// part of login_page.dart
class LoginPageState extends State<LoginPage> {
...
  @override
  void initState() {
    super.initState();

    FirebaseAuth.instance.currentUser().then((user) {
      if (user != null) {
        Navigator.of(context).pushReplacement(
          MaterialPageRoute(
            builder: (context) => FavorsPage(),
          ),
        );
      }
    });
  }
...
}
```

As you can see, if the current `Firebase` user is not `null`, we know that we can redirect the navigation to the next screen just like before.

 What would be good user feedback if the current user is `null`? Have a think and find out.

That's it for phone authentication; in the next section, we are going to store our favors on the Cloud Firestore backend.

# NoSQL database with Cloud Firestore

Cloud Firestore from Firebase is a flexible and scalable NoSQL cloud database. It helps us in the development of real-time applications with synchronization technologies between clients that make our app fast and functional.

In this chapter, we are going to make some changes to our Favors app. We will do the following:

- Transfer our Favors listing to Firebase
- See how to add rules so that a user cannot access another user's favors
- Send/store a favor request to another user/friend in Cloud Firestore

# Enabling Cloud Firestore on Firebase

The first step, if you remember, is enabling the necessary services on Firebase. In this case, we want to enable the Cloud Firestore technology on Firebase:

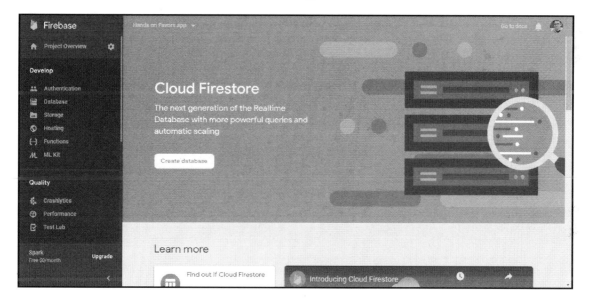

We enable it like any other Firebase service. One important thing regarding data is to do with security. Firebase provides rule mechanisms so that we can configure the level to access of any information stored in our database. In the creation prompt, this is the only thing we configure:

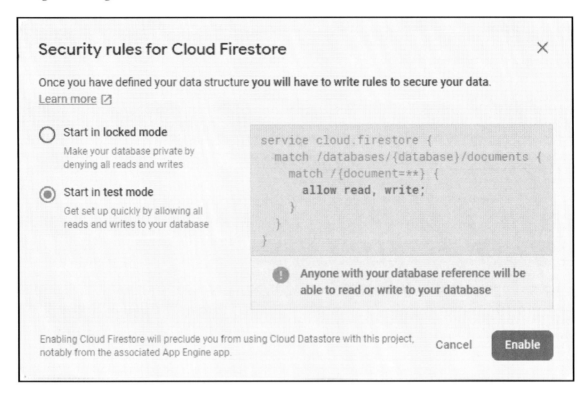

In our application, we are not going to define any rules for simplicity; that is why we chose test mode. I strongly recommend that you read more about these rules, as they are very important for real applications: https://firebase.google.com/docs/firestore/security/rules-structure?authuser=0:

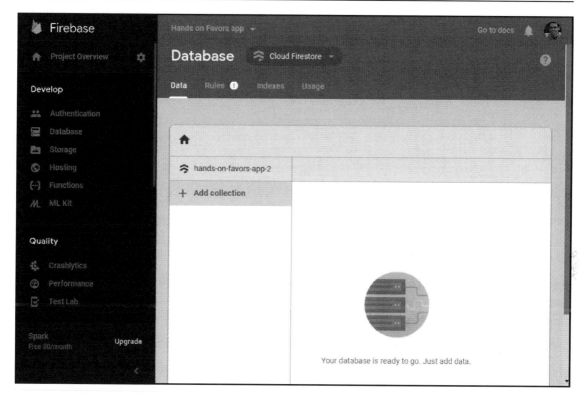

After that, we can start the development of storing and loading favors on the Cloud Firestore database.

# Cloud Firestore and Flutter

As we have seen before, `FlutterFire` provides a set of plugins for different technologies. This also is true for the Cloud Firestore plugin. So, the first step is to add their necessary dependencies to our `pubspec.yaml` as shown here:

```
dependencies:
  cloud_firestore: ^0.9.5 # Cloud Firestore
```

After getting the necessary dependencies with `flutter packages get`, we are ready to change our favors storage.

# Loading favors from Firestore

We use Firestore through the `Firestore` class from the `cloud_firestore` Dart library. In `initState()` function of the `FavorsPageState`, we add a call to `watchFavorsCollection()`.

 **Collections** are just a group of documents. In our app, we have a single collection called favors that store all of the favor documents from the app. A **document** is a record in a collection. They are commonly represented as JSON objects.

In `watchFavorsCollection()`, we start loading favors from Firebase as shown here:

```
// part of favors_page.dart watchFavorsCollection
class FavorsPageState extends State<FavorsPage> {

  @override
  void initState() {
    super.initState();
    ...
    pendingAnswerFavors = List();
    acceptedFavors = List();
    completedFavors = List();
    refusedFavors = List();
    friends = Set();

    watchFavorsCollection();
  }
  ....
  void watchFavorsCollection() async {
    final currentUser = await FirebaseAuth.instance.currentUser();

    Firestore.instance
      .collection('favors') // 1
      .where('to', isEqualTo: currentUser.phoneNumber) // 2
      .snapshots() //3
      .listen((snapshot) {}) //4
    ...
  }
}
```

A typical Firebase query can have many formats; this one does the following:

1. It starts by specifying the targeted collection—favors.
2. It add a `where` condition to filter the favors that are sent only to the current user's phone number.

3. `snapshots()` creates a stream of snapshots.

4. `listen((snapshot) {})` is where we listen for changes on the snapshots; that is, we subscribe to the snapshot changes. On every change on the database that affects the query, the function passed to `listen()` will be called. The callback code to the `listen()` function is as follows:

```
// part of watchFavorsCollection
void watchFavorsCollection() async {
final currentUser = await FirebaseAuth.instance.currentUser();

Firestore.instance
    .collection('favors')
    .where('to', isEqualTo: currentUser.phoneNumber)
    .snapshots()
    .listen((snapshot) {
        List<Favor> newCompletedFavors = List();
        List<Favor> newRefusedFavors = List();
        List<Favor> newAcceptedFavors = List();
        List<Favor> newPendingAnswerFavors = List();
        Set<Friend> newFriends = Set();

        snapshot.documents.forEach((document) {
          Favor favor = Favor.fromMap(document.documentID,
          document.data);
          if (favor.isCompleted) {
            newCompletedFavors.add(favor);
          } else if (favor.isRefused) {
            newRefusedFavors.add(favor);
          } else if (favor.isDoing) {
            newAcceptedFavors.add(favor);
          } else {
            newPendingAnswerFavors.add(favor);
          }

          newFriends.add(favor.friend);
        });

        // update our lists
        setState(() {
          this.completedFavors = newCompletedFavors;
          this.pendingAnswerFavors = newPendingAnswerFavors;
          this.refusedFavors = newRefusedFavors;
          this.acceptedFavors = newAcceptedFavors;
          this.friends = newFriends;
        });
    });
}
```

As you can see, every time the part of the collection where our query is looking changes through the insertion, editing, of deletion of a favor, the callback will be called and the following will occur:

- A new list of each favor type is created.
- A favor is created through a new `fromMap` defined constructor as shown here:

```
Favor.fromMap(String uid, Map<String, dynamic> data)
    : this(
        uuid: uid,
        description: data['description'],
        dueDate: DateTime.fromMillisecondsSinceEpoch
        (data['dueDate']),
        accepted: data['accepted'],
        completed: data['completed'] != null
            ? DateTime.fromMillisecondsSinceEpoch
                (data['completed'])
            : null,
        friend: Friend.fromMap(data['friend']),
        to: data['to'],
    );
```

The `fromMap` constructor receives an ID (the document ID) and a `Map` instance with the corresponding fields. As you can see, it's a simple usage of the default constructor with parameters from the data coming from Firebase:

 The same thing is done for the `Friend` object. Check out the `Favor` class for that example.

- Depending on the status of `favor`, it is inserted in the corresponding list.
- In addition to that, a set of friends is created, and every friend from favor is added to the set. As `Set`s allow a single occurrence of each object, no repeated friends will be present.

 Check the `Friend` class. For the proper usage in the `Set` collection the, equals operator (==) and `hashCode` method were overridden for the correct evaluation.

- At the end, the lists of the `State` instance are updated to cause a rebuild of the layout.

# Updating favors on Firebase

Before, when using mock data, we only needed to change our lists in memory. Now, we need to update our corresponding favor documents on Firebase so that this will trigger our previously defined callback, which will cause a rebuild and update our layouts.

We create a new method that will be used on every favor change, `_updateFavorOnFirebase()`:

```
void _updateFavorOnFirebase(Favor favor) async {
  await Firestore.instance
      .collection('favors') // 1
      .document(favor.uuid) // 2
      .setData(favor.toJson()); // 3
}
```

The beginning of the Firestore call is almost always the same: we get the Firestore instance, then we complete the following steps:

1. We go to the favors collection.
2. Then we get the reference of the favor document that we want to update.
3. The last step is to send the data in JSON format to be updated in the corresponding document. The `toJson()` method is a simple converter to store on Firebase.

 Check out the `hands_on_firebase` attached source code for the full code of conversions to and from Firebase.

The `_updateFavorOnFirebase` method is used on previously defined methods: `complete`, `giveUp`, `acceptToDo`, and `refuseToDo`. That's all we need to update on Firebase and reflect changes on the app layout.

# Saving a favor on Firebase

In the `RequestFavorPageState` class, we need to add the code to insert a new favor in our favor collection in Firestore. This is done on the previous `_save()` method, which, until now, did not save anything:

```
// part of request_favors_page.dart file
  void save(BuildContext context) async {
    if (_formKey.currentState.validate()) {
```

```
_formKey.currentState.save(); // 1
final currentUser = await FirebaseAuth.instance.currentUser();
//2

await _saveFavorOnFirebase(
  Favor(
    to: _selectedFriend.number,
    description: _description,
    dueDate: _dueDate,
    friend: Friend(
      name: currentUser.displayName,
      number: currentUser.phoneNumber,
      photoURL: currentUser.photoUrl,
    ),
  ),
); //3

Navigator.pop(context); //4
  }
}
```

The save process is defined as follows:

1. We validate and save the Form fields. That is, we store the value of the text fields of description, due date, and friend as variables to use later. There are other ways of getting form fields values; this one is a simple and clean one.
2. We get the current logged-in user, as we need the current user info to populate the favor request, so that the requested friend will know who is asking them for a favor.
3. We call a new _saveFavorOnFirebase() utility method that makes the Firebase call, with a new Favor instance created with the values coming from Form as shown here:

```
_saveFavorOnFirebase(Favor favor) async {
  await Firestore.instance
    .collection('favors')
    .document() // without passing any document id
    .setData(favor.toJson());
}
```

As you can see, the call is very similar to the previous update code. The only thing different is that we are not walking to a specific document on the `document()` method call. This will cause Firestore to generate a new unique ID, then map to a new document where we set data later.

4. After saving, we pop the route so that we go back to the previous screen.

 Maybe, we could have treated any errors occurring in the saving process so that the user might try again later, what do you think? This is a good time to get your hands dirty and improve the code.

With these changes, we are now storing and fetching favors from Cloud Firestore, as shown in the following screenshot:

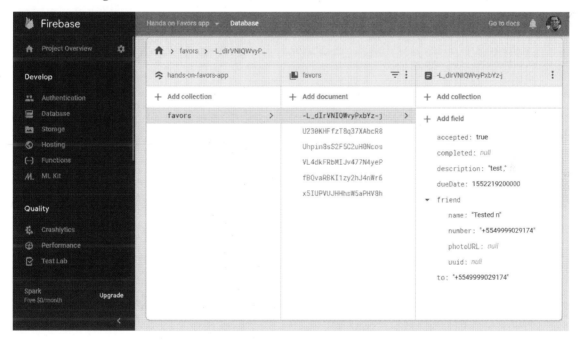

We did not write any backend code here, and as a bonus, we also have real-time changes reflected in our app, making it great for contexts involving multiple users.

# Cloud Storage with Firebase Storage

Firebase **Storage** is a great platform for storing files on the cloud. The most typical use cases are storing pictures or videos from users, but there are no limitation; you can store any kind of data needed in your application. The needs of the application are attended with this powerful storage mechanism.

## Introduction to Firebase Storage

Like previous services, Firebase **Storage** has an introductory step where it explains the need to secure data, as shown here:

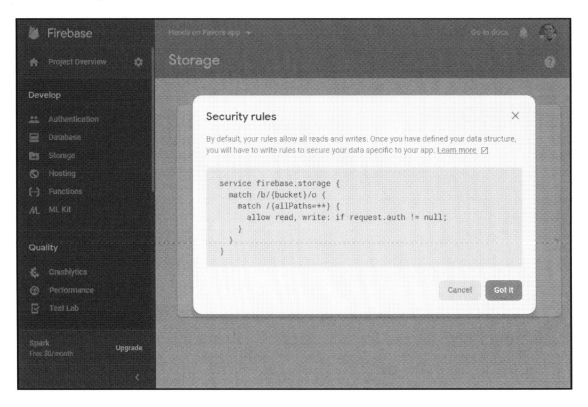

The storage service is enabled with a default rule definition, where only authenticated requests can make write and read calls. This is enough for our application.

 Again, for real-world applications, it is recommended to create the best rules you can do help to protect user-specific data: `https://firebase.google.com/docs/storage/security`.

After this introductory step, we can add Flutter-specific libraries and start the development step.

# Adding Flutter Storage dependencies

In addition to previous plugins, `FlutterFire` provides a plugin for Firebase Storage. We need to add the dependency to our `pubspec.yaml`, as shown in the following code:

```
dependencies:
    firebase_storage: ^2.1.0 # Cloud Firestore
```

After getting dependencies with `flutter packages get`, we are ready to use Firebase **Storage** in our project.

# Uploading files to Firebase

We are going to add the functionality of uploading files to Firebase Storage to our Favors app. In the **Profile** section of login process, after the user is successfully logged in, we can add a feature so the user can add an image to his/her profile.

You can check out this section of the app in the last part of the login screen, as shown in the following screenshot:

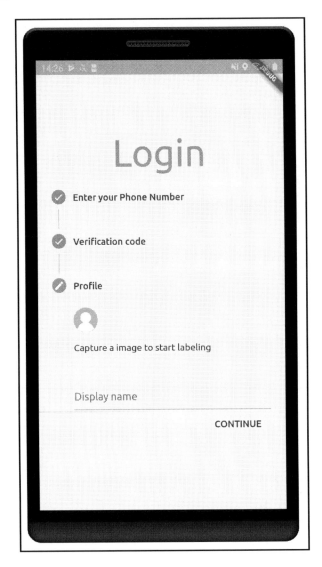

We also have added another useful library, `image_picker`, to the dependencies, so we can get an image from the camera and upload it to Firebase Storage for use as a user profile picture.

 To check the camera usage and `image_picker` plugin in detail, read Chapter 10, *Accessing Device Features from the Flutter App*, particularly *Integrating phone camera* section.

We need to change our `_saveProfile()` method in the login screen. Here, we add the code needed to upload the selected picture to Firebase Storage, and after that, we store the URL in the user's profile information as follows:

```
// part of login_page.dart

void _saveProfile() async {
  setState(() {
    _showProgress = true;
  });

  final user = await FirebaseAuth.instance.currentUser();

  final updateInfo = UserUpdateInfo();
  updateInfo.displayName = _displayName;
  updateInfo.photoUrl = await uploadPicture(user.uid);

  await user.updateProfile(updateInfo);

  Navigator.of(context).pushReplacement(
    MaterialPageRoute(
      builder: (context) => FavorsPage(),
    ),
  );
}
```

As you can see, the only thing was the change to the `updateInfo` object using its `photoUrl` property. The saving part is still the same. `uploadPicture()` is the interesting part:

```
uploadPicture(String userUid) async {
  StorageReference ref = FirebaseStorage.instance
      .ref()
      .child('profiles')
      .child('profile_$userUid'); // 1

  StorageUploadTask uploadTask = ref.putFile(_imageFile,
```

```
StorageMetadata(contentType: 'image/png')); // 2

    StorageTaskSnapshot lastSnapshot = await uploadTask.onComplete; // 3

    return await lastSnapshot.ref.getDownloadURL(); // 4
}
```

The upload task to Firebase Storage is divided into the following small steps:

1. First, we create a reference to a new object on **Storage**. As you can see, we chain `child()` calls, creating a folder called `Profiles` and a file with the user ID in its name.
2. After that, we create a storage upload task that will initialize the upload to Firebase. Note the `StorageMetadata` parameter; we create an image content type as it's an image that's being stored.
3. Here we await the `Future` reference of the upload task, getting the last snapshot of the task (the result).
4. At the end, we get the file URL; this is a download URL of the Firebase file so that we can access the file from Storage.

The list of files is accessible in the Firebase console as shown here:

In the Favors page, nothing changes. As before, the profile picture is loaded in `CircleAvatar` with `NetworkImage`, only if the friend's `photoURL` property is given (not `null`):

```
// part of favors page FavorCardItem class
        CircleAvatar(
          backgroundImage: favor.friend.photoURL != null
            ? NetworkImage(
                favor.friend.photoURL,
              )
            : AssetImage('assets/default_avatar.png'),
        ),
```

As you can see, we have a fallback for the case of a user without a profile picture. That is it for Storage in our Favors app. There are a lot of capabilities that are yet to be explored.

In the next section, we are going to explore the Firebase AdMob plugin.

# Ads with Firebase AdMob

Google AdMob is a technology of mobile publicity to generate revenue. Adding ads to applications is a common method of monetization and a good solution for free applications.

We can easily integrate AdMob into our application with the usage of FlutterFire plugins. The registration and usage of AdMob are slightly different from those for previous plugins that we have seen; we need to create another account for this.

# AdMob account

In truth, AdMob is kept separate from the Firebase console. Although we have an AdMob section in the console, we don't have more than links to AdMob documentations and the start page:

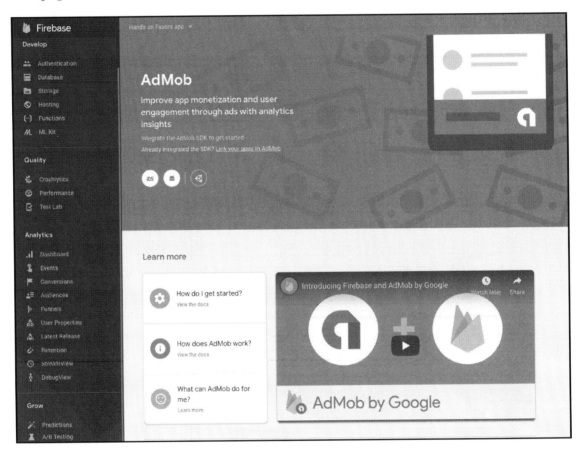

In the `apps.admob.com` page, we can create and manage all of our applications.

 Note that Firebase projects and AdMob apps are not explicitly connected until you link the application and Firebase project/app manually. This may change by the time you are reading this book. Right now, everything is all separated: apps from AdMob are registered separately from Firebase and we need to link them manually.

# Creating an AdMob account

In the previous link, we have the possibility to create our AdSense and AdMob account. You can follow the steps in the page to create a new account as follows:

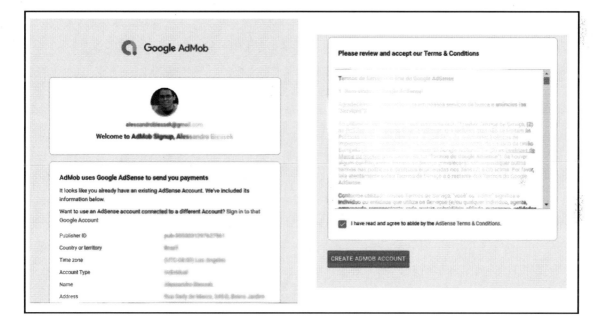

After that, we are ready to manage our applications. In the case of Flutter, we create two applications—one for Android and one for iOS:

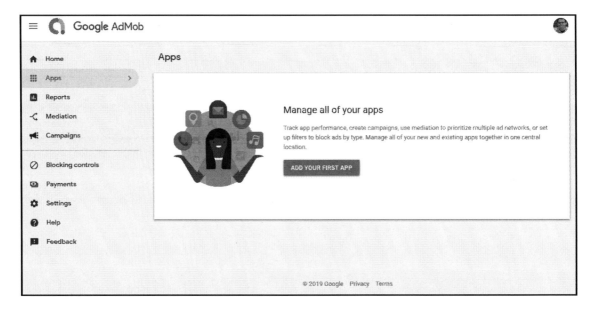

We manage our apps and we get a unique app ID for each of the applications.

 The creation of the applications in the AdMob portal is simply done by following the config steps. Make sure you create one application for each platform.

You will get the following window after successfully adding your app to AdMob:

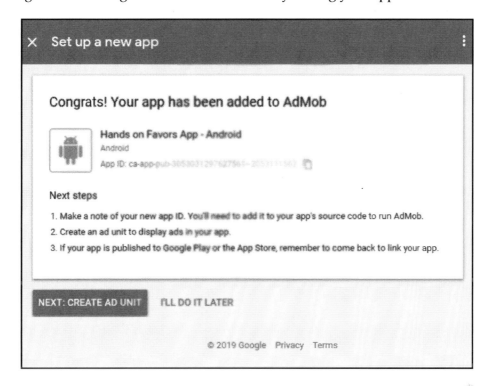

We will be using these app IDs to display banners in our application.

After creating the AdMob app, we can link the app in the on Google AdMob portal as shown here:

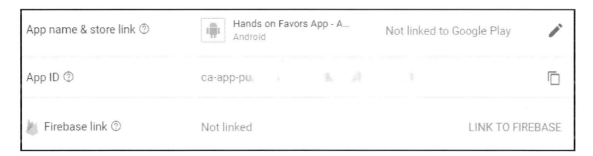

Just follow the dialog workflow and link the iOS/Android AdMob app with the corresponding Firebase app in the project, as shown in the following screenshot:

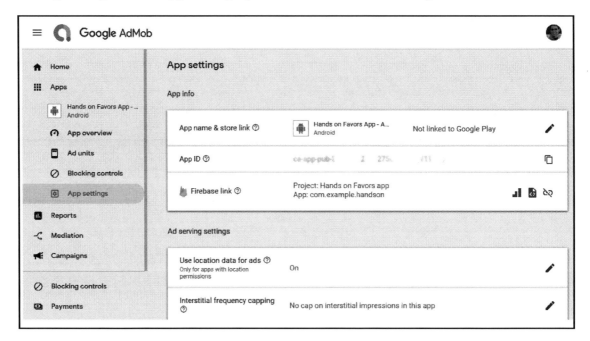

This will mean that the analytics data collected on Firebase will help your AdMob. This lets your Analytics data flow to AdMob to enhance product features and monetization.

# AdMob in Flutter

Like for previous `FlutterFire` plugins, we need to add the dependency for AdMob to our `pubspec.yaml`, as follows:

```
dependencies:
    firebase_admob: ^0.8.0+4 # AdMob
```

After getting dependencies with `flutter packages get`, we are ready to use Firebase AdMob in our project.

The `FirebaseAdMob` class is our starting point to add banners to the application. Unlike previously seen Firebase plugins that get all the information needed to run from the `google-services.json` (Android) and `GoogleService-info.plist` (iOS) files, in this case, we need an additional setting before we can use the plugin effectively.

We need to manually initialize the plugin with our application IDs. This can be done at any point. In our Favors app, for example, we can do this in the main method as shown here:

```
void main() {
  FirebaseAdMob.instance.initialize(
    appId: Platform.isAndroid
        ? 'ca-app-pub-3940256099942544~3347511713' // replace with your
Android app id
        : 'ca-app-pub-3940256099942544~1458002511', // replace with your
iOS app id
  );
  runApp(MyApp());
}
```

As you can see, we initialize the plugin by providing our registered app ID (important for release). In the previous example, we are using just test IDs. This is the same value as present in the library's `FirebaseAdMob.testAppId` property. We can test our banners in the following two ways:

- By using test ads provided by Google. With this, we use a set of mock ads, with no real traffic in our application ads.

This setting is really important, as generating invalid traffic to our apps can cause in account invalidation. So make sure you are using testing ads during development; find out more here: `https://developers.google.com/admob/android/test-ads` and after, change it to real app ID with test devices.

- By adding testing devices with our real IDs. This is the preferred option, as it means we have the real look of the ads.

When using Android emulators or iOS simulators, they are automatically configured as test devices. For real devices, the first time you run a properly configured AdMob app, the test device ID will appear in **LogCat** (Android) or **Console** log (iOS). Use this ID to mark your device as a test device. Check out more here: `https://developers.google.com/admob/ios/test-ads` and `https://developers.google.com/admob/android/test-ads`.

## Side note on Android

In Android, there is an additional step. We need to add the same AdMob app ID used to initialize the `FirebaseAdMob` plugin into `AndroidManifest.xml` with the following code:

```
<!-- AndroidManifest.xml -->
    <application>
        <meta-data
            android:name="com.google.android.gms.ads.APPLICATION_ID"
            android:value="ca-app-pub-3940256099942544~3347511713"/>
    </application>
```

This is done by adding the `<meta-data>` value containing the same app ID previously configured.

## Side note on iOS

In iOS, we also need to add the same AdMob app ID used to initialize the `FirebaseAdMob` plugin into the `Info.plist` file with the following code:

```
<!-- Info.plist -->
<plist version="1.0">
<dict>
...
  <key>GADApplicationIdentifier</key>
  <string>ca-app-pub-3940256099942544~1458002511</string> // replace with
                                                           // your iOS app
                                                           // id
...
</dict>
```

This is done by adding an entry to the `<dict>` section containing the same app ID that was previously configured for iOS.

# Showing ads in Flutter

After properly configuring the initialization of the AdMob plugin, we can start displaying different kinds of ads, like **banners** for example. Ads, unlike many Flutter views, are displayed in a different way from widgets. They do not have a node in the tree.

We will be changing our `RequestFavorPageState` to display ads. We will be displaying a `BannerAd` at the bottom of the screen and a fullscreen `InterstitialAd` after saving a request.

We need to keep a reference to ads when we show them to be capable of disposing of them later. So, first we add them as fields in our state with the following code:

```
// RequestFavorPageState class

  InterstitialAd _interstitialAd;
  BannerAd _bannerAd;
```

In the initState() function, we prepare the ads as follows:

```
    _bannerAd = BannerAd(
      adUnitId: BannerAd.testAdUnitId,
      size: AdSize.banner,
    )
      ..load()
      ..show();

    _interstitialAd = InterstitialAd(
        adUnitId: InterstitialAd.testAdUnitId,
    )..load();
```

> You can check more ad types here: https://pub.dartlang.org/
> packages/firebase_admob.

We have a few things to consider when defining the ads; see this:

- adUnitId is the main property of an ad, from the AdMob docs:

    *"An ad unit is one or more Google ads displayed as a result of one piece of the AdSense ad code."*

> We use testAdUnitId from the Ad classes to create mock ads; that is, simple test ads. You can create/configure ad units on the AdMob portal.

- The load() function is the start call of the ads; this will make the ad ready for displaying.
- The show() function makes the ad visible (waiting if load is not completed).
- Another important property is targetingInfo; it helps us to target ads. Check the MobileAdTargetingInfo class for more info. In this class, we can also define test devices (previously mentioned in *AdMob in Flutter* section).

As you can see, we display the banner ad at the start right after loading it. Later in the `save()` method, the interstitial Ad is also shown with the following code:

```
// save method
await _interstitialAd.show();
```

As you can see, the ads are displayed with a test mark; you can use real ads by creating Ad units and using test devices:

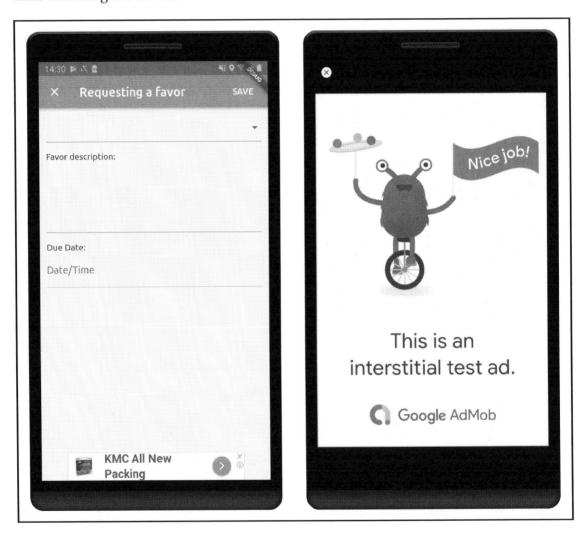

In the next section, we will be covering another technology, Firebase ML Kit, which helps us to integrate machine learning tools in our apps.

# ML with Firebase ML Kit

Firebase ML Kit helps to add ML features to our app without the need of ML experience it. There's no need to have deep knowledge of neural networks or model optimization to get started.

Firebase ML Kit provides multiple tools, which are as follows:

- **Text recognition (OCR)**: Recognize text on photos. Available as on-device and cloud-based functionality.
- **Face detection**: Detect faces in an image, identify key facial features, and get the contours of detected faces. Available as on-device functionality.
- **Barcode scanning**: Scan multiple types of barcodes. Available as on-device.
- **Image labeling**: Recognize entities in an image. Available as on-device and cloud-based functionality.
- **Landmark recognition**: Recognize well-known landmarks in an image. Available as cloud-based functionality.
- **Language identification**: Determine the language of a string of text. Available as on-device functionality.
- **Custom model inference**: Use a custom TensorFlow Lite (`https://www.tensorflow.org/lite`) model with ML Kit. Available as on-device functionality.

The on-device tools are APIs that run offline and process data quickly. Cloud-based APIs, on the other hand, rely on Google Cloud Platform to provide results with high accuracy.

# Adding ML Kit to Flutter

Like for previous `FlutterFire` plugins, we need to add the dependency for ML Kit to our `pubspec.yaml` as follows:

```
dependencies:
    firebase_ml_vision: ^0.6.0 # ML Vision
```

After getting the dependencies with `flutterpackages get`, we are ready to use Firebase ML Kit in our project.

# Using the label detector in Flutter

As we have seen, we have multiple tools provided by Firebase ML Kit; in this example, we will be running the label detector on image, so that the image will be interpreted and the library will give us info about what the image might be of. This can be useful for the preprocessing and filtering of images.

Depending on the service we want to use, we need to add specific libraries at system level. For image labeling, we need to add a labeling library (OCR) at the native level of our project.

In Android, this is done in the `android/app/build.gradle` file, basically, by downloading the native code that allows the entity resolution in an image as follows:

```
dependencies {
    ...
    api 'com.google.firebase:firebase-ml-vision-image-label-model:16.2.0'
}
```

This is another step, but it's optional. We can add this to `AndroidManifest.xml` like so:

```
<application ...>
  ...
  <meta-data
    android:name="com.google.firebase.ml.vision.DEPENDENCIES"
    android:value="ocr" />
  <!-- To use multiple models: android:value="ocr,label,barcode,face" -->
</application>
```

In iOS, the basis is the same, we add this through `pods` (pods are equivalent to plugins in Flutter).

In the `ios` directory, run `pod init` if you do not have a `Podfile` file on it.

 Note: `Podfile` would be likely to exist if you try to run the Flutter app on iOS, as during build, it will get the corresponding pods for Flutter plugins. So, `Podfile` might already have some contents.

Then add the dependency for image labeling in `Podfile` with the following code:

```
pod 'Firebase/MLVisionLabelModel'
```

Then, execute with the following command:

```
pod install
```

All the needed configuration for each technology can be seen in detail on the plugin page: `https://pub.dartlang.org/packages/firebase_ml_ vision`.

After the dependencies are added, we can detect entities in an image.

As a simple case, we will be detecting the labels for the user profile image. This is done by changing the behavior of the capture button; after capturing the image, we run the code of `_labelImage()`.

The `_labelImage()` method looks like this:

```
// part of login_page.dart

_labelImage() async {
    if (_imageFile == null) return;

    setState(() {
      _labeling = true;
    });

    final FirebaseVisionImage visionImage =
        FirebaseVisionImage.fromFile(_imageFile); //1

    final LabelDetector labelDetector =
    FirebaseVision.instance.labelDetector(); //2

    List<Label> labels = await labelDetector.detectInImage(visionImage);
    //3

    setState(() {
      _labels = labels;
      _labeling = false;
    });
}
```

To make the entities detection, we run a few steps:

1. We instantiate `FirebaseVisionImage` from the captured image
2. Then we instantiate a Firebase `LabelDetector`
3. We process the image with `LabelDetector`; this will return a collection of `Label` objects that are displayed later

Remember, all the processed info has a confidence value associated with it.

Capturing a simple image from the Android emulator camera app with a room and some furniture, we get a few labels, as shown here:

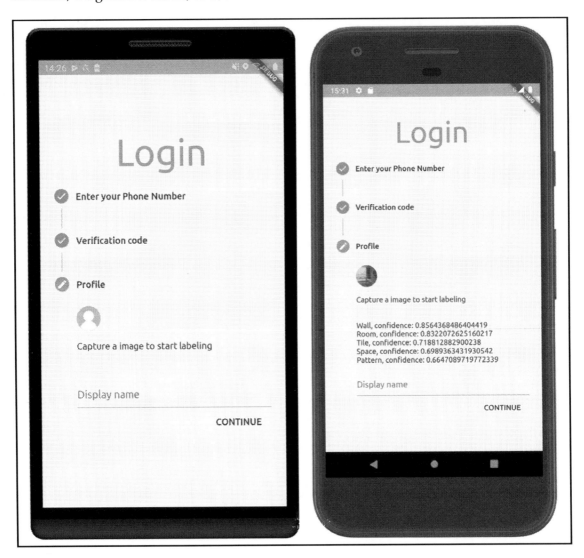

As you can see, it detects many of the entities in the image with a high confidence value. This is important info in machine learning; all calculated values have a confidence value.

With this, we conclude the integration of image labeling in our app.

# Summary

In this chapter, we have seen the great Firebase tools that help us to develop fully featured apps with advanced technologies. We have added authentication via phone with SMS code validation to our app by using the Firebase `auth` plugin. Later, we changed the favors list and made it so that requests are sent to the Cloud Firestore service. The Firebase Storage plugin was used to send user profile images to the Firebase Storage backend, where we can store any kind of files for usage in our applications. As a bonus, we had an introduction to the AdMob service with the Firebase AdMob plugin and to ML Kit through the Firebase ML vision plugin. We have seen how to configure and manage our apps in the Firebase console and the AdMob portal.

We can also create our own plugins to use in our Flutter applications. In the next chapter, we will check out the process of plugin creation, from implementation to publication in the `pub` repository.

# 9
# Developing Your Own Flutter Plugin

Like using community plugins, a developer may want to share some usable modular code with the community or have it in their own toolbox. This way, the creation and sharing of packages is totally facilitated with the Flutter framework. In this chapter, you will learn how to create a small plugin project to learn the fundamentals of the process, add some documentation, and publish it to contribute to the community.

The following topics will be covered in this chapter:

- Creating a package/plugin project
- Plugin project structure
- Documentation in packages
- Publishing a package
- Plugin development recommendations

## Creating a package/plugin project

As we have seen, developing full-featured Flutter apps relies on using one or more packages shared by the community in the **Flutter/Dart** ecosystems. Developing everything from scratch would be impractical for most applications, as we would have to repeatedly develop platform-specific code, which makes the development cycle longer and slower.

The Flutter and Dart ecosystems provide tools to help this contribution occur with no difficulties. The process of developing and publishing a package is done in the Flutter environment.

In this chapter, we are going to generate a simple Flutter plugin project and analyze its structure. The generated plugin contains a Flutter example that has a single method to get the platform version, that is, the currently running operating system version. This is a simple plugin that does not have anything special, but is a good introduction to the plugin projects.

# Flutter packages versus Dart packages

In Chapter 2, *Intermediate Dart Programming*, we have seen how Dart packages look and how they are managed by the pub tool. In Flutter it's no different; Flutter packages are nothing more than Dart packages that may contain Flutter-specific functionality and thus have a dependency on the Flutter framework.

There are two kinds of Flutter package:

- **Dart packages**: There are simple Dart packages that may provide useful libraries that do not depend on the Flutter framework and therefore can be used in any Dart environment: web, desktop, server, and so on. Flutter-specific packages that have a dependency on Flutter framework can only be used in a Flutter context.
- **Plugin packages**: There are packages that contain platform-dependent implementations (Java/Kotlin in Android and ObjC/Swift in iOS) of its features, and the Dart part is nothing more than an API that translates calls to the Flutter level of the application. If you inspect the packages used in our Favors application, such as the Firebase packages or image_picker, you will see they are plugin packages that contain platform-native implementations with an API written in Dart.

# Starting a Dart package project

To create a Dart package in Flutter, we will use the well-known Flutter create tool. One of the arguments of this tool (--template) determines the kind of package that we are creating: an app package, a Dart package, or a plugin package. We use the --template argument to create a new Dart package:

```
flutter create --template=package simple_package
```

This will generate a project called `simple_package` that contains a simple Dart package project. The generated project structure is as simple as a Dart package and does not have anything specific to Flutter:

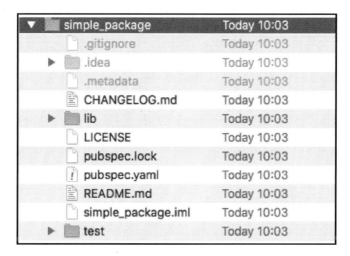

As you can see, it does not contain the typical `android` and `ios` folders, as we do not need them for simple Dart packages.

Even `pubspec.yaml` does not have anything special, except for the Flutter `sdk` dependency:

```
name: simple_package
description: A new Flutter package project.
version: 0.0.1
author:
homepage:

environment:
  sdk: ">=2.1.0 <3.0.0"

dependencies:
  flutter:
    sdk: flutter

dev_dependencies:
  flutter_test:
    sdk: flutter

flutter:
...
```

If we wanted to make the package so that it wasn't Flutter-specific, we could remove the Flutter framework part and work on it as a Dart package. Like the `flutter_test` dependency, for example, it is not really necessary for Dart-only packages.

 Remember: for simple Dart packages, you can use the `https://github.com/dart-lang/stagehand` Dart project generator. So, when writing simple Dart packages, we would use stagehand, Flutter- specific packages, and we use the Flutter `create` tool.

We will not be going into detail regarding the implementation of this kind of package, as it's a simple Dart package.

Now let's discuss plugin packages.

## Starting a Flutter plugin package

To create a plugin package in Flutter, we again use the Flutter `create` tool with the `plugin` template this time:

```
flutter create --template=plugin hands_on_platform_version -a kotlin -i
swift
```

 By default, the `plugin` template uses ObjC for iOS and Java for Android. Remember: to change to Swift or Kotlin, you can specify the iOS language using the `-i` argument and the Android language using `-a`.

This will generate a project called `hands_on_platform_version` that contains a Flutter package project. The generated project structure is similar to a Flutter app package.

# A plugin project structure

In the previous section, we generated a plugin project to start analyzing. Now let's take a look at specific parts of it. The project is the default plugin example from Flutter; the only thing it does is return the platform OS version of the running device.

There are some differences, though:

- The contents of the ios/ and android/ folders does not contain native applications that start the Flutter runtime. Instead, it simply contains native classes that are entry points to specific native implementations. We will check this in detail later.
- The example/ directory is a simple Flutter application package—yes, a subpackage inside the plugin package.
- lib/hands_on_show_toast.dart is a Dart API for the plugin:

```
// pubspec.yaml

name: hands_on_platform_version
description: A new flutter plugin project.
version: 0.0.1
author:
homepage:

environment:
  sdk: ">=2.1.0 <3.0.0"

dependencies:
  flutter:
    sdk: flutter

dev_dependencies:
  flutter_test:
    sdk: flutter

flutter:
 plugin:
 androidPackage: com.example.hands_on_platform_version
 pluginClass: HandsOnPlatformVersionPlugin
```

As you can see, the pubspec file is also similar to a simple Flutter application package. The difference is in the plugin section inside the flutter section. This part defines the package as a plugin package identifying the native code that will compose the real implementation in a specific platform context.

# MethodChannel

Flutter communication between the client (Flutter) and the host (native) application occurs through platform channels. The `MethodChannel` class is responsible for sending messages (**method invocations**) to the platform side. On the platform side, `MethodChannel` on Android (API) and `FlutterMethodChannel` on iOS (API) enable receiving method calls and sending a result back:

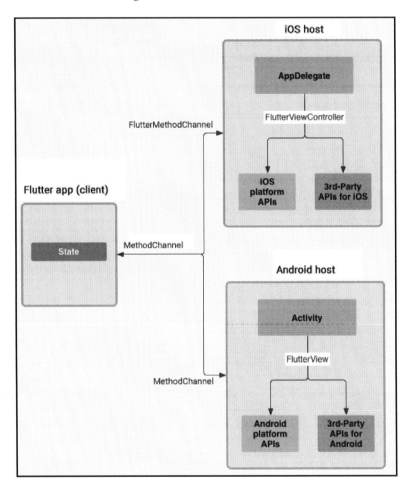

The platform channel technique allows the decoupling of the UI code from the platform-specific code. The host listens on the platform channel, and receives a message. It can use platform APIs to make the implementation of logic and sends back a response to the client, the Flutter portion of the app.

To understand how the message exchange occurs, you can check out the `https://flutter.dev/docs/development/platform-integration/platform-channels` page. It contains examples on platform channels and message types.

# Implementing the Android plugin

As we have seen, the default project template generates a small code that gets the platform version. Let's take a look at the generated code in `HandsOnPlatformVersionPlugin.kt`, which is in the Android subproject `com.example.hands_on_platform_version` package. This single file is the entrypoint of the plugin:

```kotlin
// HandsOnPlatformVersionPlugin.kt

class HandsOnPlatformVersionPlugin: MethodCallHandler {
  companion object {
    fun registerWith(registrar: Registrar) { // 1
      val channel = MethodChannel(registrar.messenger(),
      "hands_on_platform_version")
      channel.setMethodCallHandler(HandsOnPlatformVersionPlugin())
    }
  }

  override fun onMethodCall(call: MethodCall, result: Result) { // 2
    if (call.method == "getPlatformVersion") { // 3
      result.success("Android ${android.os.Build.VERSION.RELEASE}")
      //4
    } else {
      result.notImplemented() // 5
    }
  }
}
```

The invocation of a plugin method runs as follows:

1. This first static method is used by the Flutter framework to prepare the plugin to be accessible from a Dart context. It basically creates a `MethodChannel` instance and sets the method handler as the current class. In summary, it sets up the linkage between Dart and native code.

We will check the MethodChannel type in detail in Chapter 13, *Improving User Experience*, where we will see how to add native codes to application projects, not only plugin packages.

2. The onMethodCall method is called whenever the corresponding Dart API needs the native code to run; that is, on the Dart side, it will request the framework to run a native code with a specific registered name and parameters. There are two arguments in the method:
   - MethodCall: Describes the request
   - Result: Passes back results to a Dart context
3. The first step to run a specific code is to check what the caller wants to be executed. In this case, there is a check by the method name. A plugin might have many methods; that is why it is needed.
4. Using the Result object, we deliver the result of the method, using the success callback to pass back the requested value.
5. The notImplemented() callback, also from the Result class, can be used to notify the caller that the requested method does not have a corresponding implementation. In the same way, there is the error callback for handling errors.

# Implementing the iOS plugin

On the iOS side, the Swift code looks similar to the Kotlin code:

```swift
// SwiftHandsOnPlatformVersionPlugin.swift

public class SwiftHandsOnPlatformVersionPlugin: NSObject, FlutterPlugin {
  public static func register(with registrar: FlutterPluginRegistrar) {
  // 1
    let channel = FlutterMethodChannel(name: "hands_on_platform_version",
    binaryMessenger: registrar.messenger())
    let instance = SwiftHandsOnPlatformVersionPlugin()
    registrar.addMethodCallDelegate(instance, channel: channel)
  }

  public func handle(_ call: FlutterMethodCall, result: @escaping
  FlutterResult) {
    result("iOS " + UIDevice.current.systemVersion)
  }
}
```

The process looks similar to Android, but there are some small differences:

- The `handle` method is the iOS equivalent of `onMethodCall` in Kotlin. Note that it does not check the method call from the `FlutterMethodCall` argument. Although it is alright for a single method plugin, it is always good to check the caller method to make it clear what this is handling.
- `FlutterResult` is used to send data back to Dart context. There are also constant types for equivalent error, and not implemented cases: `FlutterError` and `FlutterMethodNotImplemented`.

# The Dart API

So, now that we have checked the native implementation of the plugin, we need to understand how Flutter communicates with it from the Dart context. The generated Dart API file `lib/hands_on_platform_version.dart` is the entry point for costumer apps. The consumer packages will import this library to use the plugin. Let's check the API file:

```
// hands_on_platform_version.dart

class HandsOnPlatformVersion {
  static const MethodChannel _channel =
      const MethodChannel('hands_on_platform_version'); // 1

  static Future<String> get platformVersion async { // 2
    final String version = await
_channel.invokeMethod('getPlatformVersion'); // 3
    return version;
  }
}
```

The `HandsOnPlatformVersion` class is public, as you can see, and it contains a single method that exposes native implementations:

1. The first thing that is created is `MethodChannel`—the bridge between Dart and native platform code.
2. The `platformVersion` method is exposed to consumers.
3. The `invokeMethod()` of `MethodChannel` is used to call a specific method by name, `getPlatformVersion` in this case. This method resolves to a `Future` with the result from the native code.

# An example of plugin package

The `example/` directory contains a simple Flutter application that depends on the created plugin. Check out the `pubspec.yaml` file:

```
// example/pubspec.yaml

name: hands_on_platform_version_example
description: Demonstrates how to use the hands_on_platform_version plugin.
publish_to: 'none'

environment:
  sdk: ">=2.1.0 <3.0.0"

dependencies:
  flutter:
    sdk: flutter

  cupertino_icons: ^0.1.2

dev_dependencies:
  flutter_test:
    sdk: flutter

  hands_on_platform_version:
    path: ../

flutter:
  uses-material-design: true
```

It is a common Flutter application `pubspec.yaml` file, except for the last item on the `dev_dependencies` list. There is a dependency on the `hands_on_platform_version` plugin with the `path` specification variant.

 As we have seen in `Chapter 2`, *Intermediate Dart Programming*, remember that you can specify a plugin dependency from the `pub` repository, paths, or source repositories.

# Using the plugin

To use the plugin package, we start by importing it into our Dart libraries, like any other plugin:

```
import 'package:hands_on_platform_version/hands_on_platform_version.dart';
```

The usage follows with the plugin method invocation:

```
await HandsOnPlatformVersion.platformVersion;
```

The full example retains the platform version in the _platformVersion field and calls the native code in the initPlatformState() method:

```
Future<void> initPlatformState() async { // 1
  String platformVersion;
  try { // 2
    platformVersion = await HandsOnPlatformVersion.platformVersion;
  } on PlatformException {
    platformVersion = 'Failed to get platform version.';
  }

  if (!mounted) return; // 3

  setState(() {
    _platformVersion = platformVersion; // 4
  });
}
```

We can highlight some points here:

- The method calling is async as platform messages are asynchronous
- Platform messages may fail, so we use a try/catch PlatformException that helps to inspect errors
- This check helps discarding the result from the platform if the widget is removed from the tree by then
- The state is updated so the widget is rebuilt and displays the retrieved platform version from the plugin

# Adding documentation to the package

Flutter plugins are important pieces in app development. The Flutter ecosystem is growing and, day by day, brand-new useful plugins are shared with the community. However, useful plugins must clearly describe how they should be used properly. This is done with concrete documentation.

# Documentation files

If you check out the `pub` repository site (`pub.dev`), you will see important information about the package. This information is collected from specific files present in the project:

- `pubspec.yaml`: This file contains details about the package:

```
name: hands_on_platform_version_example
description: Demonstrates how to use the hands_on_platform_version
plugin.
version: 0.0.1
author: Alessandro Biessek <alessandrobiessek@gmail.com>
# homepage: the plugin homepage
....
```

This info is useful so that clients of the library know who created it and what it does.

- `README.md`: This is short documentation about the usage of the package and important things
- `LICENSE`: This is the license for the usage of the package
- `CHANGELOG.md`: This logs the changes in each version of the package
- `example/`: This is a practical example on how to use the package

# Library documentation

Another important piece of package documentation is on the Dart level. The consumer needs to know every available method, its arguments, and return types to know how to take the maximum from the library.

We will create library documentation in Dart APIs by adding documentation comments in libraries directives (see `Chapter 2`, *Intermediate Dart Programming*) with the `///` syntax:

```
/// This is a doc comment and may be added to any member of a library.
```

This can be applied to library members as well, such as methods, variables, and classes. Even *private members* may have documentation comments that may be helpful for understanding different pieces of the library.

 Check out the official tips for writing good documentation for your Flutter packages: `https://www.dartlang.org/guides/language/effective-dart/documentation`.

# Generating documentation

When you publish a package, API documentation is automatically generated (as long as you use the comment type mentioned earlier) and published to `dartdocs.org`. You can, if necessary, generate the API documentation locally.

First, configure the Flutter root environment in the following way:

```
export FLUTTER_ROOT=~/dev/flutter (on macOS or Linux)

set FLUTTER_ROOT=~/dev/flutter (on Windows)
```

You can generate a package documentation by running the following:

```
cd ~/dev/mypackage

$FLUTTER_ROOT/bin/cache/dart-sdk/bin/dartdoc (on macOS or Linux)

%FLUTTER_ROOT%\bin\cache\dart-sdk\bin\dartdoc (on Windows)
```

 During the writing of this book, there is an open issue regarding the previous command on Windows; please do have a look: `https://github.com/dart-lang/dartdoc/issues/1949`.

By default, the documentation is generated under the `doc/api` directory as static HTML files.

# Publishing a package

Publishing a package is the last step to make it available to the Flutter community. All the publication is done by the pub tool. The command to make the publication is as follows:

```
flutter packages pub publish --dry-run
```

The --dry-run argument works like a pre-publication step, where the pub tool will make a validation process but does not actually upload the package. After everything is good, we can remove the --dry-run part:

```
flutter packages pub publish
```

This will effectively publish the package to the pub site so that every source code is published to the pub repository. Only hidden files and ignored ones (in case of using Git) are not uploaded.

 You can see more about the publish command here: https://www. dartlang.org/tools/pub/publishing.

# Plugin project development recommendations

Flutter plugins are great for accelerating app development. Contributing to the community by sharing a plugin is also great; however, there are few points to consider when planning to publish a plugin to make it really useful and accepted:

- **Support multiple platforms**: Plugins that target a single platform go wrong from the start. Since Flutter is a cross-platform framework, we need to think this way, since the plugins will be used to create applications that will run on multiple platforms.
- **Write good documentation**: Flutter provides tools to make it easy to create and publish a package with all the documentation; the only task required is to write this document.
- **Search for existing plugins first:** Maybe you are thinking of developing another plugin on Flutter, but you should search in pub first to check whether it's already developed by other developers so that you can use and even contribute to it:

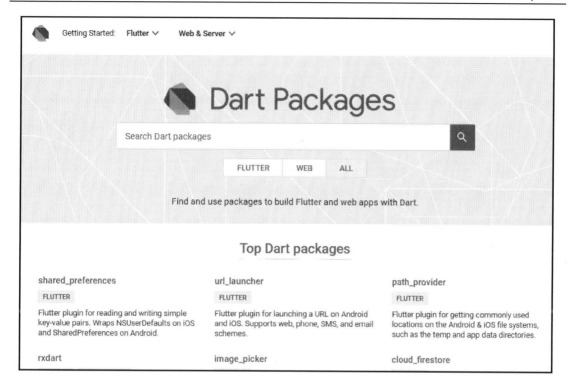

Writing a good, focused plugin can be really helpful to other developers. Do not hesitate to check out the existing plugin source code and learn how to make great tools for the community.

# Summary

In this chapter, we have seen how a Flutter plugin package looks and how it is different than the Flutter application and simple Dart packages. We have seen that Flutter plugins go down to native code by using `MethodChannels`, which provide good mechanisms to interop with the system directly.

We saw how to start a plugin package project in Flutter and how to properly document it to make it useful and understandable for the community. And lastly, we learned how to make a package public on the `pub` repository so that other developers can make use of it.

In the next chapter, we are going to continue diving into specific platform code by integrating different features that are unique to each system, such as importing a contact, using the camera, and managing app permissions.

# 10
# Accessing Device Features from the Flutter App

Mobile applications do not live alone in the device and user context, and this is true for every level of applications, from simpler single-purpose applications to more complex ones. An application may need to access hardware features such as Bluetooth, the camera, import a contact to let the user interact with friends, or share content to other apps and users. So, a developer needs to make the application aware of the user and the device.

In this chapter, you will learn how to integrate an app to the user context, such as displaying and launching a URL, managing platform permissions, launching a phone's camera, and importing a contact.

The following topics will be covered in this chapter:

- Launching a URL from the app
- Managing app permissions
- Importing a contact from a phone
- Integrating the phone's camera

## Launching a URL from the app

Until now, we have seen how we can use Flutter plugins to add specific features to apps. In the Favors app, for the user profile picture, for example, we have used a plugin that launches the camera app and awaits for an image file: the `image_picker` plugin. This plugin acts as a bridge for us, and the camera app is independent from the underlying system, as we do not need to know how to launch the camera app and how to take the image file, we just ask it to do the hard work for us.

Taking a profile picture is a good use of a plugin, as in a future version of the app, we could allow the user to import the image from the gallery and use it in the same way. The `image_picker` plugin used does this job as well.

Now let's imagine another use case: a user asks a favor from another user that involves accessing a URL to get more context about the favor. For example, if someone asks you to buy a product from an e-commerce website, it's good to share the link to the product so that there isn't any misunderstanding.

Adding the *open link* functionality to the app can be made with the help of a plugin, `url_launcher`. The point is, for many features of our apps, we do not need to know how the platform works under the hood, as there are many useful Flutter plugins available to us.

 Check out the code for launching URLs from the app on GitHub in the `Chapter11|hands_on_url_handler` directory.

# Displaying a link

First of all, the user must identify the link in a text to click on. In a mobile context, we need to make the things as simple as possible, so, as you may know, it is not suitable to add another field to the favors request to add a link to the favor. Take a look at a chat app you may be using right now; you can type a URL into it, and when you send it to another user, it automatically appears as clickable text, and you do not need to perform any action; you just type.

The best way we can do in the app is the URL links added to a favor description can be turned into clickable links in the favors cards. You may be thinking to write the code with this functionality, as it would not be hard to do the following:

- Parse the favor description to the found links.
- Create multiple `TextSpans` to change its styling.
- Handle taps with Flutter gestures.

 `TextSpans` can be used when we want to apply different styles to parts of text. Check the `TextSpan` widget documentation for more details: `https://api.flutter.dev/flutter/painting/TextSpan-class.html`.

Although it's simple, coding this will take time that you could be investing in the app. That's why it is good to use plugins whenever possible: it increases *productivity*.

# The flutter_linkify plugin

There is, of course, a plugin that does the job of styling links in text for us, `flutter_linkify`. It does the job described in the previous section and presents this to us through the `Linkify` widget. It parses a text looking for links, and uses spans to differentiate between simple text and links, and, as a bonus, it exposes useful features:

- The `onOpen` property, which expects a callback to handle a click on a link
- The `humanizing` property, which displays a link without HTTP/HTTPS

We have changed our Favors app to show the links from the description of the request in the favor cards.

 The request part doesn't need any modification, as the user types the link normally in the text.

The changes to make the links appear and be clickable are minimal:

1. First, we add the plugin as a dependency:

```
dependencies:
    flutter_linkify: ^2.1.0 # Flutter Linkify plugin
```

2. After that, in the `FavorCardItem` widget, we swap its description `Text` child to the new `Linkify` widget

This is what it looked like before:

```
// in the build method of FavorCardItem class, favor description
    Text(
        favor.description,
        style: bodyStyle,
    ),
```

This is what it looked like now:

```
import 'package:flutter_linkify/flutter_linkify.dart'; // import plugin
library

// in the build method of FavorCardItem class, favor description
```

```
Linkify(
    text: favor.description,
    humanize: true,
),
```

This will make the link clickable and with a distinct style:

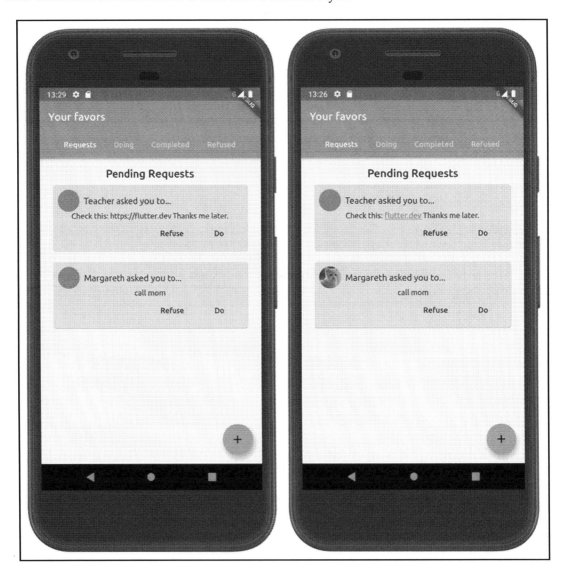

Text that starts with `http://` or `https://` appears as a link and is clickable. The next step is to handle the click to open the target URL.

# Launching a URL

Now that we have the links displaying and actionable in the app, we need to make them work properly. If you are an Android or iOS developer, you may know how to launch a URL, the valid schemes, and how to achieve this. In Flutter, as you may expect, this functionality must be handled in platform-specific ways.

 You can check out the supported URL schemes for each platform for iOS at: `https://developer.apple.com/library/archive/featuredarticles/iPhoneURLScheme_Reference/Introduction/Introduction.html` and for Android at: `https://developer.android.com/guide/components/intents-common.html`.

Again, thanks to the work of the Flutter community, we can do this level of integration with the help of the previously presented `url_launcher` plugin.

## The url_launcher plugin

The `url_launcher` plugin acts as a bridge to the platform-native link handlers so that we do not need to worry about platform-level details.

The usage of the plugin is reduced to few functions, `launch(url)` being the main one. The launch function retrieves a URL as an argument and takes care of the launching that's particular to each system.

In Android, it will build an intent for the system to handle through a browser app (or display a webview for web schemes if `forceWebView` is set to `true`). In iOS, web-scheme URLs are handled by default in a view controller owned by the app.

We integrate the plugin in the `FavorCardItem handleLinkClick` function, where we simply call the `launch(url)` function, passing the URL that comes from the `Linkify` callback:

```
// description element
Linkify(
    text: favor.description,
    humanize: true,
    onOpen: handleLinkClick,
),
...
// click handling
handleLinkClick(LinkableElement link) async {
    if (await canLaunch(link.url)) { // 1
```

```
        await launch(link.url); // 2
    }
}
```

As you can see, the plugin abstracts much of the work for us. We just need to call its function with the right argument:

1.  First, we check whether the device is capable of launching the URL with the `canLaunch` function. This will assert that the device has an app installed that's able to handle the URL scheme.
2.  Last, and if possible, we launch the URL; this will dispatch the intention to the corresponding platform.

 To have an idea of what is implemented under the hood for each system, I recommend you take a look at the native part of the plugin source code.

# Managing app permissions

Android and iOS systems have their own security policies involving user information or device hardware. The purpose of permission is to protect the privacy of a user. An app, whether native or not, must request permission to access user data, such as the camera, for example.

In iOS's recent versions, you must include the usage description in the `ios/Runner/Info.plist` file keys for the types of data the app needs to access, or it will crash. To access the camera, for example, it must include `NSCameraUsageDescription`.

 You can check out the available permissions for iOS here: `https://developer.apple.com/library/archive/documentation/General/Reference/InfoPlistKeyReference/Articles/CocoaKeys.html#//apple_ref/doc/uid/TP40009251-SW1`.

In Android, the `android/app/src/main/AndroidManifest.xml` file is where permissions are listed. Android has the concept of system permissions besides user ones; for your app to access the internet, for example (to fetch data from Firebase), it must have `android.permission.INTERNET` added by default on the Flutter template.

Check out the official Android guide on permissions to learn more about how they work on the system here: `https://developer.android.com/guide/topics/permissions/overview`.

So, the key difference is, in Android, every user-based resource has permission, and you must add it to the `manifest` file, and also request the permission using the system provided APIs. In iOS, you need to add a description to every user-sensitive resource in `Info.plist` so that a prompt will be shown by the system for the user to accept or deny it.

# Managing permissions on Flutter

As both systems have their own permission management, we need to take this into account when making use of protected resources. In Flutter, we need to go down to the platform level to request the necessary permissions.

As you have seen in our Favors app, we have not worried with permissions until now; the only existing setting regarding this is the link in the `AndroidManifest.xml` file:

```
<manifest xmlns:android="http://schemas.android.com/apk/res/android"
    package="com.example.handson">
    <uses-permission android:name="android.permission.INTERNET"/>
    ...
</manifest>
```

The internet permission is not added by default in the `AndroidManifest` file. The Flutter framework uses this for debugging and hot reloading.

Thanks to the Flutter community, we have a few plugins to help us with this task. A good example is the `permission_handler` plugin.

## Using the permission_handler plugin

The permission_handler plugin provides a high-level API to request and check the status of permissions. The plugin exposes a set of permissions in the PermissionGroup enum and makes a simplification over each one on its respective platform. Each permission group is mapped down to the corresponding permission in the system. The main provided methods from the plugin are as follows:

- requestPermissions: To request access to a particular resource
- checkPermissionStatus: To check the access status to a particular resource
- openAppSettings: To open the app settings so the user can see/change a particular resource

For Android, there is also the shouldShowRequestPermissionRationale method.

 You can check out the available methods and the map of permissions in the plugin page here: https://pub.dartlang.org/packages/permission_handler.

# Importing a contact from the phone

From the user perspective, inserting a phone number manually to make a favor request is not the preffered method, as it is susceptible to mistakes.

Importing a contact from the user's phone is a platform-specific task that, of course, has similarities. The final point is to launch the platform's contact selector and get a single contact from it.

The pub repository contains a set of plugins that help with this task. Some of them are as follows:

- contact_picker: Supports picking a phone number from the phone's contact list
- contacts_service: Provides an API that allows us to pick a contact and also manage them

If you remember, our Favors app allows the user to request a favor from another user by adding the phone number of the targeted friend. Importing the contact from the phone's contact list is the best way to do it.

# Importing a contact with contact_picker

The `contact_picker` plugin is suitable for the task, and we will be using this to import contact into the favor request phase.

The first step is to include the plugin as a dependency in `pubspec.yaml` file and run the `flutter packages get` command as well:

```
dependencies:
    contact_picker: ^0.0.2
```

Then, we need to change the **Request a favor** screen. We add an **Import** button to the right side of the friend's drop-down list:

In the `onPressed` action of the import button, we are going to redirect the user to the contacts screen so they can select a contact.

Let's take a look at the code. First, we add two fields to the `RequestFavorPageState` class:

```
// request_favors_page.dart

class RequestFavorPageState extends State<RequestFavorPage> {
  final ContactPicker _contactPicker = ContactPicker();
  Friend _importedFriend;
  ...
}
```

Here is what the two fields will help us with:

- `_contactPicker` provides the plugin functionality.
- `_importedFriend` stores the imported friend from the contacts, if any.

With this, we will be able to import a contact easily. After that, we add the `onPressed` callback for the **Import contact** button:

```
onPressed: () {
    _importContact();
},
```

Then we import a contact using the `_importContact()` method:

```
void _importContact() async {
    Contact contact = await _contactPicker.selectContact(); // 1
    if (contact != null) {
      setState(() {
        _importedFriend = Friend(
          name: contact.fullName,
          number: contact.phoneNumber.number,
        ); // 2
      });
    }
}
```

The import of a contact is carried out in a few steps:

1. First, we launch the contact selector by using the `selectContact` method from the `ContactPicker` class from the plugin.
2. After checking that the user has selected a contact (`contact != null`), we create a new `Friend` instance based on the selected contact info.

The final step is handling the saving of the favor where we need to get the friend's info from _importedFriend, as we did with _selectedFriend from the friend's drop-down list:

```
void save(BuildContext context) async {
    ...
    await _saveFavorOnFirebase(
        Favor(
            to: _importedFriend?.number ?? _selectedFriend?.number,
            ...
        )
    )
    ...
}
```

The only needed modification was in the 'to' property of the new Favor that will point to the _importedFriend or _selectedFriend value.

As you may be thinking, phone contacts are a user resource, and are therefore protected information. The user must allow the application to read or write contacts.

# Contact permission with permission_handler

Although contacts info is a user-protected resource, we do not need any specific permission to import a contact by using the contact_picker plugin because we are not reading it directly, but through platform-specific APIs.

We are going to see, however, how request permission to use contacts, as this can be useful in the future.

If you remember, each platform has its own way to handle permissions, and we need to implement permission requests based on this.

## Contact permission on Android

In Android, we need to add the contact permission request in AndroidManifest file, so let's change the android/app/src/(main|debug|profile)/AndroidManifest.xml file:

```
<manifest xmlns:android="http://schemas.android.com/apk/res/android"
    package="com.example.handson">
  ...
  <uses-permission android:name="android.permission.READ_CONTACTS" />
```

```
<uses-permission android:name="android.permission.WRITE_CONTACTS" />
</manifest>
```

By adding READ_CONTACTS permission, we declare to the Android system that we need to access the user contacts list; WRITE_CONTACTS, as you might have deduced, declares the need to write new contacts to the system.

 The behavior of this record depends on the version of the system the app is installed on. Check out this here: https://developer.android.com/training/permissions/requesting.

## Contact permission on iOS

In iOS, we need to provide an appropriate description of the Info.plist file so that the user knows why the app needs the requested permission. This is done in the ios/Runner/Info.plist file:

```
<dict>
  ...
  <key>NSContactsUsageDescription</key>
  <string>You can import a friend from a list of contacts.</string>
</dict>
```

When the app tries to access contacts in iOS, the system will ask the permission to the user showing the provided description to help on the acceptance.

## Checking and requesting permission in Flutter (permission_handler)

Suppose our app needs permission to access contacts in order to make a favor request (that is, this would be true if we wanted to display all the contacts inside our app for the user to select one). We create the _checkPermissions function to check and request the permission, if needed, and follow these steps:

1. First, we get the status of the permission from the API:

```
void _checkPermissions() async {
    PermissionStatus status = await PermissionHandler()
        .checkPermissionStatus(PermissionGroup.contacts);
```

2. Then, we test whether the status is different than granted, that is, it has not already granted by the user:

```
if (status != PermissionStatus.granted)
```

3. Lastly, if the permission is not granted (`status !=
PermissionStatus.granted`), we request it:

```
await
PermissionHandler().requestPermissions([PermissionGroup.contacts]);
}
```

In summary, `_checkPermissions` will get the current permission status, and if it is not granted, it will request it. A suitable place to call this function is in the **Contact import** button, before we import the contact:

```
void _importContact() async {
  await _checkPermissions();
  ...
}
```

In our case, the result of the `_checkPermissions()` is only illustrative, as we do not need the permission.

# Integrating the phone's camera

The camera feature is present in many apps, and integrating with it can be done in few ways. We could, for example, implement the code on our own, but thanks to the community, Flutter provides multiple plugins to access the camera. Some of the most well-known plugins are as follows:

- `camera`: With this plugin, we can display the camera preview directly on Flutter, take photos, or record video.
- `image_picker`: This plugin tries to simplify the task a lot; we only ask it to give us a photo from the camera or gallery, and it takes care of the rest.

If you remember, in Chapter 8, *Firebase Plugins*, we managed to send a user profile picture to Firebase Storage, and we have used the `image_picker` plugin to get an image file from the camera. So, let's review how this works in detail.

# Taking pictures with image_picker

Flutter does not communicate with the camera API directly, as this is a platform-level resource. The `image_picker` plugin, as its name suggests, helps with picking an image. It enables importing image files from the gallery and taking new pictures using the camera.

First, we add the dependency to the `pubspec.yaml` file and get it with the `flutter packages get` command:

```
dependencies:
  image_picker: ^0.5.0 # Image picker
```

We control image picking in the same place as the user enters their display name after login, in the final step of the `Stepper` widget. When the user presses the small avatar image, the camera opens to take a picture:

```
// login_page.dart

// part of LoginScreenState class
void _importImage() async {
    final image = await ImagePicker.pickImage(source: ImageSource.camera);
    setState(() {
      _imageFile = image;
    });
}
```

This is done with the `ImagePicker` class. We use its `pickImage()` method to start the camera and take a picture (all managed by the plugin) that resolves the captured image to a file for our usage.

 You can find the source code of `login_page.dart` on GitHub for a full example on how to use the `image_picker` plugin's. Also, it is important that you check the plugin's documentation, at `https://pub.dartlang.org/packages/image_picker`, as it requires some configuration to work.

# Camera permission with permission_handler

The plugin by itself handles permission requesting, but, in this case, we will again use the `permission_handler` plugin to check and ask the camera for permission.

# Camera permission on Android

In Android, we need to declare the camera permission in `AndroidManifest` file as we did for the contacts, so we change
the `android/app/src/(main|debug|profile)/AndroidManifest.xml` file:

```
<manifest xmlns:android="http://schemas.android.com/apk/res/android"
    package="com.example.handson">
  ...
  <uses-permission android:name="android.permission.CAMERA" />

</manifest>
```

By adding the `CAMERA` permission, we declare to the Android system that we need to access the camera. Additionally, we can use another Android `manifest` tag:

```
<manifest ...>
  <uses-feature
      android:name="android.hardware.camera"
      android:required="false" />
</manifest>
```

The `uses-feature` tag will declare that our app needs the camera to work properly (again, in our case, this is not really true. The required argument can be set to `true` if needed). If `true`, the app will only be available to devices that contains camera available.

# Camera permission on iOS

As we did for contacts, in iOS, we need to provide an appropriate description in the `Info.plist` file so that the user knows why the app needs the camera permission. Refer the code from the `ios/Runner/Info.plist` file:

```
<dict>
  ...
  <key>NSCameraUsageDescription</key>
  <string>You can add a profile picture right from the camera</string>
  <key>NSPhotoLibraryUsageDescription</key>
  <string>This app requires access to the photo library.</string>
  <key>NSMicrophoneUsageDescription</key>
  <string>This app does not require access to the microphone.</string>
</dict>
```

When the app tries to access the camera in iOS, the system will ask the uses for permission, showing the provided description so that the user will give permission to access the camera.

# Requesting camera permission in Flutter (permission_handler)

In the profile setting after login, we can add a profile picture. To request permission to access the camera, the process is very similar to requesting access to the user's contacts.

We create a function to check and request permission, if needed:

```
void _checkPermissions() async {
  PermissionStatus status = await PermissionHandler()
      .checkPermissionStatus(PermissionGroup.camera); // 1
    if (status != PermissionStatus.granted) { // 2
    await PermissionHandler().requestPermissions([PermissionGroup.camera]);
    // 3
   }
  }
```

The method is very similar to the check completed in the contact import example:

1. We get the status of the camera permission from the API.
2. We test whether the status is different than granted (if the permission was already granted by the user).
3. Lastly, if the permission is not granted, we request it.

A suitable place to call this function is in the profile image picking a stage, inside the _importImage() method:

```
void _importImage() async {
await _checkPermissions();
  ...
}
```

Although we need the camera permission, the image_picker plugin has already requested it for us, so it will work as well.

# Summary

In this chapter, we saw how to use plugins to utilize phone features such as camera, contacts, and launching a URL. We have seen that the Flutter community provides a set of plugins for all of the features needed.

We used the `url_launcher` and `flutter_linkify` plugins to show a link to the user in the Favor app's description. After this, we added the `permission_handler` plugin to manage app permissions. We also used the `contact_picker` plugin to import a contact from the user's contacts list, and, by using the `permission_handler` plugin, we added a contact permission check and request.

Later, the `image_picker` plugin was used in the same way to retrieve the user's profile picture on login, and, again, we used the `permission_handler` plugin to check and request camera permission.

In `Chapter 11`, *Platform Views and Map Integration*, we will continue to integrate Flutter plugins. This time, we will see how to use maps, so keep reading to check out map integration with Flutter apps.

# Platform Views and Map Integration

**11**

Displaying maps is a feature that appears frequently in apps nowadays because many mobile applications rely on user positioning and the location of places to provide tools to assist in many tasks and activities, such as finding specific places, driving, cycling, transportation, and transit. In this chapter, you will learn how to integrate Google Maps in Flutter applications in order to add markers and interactions to make them fully interactable with interesting places by using the Google Places API.

The following topics will be covered in this chapter:

- Displaying a map
- Adding a marker to the map
- Adding map interactions
- Using the Google Places API

# Displaying a map

Displaying a map in the application is the first step to make it a map-based application, so let's start by creating an application that displays a map and we will later add features to it. The Flutter framework does not contain a map widget directly in its core SDK; this is supported instead with the official `google_maps_flutter` plugin, which we will use to display a map like this:

At the time of writing this book, google_maps_flutter is in *developers' preview*; that is, the plugin *relies* on Flutter's new mechanism for embedding Android and iOS views and, as that mechanism is currently in developers' preview, this plugin should also be considered in developers' preview.

Displaying a map in Flutter apps requires some adjustments to the default application. So, let's begin by understanding what these adjustments are and then add support to platform views.

# Platform views

Flutter's PlatformView is a widget that embeds an Android/iOS native view and integrates it in the Flutter widget tree. Platform views are stateful widgets that control the resources associated with the platform's native view. As for embedding, this kind of view is an expensive task, so it should be used with caution, and only if really necessary. You can use it to display maps, for example, as Flutter does not have an equivalent widget that displays a map on its own.

Platform views are important pieces in frameworks such as Flutter, as they enable you to fill some gaps during the evolution of the framework. However, there are some points associated with this that you may need to consider before using it:

- On Android, it requires API level 20 or greater
- On iOS, it requires some additional steps to set up the feature (*see the following sections*)
- Again, embedding views is expensive for the framework and should be avoided whenever possible
- PlatformView fills up all of the available space of the parent, similar to the container widget
- PlatformView takes part in the widget tree like any other widget

 This feature was presented during the Flutter 1.0 release and, at the time of writing, is still evolving on both Android and iOS platforms, so keep following its status on Flutter repository-related issues: https://github.com/flutter/flutter/labels/a%3A%20platform-views.

# Enabling platform views on iOS

In the early versions of the platform views features, it was only supported on Android. At the time of writing this book, the iOS implementation of embedding `UIKitView` is still in *release preview*. So, we need to change the application's `ios/Runner/Info.plist` file and add a specific setting:

```
<plist version="1.0">
<dict>
  ...
  <key>io.flutter.embedded_views_preview</key>
  <string>YES</string>
</dict>
</plist>
```

This will enable the functionality for iOS apps so that we can use the preview feature in our application.

A list of open issues about embedding iOS views is available on GitHub: `https://github.com/flutter/flutter/issues?q=is%3Aopen+is%3Aissue+label%3A%22a%3A+platform-views%22+label%3A%22%E2%8C%BA%E2%80%AC+platform-ios%22`.

# Creating a platform view widget

When we create a platform view widget, we basically create a Flutter wrapper of a native iOS/Android view. The process of creating a platform view is similar to plugins and requires adding native code to an application.

To keep things simple, we create a plugin project; see Chapter 9, *Developing Your Own Flutter Plugin*, to remember how to create a plugin project. In this project, we define a new view, `HandsOnTextView`, which is a native text displaying view; `TextView` on Android and `UITextView` on iOS.

Check, the `hands_on_platform_views` file on GitHub for the complete plugin code.

To begin with, after the plugin project is created, we define the Dart API. This is the code that makes the bridge from Dart to native code. We create a `HandsOnTextView` widget.

As you can see, its build method has the following important parts:

- Depending on the platform type, `Theme.of(context).platform`, we instantiate a `AndroidView` or `UiKitView` widget.
- Their properties are similar, and we define the `viewType` widget we want to create, its parameters (`creationParams`), and the parameters codec (`creationParamsCodec`):
  - `viewType`: A view type is used by the Flutter platform view system to indicate which native view we are intending to use, similar to a plugin system.
  - `creationParams`: These are the arguments that we want to pass down to the native view creation—the `text` to be shown, in our case.
  - `creationParamsCodec`: This defines which method of parameter data transfer will occur while sending `creationParams` to the native code.

This is all for the Dart side of the platform view. Now we need to define the view in corresponding platforms.

In `Chapter 13`, *Improving User Experience,* we will check how to add native code to the application. You may also find some helpful information there to helps you understand how the platform view works.

# Creating an Android view

Creating and registering platform views on each platform is a very similar process; we just need to manage the differences in languages and native view APIs. The simplest way to start platform view creation is to register it into the platform views registry, very similar to what is done when creating a Flutter plugin. Also, as we are dealing with a plugin project, this is done together with the plugin registration:

```
class HandsOnPlatformViewsPlugin{
    companion object {
        @JvmStatic
        fun registerWith(registrar: Registrar) {
            registrar
                .platformViewRegistry()
```

```
                    .registerViewFactory(
                        "com.example.handson/textview",
                        HandsOnTextViewFactory());
            }
        }
    }
```

We register a view factory identifying it with a *type/key*, so that, when instantiating a platform view, the Flutter engine is able to find the corresponding factory and delegate the view creation to it. The view factory, by the way, is responsible for instantiating views from specific types. As you can see, we registered a view factory for the com.example.handson/textview type. We get the PlatformViewRegistry instance with the platformViewRegistry() method, and through it, we added our factory to the registry so when someone asks for the registered type, the construction will be delegated to this HandsOnTextViewFactory factory instance.

HandsOnTextViewFactory looks as follows:

```
class HandsOnTextViewFactory :
PlatformViewFactory(StandardMessageCodec.INSTANCE) {

    override fun create(context: Context, id: Int, args: Any): PlatformView
{

        val params = args as Map<String, Any> // 1

        val text = if (params.containsKey("text")) { // 2
            params["text"] as String? ?: ""
        } else ""

        return HandsOnTextView(context, text) // 3
    }
}
```

The factory class must extend PlatformViewFactory and implement the create method. This method is responsible for the creation of the specified view type, which goes as follows:

1. It receives args as a parameter and can use this to configure the view
2. It gets the text value from a Map received in the parameter
3. Finally, it returns a HandsOnTextView instance

Notice the StandardMessageCodec.INSTANCE value passed to the parent class of the factory. This must have the same type of creationParamsCodec defined in Dart, so the framework is able to transfer the arguments from Dart-side to native.

The `HandsOnTextView` class is the native view class:

```
class HandsOnTextView internal constructor(context: Context, text: String)
: PlatformView {
    private val textView: TextView = TextView(context)

    init {
        textView.text = text
    }

    override fun getView(): View {
        return textView
    }

    override fun dispose() {}
}
```

As you can see, it must implement the framework's `PlatformView` interface. The interface requires two methods, `getView` and `dispose`:

- `getView()` must return an Android view to be embedded in the Flutter context.
- The `dispose()` method is called when the view is detached from the Flutter context. We can use this to clear any resource or reference to prevent memory leaks.

# Creating an iOS view

In iOS, the process is very similar to Android, but there are a few points on syntax that differ. We register the factory like we did earlier, in the *Creating an Android view* section:

```
public class SwiftHandsOnPlatformViewsPlugin: NSObject, FlutterPlugin {
    public static func register(with registrar: FlutterPluginRegistrar) {
        let viewFactory = HandsOnTextViewFactory()
        registrar.register(viewFactory, withId: "com.example.handson/textview")
    }
}
```

Then, we make the `HandsOnTextViewFactory` class able to return the iOS version of the view:

```
public class HandsOnTextViewFactory: NSObject, FlutterPlatformViewFactory {

    public func create(
        withFrame frame: CGRect,
        viewIdentifier viewId: Int64,
```

```
        arguments args: Any?
        ) -> FlutterPlatformView {
        return HandsOnTextView(frame, viewId: viewId, args: args)
    }

    public func createArgsCodec() -> FlutterMessageCodec & NSObjectProtocol
{
        return FlutterStandardMessageCodec.sharedInstance()
    }
}
```

Here, the factory must implement the `FlutterPlatformViewFactory` protocol, with both the `create` and `createArgsCodec` methods:

- `create()` must return an iOS view to be embedded in the Flutter context, like `getView()` from the Android version.
- `createArgsCodec()` must return the corresponding `creationParamsCodec` version. As we did earlier, we use the standard codec, `FlutterStandardMessageCodec.sharedInstance()`, in iOS.

In our case, as we are passing just a string to the native side. We could have used `StringCodec` as the message codec but, for the sake of our example, we used the standard codec instead.

 Check the message codec document, `https://docs.flutter.io/flutter/services/MessageCodec-class.html`, for all of the possible codec types.

Now, let's have a look at how to use platform widget.

# Usage of a platform view widget

The usage of a platform widget is as simple as using an ordinary widget. Apart from the specific configuration previously provided for the iOS platform, there is nothing more needed. We just use it as a normal widget:

```
@override
Widget build(BuildContext context) {
  return MaterialApp(
    home: Container(
      alignment: Alignment.center,
      color: Colors.red,
      child: SizedBox(
```

```
        height: 100,
        child: HandsOnTextView(
          text: "Text from Platform view",
        ),
      ),
    ),
  );
}
```

 Check the `hands_on_platform_views` example on GitHub for the complete plugin code.

After that, the platform widget looks like any other widget:

Wrapping the platform view into `SizedBox` limits its dimensions; otherwise, it would take all of the available space. However, this is not mandatory; the `AndroidView` and `UiKitView` classes are responsible for making the platform views present into the widget hierarchy in other widgets.

 It is important to note that embedding platform views is an expensive operation as the Flutter engine needs to manage the resources required by each of them. So, using platform views should be avoided when a Flutter equivalent is possible.

# Getting started with the google_maps_flutter plugin

As said before, the `google_maps_flutter` plugin relies on the platform views to display maps on Flutter apps, as you have seen in the previous section.

 Like platform views feature, this plugin is still under active evolution, so you may need to check for changes in the plugin page: `https://pub.dartlang.org/packages/google_maps_flutter`.

The plugin exposes the `GoogleMap` widget, and that is all this is about. Besides that, the widget exposes common map functionalities that are important to make it fully customizable and interactive. The main ones are as follows:

- `mapType`: This is to change the style of map tiles to display, for example, `MapType.normal` displays traffic and terrain information and `MapType.Satellite` displays aerial photos.

 Check all of the available types in the `MapType` documentation page: `https://pub.dartlang.org/documentation/google_maps_flutter/latest/google_maps_flutter/MapType-class.html`.

- `markers`: This allows us to add markers on top of the map (see the *Adding markers to the map* section).
- `myLocationEnabled`: This is to enable the **My Location** layer on the map. It enables the possibility to show an indicator at the current device location, as well as a **My Location** button for the user to be capable of focusing on the current known location, if possible.

 Enabling the **My Location** requires us to also add location permissions to both native platforms of our app. Check the previous chapter's *Managing app permissions* section to remember how to do it.

- `initialCameraPosition`: This is to configure the initial visible portion of the map.
- `cameraTargetBounds`: This is to change the geographical bounding box for the camera target, that is, the focused part of the map.
- `rotateGesturesEnabled`, `scrollGesturesEnabled`, `tiltGesturesEnabled`, and `zoomGesturesEnabled`: These enable/disable corresponding gestures.

This plugin also exposes some callbacks for us to be able to respond to specific map events:

- `onMapCreated`: Called when the map is structurally ready
- `onTap`: Called when a tap occurs on the map
- `onCameraMoveStarted`, `onCameraMove` and `onCameraIdle`: Called on corresponding camera events

 You can check all of the available properties of the `GoogleMap` class on https://pub.dartlang.org/documentation/google_maps_flutter/latest/google_maps_flutter/GoogleMap-class.html.

# Displaying a map with the google_maps_flutter plugin

The `GoogleMaps` plugin can be to display a map in Flutter, like this:

The first step needed is to add the plugin dependency in the `pubspec.yaml` file and install it with the `flutter packages get` command:

```
dependencies:
  ...
  google_maps_flutter: ^0.5.3
```

# Enabling the Maps API on Google Cloud Console

Before using the `GoogleMap` widget, we need to get a valid Maps API key from the Google Maps platform. The process is done in the Maps Platform on Google Cloud Console, `https://cloud.google.com/maps-platform`:

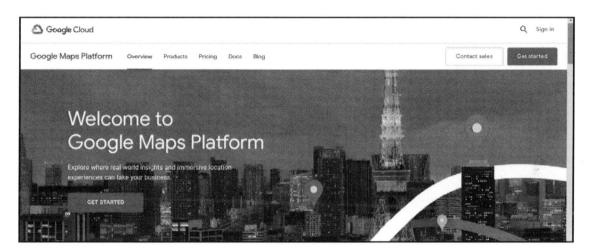

Let's see how the process works:

1. Select the **GET STARTED** option. We are guided through the process of enabling the API. First, we select the APIs we want to enable:

2.  And then, we select the project for which we want to enable the Maps API:

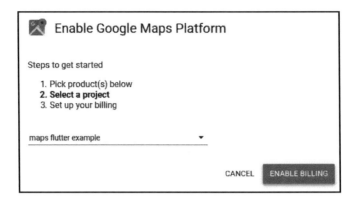

3.  After that, we need to enable billing for the project. Google Maps Platform is free to use but needs a billing account to be linked to the project. After creating/enabling the billing account for the project, we enable the API:

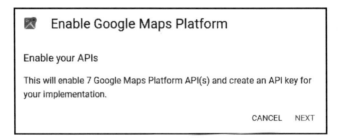

4.  And finally, we get the API key to be used in our mobile application:

The API key can be accessed later, on the API's explorer on Google Cloud Console.

This key is used to initialize the map plugin on both platforms, in a similar way to how we did it before for AdMob and Firebase.

## Google Maps API integration on Android

For the Android platform, we need to change the `android/src/main/AndroidManifest.xml` file and add a `meta-data` tag containing the API key we got from the Maps Console:

```
<manifest xmlns:android="http://schemas.android.com/apk/res/android"
    package="com.example.hands_on_maps">
  <application ... >
    <meta-data android:name="com.google.android.geo.API_KEY"
    android:value="YOUR KEY HERE"/>
  </application>
</manifest>
```

## Google Maps API integration on iOS

In iOS, we change the `ios/Runner/AppDelegate.swift` file by adding the code responsible for setting the API key on the plugin:

```
import UIKit
import Flutter
import GoogleMaps

@UIApplicationMain
@objc class AppDelegate: FlutterAppDelegate {
  override func application(
    _ application: UIApplication,
    didFinishLaunchingWithOptions launchOptions:
    [UIApplicationLaunchOptionsKey: Any]?
  ) -> Bool {
    GMSServices.provideAPIKey("YOUR KEY HERE")
    GeneratedPluginRegistrant.register(with: self)
    return super.application(application, didFinishLaunchingWithOptions:
    launchOptions)
  }
}
```

Remember, on iOS we need to opt-into the embedded views preview version by adding the specific setting on the Info.plist file (see the previous *Platform views* section).

## Displaying a map on Flutter

After properly initializing the plugin on either platform, we can use the GoogleMap widget on our app. In a minimal implementation, we just need to add it to our layout:

```
// part of MapPage widget
@override
Widget build(BuildContext context) {
  ...
  return GoogleMap(
    initialCameraPosition: CameraPosition(
    target: LatLng(51.178883, -1.826215),
      zoom: 10.0
    ),
  );
  ...
}
...
```

The only mandatory property to be set in the GoogleMap widget is initialCameraPosition, which will position the visualization of the map in a target location defined in the CameraPosition instance. The CameraPosition class also supports the zoom, tilt, and bearing properties.

With this set up, we can see `GoogleMap` in action:

As you can see again, the widget fills up all of the available space, a behavior defined by `PlatformView`. Also, by default, map interactions such as zoom and move are enabled. We can change these with the previously seen gesture-related `GoogleMap` widget properties.

# Adding markers to the map

Displaying a map in the application is just the start point of creating a map-based app. Adding information about places, for example, is one of the most common tasks when working with maps. Let's see how we can add markers to the previously created map by using the `Marker` class provided by the plugin.

# The Marker class

`Marker`, as mentioned in the documentation, simply marks a geographical location on the map. It adds context information over the map, such as identifying a place, checkpoint, or point of interest.

Markers typically are defined with an icon and single or multiple actions in its `click` event. The following properties are some of the most used when adding markers to a map:

- `position`: Although not mandatory by the plugin itself, it identifies the geographical location of the marker on the map, so it is almost always required
- `icon`: This is a marker icon in the `BitmapDescriptor` format

 Check out more information about the `BitmapDescriptor` class on the plugin documentation page: https://pub.dartlang.org/documentation/ google_maps_flutter/latest/google_maps_flutter/BitmapDescriptor- class.html.

- `markerId`: This is a unique identifier of the marker on the map
- `infoWindow`: This is the Google Maps information window that is displayed when the marker is tapped

Note from the documentation:

> *"A marker icon is drawn oriented against the device's screen rather than the map's surface, that is, it will not necessarily change orientation due to map rotations, tilting, or zooming."*

# Adding markers in the GoogleMap widget

As we have seen before, the `GoogleMap` widget exposes the `markers` property, which expects a `Set` collection of `Marker` instances to be passed to it. Let's see how to add markers by setting the `markers` property:

1. First, we add a `_markers` field to the `MapPage` class to hold a random set of markers (`Marker` instances):

```
class MapPage extends StatelessWidget {
  final _markers = {
    Marker(
      position: LatLng(51.178883, -1.826215),
      markerId: MarkerId('1'),
      infoWindow: InfoWindow(title: 'Stonehenge'),
      icon: BitmapDescriptor.defaultMarker
    ),
    Marker(
      position: LatLng(41.890209, 12.492231),
      markerId: MarkerId('2'),
      infoWindow: InfoWindow(title: 'Colosseum'),
      icon: BitmapDescriptor.defaultMarker
    ),
    Marker(
      position: LatLng(36.106964, -112.112999),
      markerId: MarkerId('3'),
      infoWindow: InfoWindow(title: 'Grand Canyon'),
      icon: BitmapDescriptor.defaultMarker
    ),
  };
  ...
}
```

2. And then, we just need to set the `markers` property on the `GoogleMap` widget:

```
@override
Widget build(BuildContext context) {
  return GoogleMap(
    initialCameraPosition:
        CameraPosition(target: LatLng(51.178883, -1.826215),
        zoom: 10.0),
    markers: _markers,
  );
}
```

If we tap on a marker, the corresponding `InfoWindow` object is displayed with the *title* set:

As you saw, adding markers to the `GoogleMap` widget is as simple as displaying the map itself, as it follows the Flutter paradigm of rebuilding the widget with the description provided in its construction (that is, `markers`).

 Note for the curious: These markers are some of the 17 stunning places to visit with Google Maps found on `lifehack.org`: `https://www.lifehack.org/articles/lifestyle/17-stunning-places-visit-with-google-maps.html`.

# Adding map interactions

Adding markers to the map helps to enrich the contextual information involved in it; however, this is far from enough for a real map-based app. Handling events or changing the map according to user needs is also fundamental. Let's see how we can add markers dynamically to the map and use the GoogleMapController class to interact with the map camera programmatically.

# Adding markers dynamically

As said before, we need to pass the markers during the GoogleMap widget construction, so the first step is to make our MapPage widget a StatefulWidget widget and rebuild its subtree every time we want to add a new marker.

After that, we have added a button to the layout so that we can add the marker after the initial build. The button onPressed callback calls _addMarkerOnCameraCenter, which works as follows:

```
void _addMarkerOnCameraCenter() {
  setState(() {
    _markers.add(Marker(
      markerId: MarkerId("${_markers.length + 1}"),
      infoWindow: InfoWindow(title: "Added marker"),
      icon: BitmapDescriptor.defaultMarker,
      position: _cameraCenter,
    ));
  });
}
```

As you can see, it uses the setState method to cause a rebuild of the widget and adds Marker to the _markers set. The only new part here is the position: _cameraCenter assignment on Marker.

The _cameraCenter value is a property in the state that tracks the center location of the camera in the GoogleMap widget. It is retrieved using the onCameraMove callback of the widget, as follows:

```
GoogleMap(
    ...
    onCameraMove: _cameraMove,
),
```

And the value is simply stored, as mentioned previously:

```
void _cameraMove(CameraPosition position) {
  _cameraCenter = position.target;
}
```

This way, every time the user presses the button, a marker is added at the center target location on the map. Although it's not a real-world use case, this is a practical starting point of interacting with the map.

 Take a look at the hands_on_maps example on GitHub to check MapPage as stateful widget code and the small layout changes to display a button.

# GoogleMapController

Another level of interaction we can do is provided by the GoogleMapController class, which works in a very similar way to well-known controllers, such as TextEditingController.

The GoogleMapController class aims to expose control methods of the GoogleMap widget. Right now, the only available methods are the following:

- animateCamera: This starts an animated change of the map camera position
- moveCamera: This changes the map camera position without animating

# Getting GoogleMapController

In contrast with other controllable widgets, we do not provide a controller to the GoogleMap widget by ourselves. Instead, this will be provided to us through the previously seen onMapCreated callback. So, we just need to store it, as follows:

```
GoogleMap(
  ...
  onMapCreated: (controller) {
    _mapController = controller;
  },
),
```

_mapController is an instance field of the MapPage widget that we will be using to interact with the map camera.

# Animating a map camera to a location

We have added a row of buttons where the user can press to focus on a specific place. By tapping on one of these buttons, a new method will be called, _animateMapCameraTo, for Stonehenge, for example:

```
RaisedButton(
    child: Text("Stonehenge"),
    onPressed: () {
        _animateMapCameraTo(_stonehengePosition);
    },
),
```

The new method is responsible for requesting the camera update:

```
void _animateMapCameraTo(LatLng position) {
    _mapController.animateCamera(CameraUpdate.newLatLng(position));
}
```

As you can see, through the GoogleMapController instance retrieved before, we can dispatch a camera animation to a new location on the map.

 The code for other buttons are very similar. Again, check hands_on_maps on GitHub for full details of the map integration example.

# Using the Google Places API

From the official website (https://developers.google.com/places/web-service/intro), we can see the following:

*"The Places API is a service that returns information about places using HTTP requests. Places are defined within this API as establishments, geographic locations, or prominent points of interest."*

This service can be used in several ways to get information about places:

- Get a list of places based on a user's location or a search string
- Get detailed information about a specific place, including user reviews

- Access to the millions of place-related photos stored in Google's Place database
- Query prediction service for text-based geographic searches, returning suggested queries as users type and automatically filling in the name and/or address of a place as users type

In this section, we will be using the API to get detailed information (that is, the name) of a place added by the user through our previously created **Place marker** button.

# Enabling the Google Places API

Like the Google Maps SDK, the Places API needs to be enabled on the Google Developer Console, `https://console.developers.google.com/apis/library/places-backend.googleapis.com`:

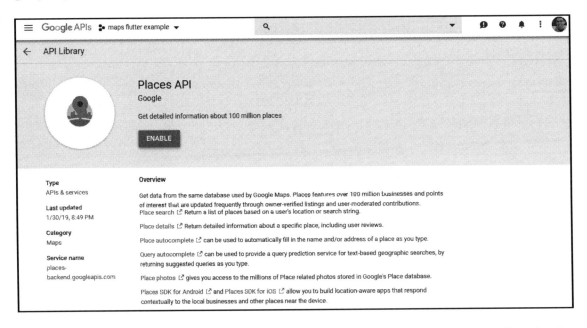

Check out that you are in the right project and click the **ENABLE** button. This will make the Places API available through the same API key used before.

# Getting started with the google_maps_webservice plugin

The `google_maps_webservice` plugin is a Dart community plugin that offers a client the Google Places API. With this plugin, we can make calls to the Google web service without the need to create the requests by ourselves.

The plugin exposes the calls as methods of its `GoogleMapsPlaces` class. This class offers methods such as `getDetailsByPlaceId`, for example, which calls the `details` endpoint of the web service and wraps the response in a `PlacesDetailsResponse` class.

> Check the plugin page to learn about all of the available methods of the web service: `https://pub.dartlang.org/packages/google_maps_webservice`.

# Getting a place address using the google_maps_webservice plugin

First of all, we need to add the plugin as a dependency in our project's `pubspec.yaml` file and get it with the `flutter packages get` command:

```
dependencies:
  google_maps_webservice: ^0.0.12
```

After that, we can start using the plugin. The first thing we need to do is create a `GoogleMapsPlaces` class instance so that we have access to the provided methods:

```
@override
void initState() {
  super.initState();

  _googleMapsPlaces = GoogleMapsPlaces(
    apiKey: 'API_KEY',
  );
}
```

We do this in the `initState` method so that we can use it right after the map is displayed to the user. `_googleMapsPlaces` is a `field` inside the state of the `MapPage` widget.

Then, we define a method that will query a place name based on a `latitude/longitude` pair:

```
Future<PlacesSearchResponse> _queryLatLngNearbyPlaces(LatLng position)
async {
    return await _googleMapsPlaces.searchNearbyWithRadius(
      Location(position.latitude, position.longitude),
      1000,
    );
}
```

The method uses the `searchNearbyWithRadious` method of
the `GoogleMapsPlaces` class that queries on the Google web service for places near the
location, ranked by their prominence/importance, that is, the closest places come first.

To use the created method, we change our `_addMarkerOnCameraCenter` function to query
the place's address before adding it to the map:

```
void _addMarkerOnCameraCenter() async {
    final places = await _queryLatLngNearbyPlaces(_cameraCenter);
    final firstMatchName =
        places.results.length > 0 ? places.results.first.name : "";

    setState(() {
      _markers.add(Marker(
        markerId: MarkerId("${_markers.length + 1}"),
        infoWindow: InfoWindow(
          title: "Added marker - $firstMatchName"
        ),
        icon: BitmapDescriptor.defaultMarker,
        position: _cameraCenter,
      ));
    });
}
```

As you can see, there are few modifications from the previous version. Here are the
modifications:

- The method is now `async`, as the plugin returns a `Future` result and we want to
  `await` it
- We get the first match of the query (only its address), if any
- We add the name information in the `InfoWindow` title property

And, after we add a marker to the map, it now contains the name of the location:

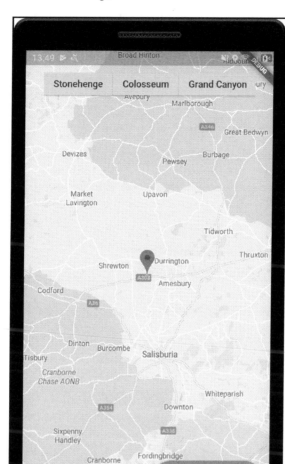

There are many more ways to integrate the Google Places API into an application: this was just a simple one. With this, we finish map integration on Flutter apps. Keep following the plugin updates as this feature is still evolving with the framework.

# Summary

In this chapter, we have seen the basics of using maps in Flutter with the great google_maps_flutter plugin. We have seen that it relies on the platform view feature that comes to enable us to display native views inside the Flutter context. We have seen how we can create these views by ourselves using the framework structure.

We have seen the available properties of the GoogleMap widget and how to manipulate it to display markers on it and move the camera using the GoogleMapController class.

Finally, we used the Google Places API to get information about a location and display it on the marker using an InfoWindow class.

In the next chapter, we will take a look at Flutter's available tools for advanced app development.

# Section 4: Advanced Flutter - Resources to Complex Apps

**4**

Complex and unique apps involve features that the developer needs to understand how to achieve, such as writing platform-native code and customizing framework resources according to their needs.

The following chapters are included in this section:

- Chapter 12, *Testing, Debugging, and Deployment*
- Chapter 13, *Improving User Experience*
- Chapter 14, *Widget Graphic Manipulations*
- Chapter 15, *Animations*

# 12
# Testing, Debugging, and Deployment

Flutter provides great tools to help the developer to reach his/her objectives on the platform, from test API to IDE tools and plugins. In this chapter, you will learn how to add tests to create a bug-free app, debug to find and solve specific issues, profile your app performance to find bottlenecks, and inspect the UI widgets. Also, you will learn how to prepare the app for deployment on App Store and Google Play.

The following topics will be covered in this chapter:

- Testing Flutter widgets
- Debugging Flutter apps
- Performance profiling of Flutter apps
- Inspecting the Flutter widget tree
- Preparing app for deployment

## Flutter testing – unit and widget testing

Testing mobile apps manually is fundamental as long as we need to add features to an app continuously. There are multiple ways to test a Flutter app, each one with some level of benefit involved and they do not differ too much from testing other software applications.

The well-known unit and integration tests are possible with Flutter. Additionally, we can write widget tests to test widgets in isolation. Let's see how we can write widget and integration tests to make sure our applications are working right.

 You can review Chapter 2, *Intermediate Dart Programming*, *Writing unit tests* section, as Flutter unit tests are nothing more than Dart unit tests.

# Widget tests

Widget tests are used to validate widgets in an isolated way. They look very similar to unit tests but focus on widgets.

The main goal is to check widget interactions and whether widgets look as expected. As widgets live in the widget tree inside the Flutter context, widget tests require the framework environment to be executed. That is why Flutter provides tools for writing widget tests through the `flutter_test` package.

# The flutter_test package

The `flutter_test` package is shipped with the Flutter SDK, is built on top of the test package, and provides a set of tools for helping us to write and run widget tests.

As said before, widget tests need to be executed in the widget environment and Flutter helps with this task with the `WidgetTester` class. This class encapsulates the logic for us to build and interact with the widget being tested and the Flutter environment.

We do not need to instantiate this class by ourselves as the framework provides the `testWidgets()` function. The `testWidgets()` function is similar to the Dart `test()` function seen before in *Chapter 2*, *Intermediate Dart Programming*, *Writing unit tests* section. The difference is the Flutter context, this function sets up a `WidgetTester` instance to interact with the environment, as mentioned earlier.

### The testWidgets function

This function is the entry point of any widget test in Flutter:

```
void testWidgets(String description, WidgetTesterCallback callback, { bool
skip: false, Timeout timeout })
```

We will be checking it in action using a few steps. First, let's check its signature:

- `description`: This helps to document the test; that is, it describes what widget features are being tested.
- `callback`: This is `WidgetTesterCallback`. This callback receives a `WidgetTester` instance so that we can interact with the widget and make our validations. This is the *body* of the test, where we write our test logic.
- `skip`: We can skip the test when running multiple tests by setting this flag.
- `timeout`: This is the maximum time the test callback can run.

# Widget test example

When we generate a Flutter project, we have the `flutter_test` package dependency added for us automatically and a sample test is generated in the test/directory. Let's check it out.

First, in `pubspec.yaml`, there is the `flutter_test` package dependency added:

```
dev_dependencies:
  flutter_test:
    sdk: flutter
```

 Note that the package version is not specified. Also, the origin is configured as the Flutter SDK.

Then, we can check the basic widget test in the `test/widget_test.dart` file:

```
void main() {
  testWidgets('Counter increments smoke test', (WidgetTester tester) async
{
    await tester.pumpWidget(MyApp());
    expect(find.text('0'), findsOneWidget);
    expect(find.text('1'), findsNothing);

    await tester.tap(find.byIcon(Icons.add));
    await tester.pump();

    expect(find.text('0'), findsNothing);
    expect(find.text('1'), findsOneWidget);
  });
}
```

This sample widget test validates the behavior of the famous Flutter counter app. The test goes as follows:

- The test is defined with a description and the previously seen `WidgetTesterCallback` property. Also, note the callback has the `async` modifier, like the `WidgetTester` methods as it returns a `Future` type.
- It all begins with a widget; `await tester.pumpWidget(MyApp());` renders the UI from the given widget— `MyApp`, in this case.
- If we need to rebuild the widget at some point, we can use the `tester.pump()` method.

- In widget tests, two additional pieces are important and very common, `find` and `expect()`:
  - The `Finder` class is what allows us to search specific widgets in the tree. The `find` constant provides tools (`Finders`) for us to search and look upon the widget tree for specific widgets.

Check all available `Finders` provided by `find`: `https://api.flutter.dev/flutter/flutter_driver/CommonFinders-class.html`.

  - The `expect()` method is used in conjunction with `Matchers` to make assertions on widgets found with the help of `Finders`. `Matcher` helps to validate the found widget characteristic with an expected value.

Let's analyze the previous widget test assertions:

1. At the beginning, there is an assertion for the presence of a single widget with the 0 text and none with 1:

```
expect(find.text('0'), findsOneWidget);
expect(find.text('1'), findsNothing);
```

2. Then, `tap()` is executed, followed by a `pump()` request. The tap occurs on a widget that contains the `Icons.add` icon:

```
await tester.tap(find.byIcon(Icons.add));
await tester.pump()
```

3. The final step is to verify the correct text is shown again. But this time, the `findsOneWidget` constant is used to verify that only the text, 1, is visible:

```
expect(find.text('0'), findsNothing);
expect(find.text('1'), findsOneWidget);
```

Like the `find` constant, multiple `Matchers` are available; `findsNothing` and `findsOneWidget` are only some of them.

 Check all available `Matchers` in the `flutter_test` library documentation: `https://api.flutter.dev/flutter/flutter_test/` `flutter_test-library.html`.

# Debugging Flutter apps

Debugging is an important piece of software development. Small mistakes, strange behaviors, and complex bugs can be solved with the help of debugging. With this, we can do the following:

- Make logic assertions
- Determine needed improvements
- Find memory leaks
- Make flow analysis

Flutter, as well, provides multiple tools to help with this task. As we have seen previously in `Chapter 1`, *An Introduction to Dart*, Dart contains a set of tools to help with the developer's job.

We are not evaluating a specific IDE for Flutter development and you may guess that debugging is not possible without it. However, the Dart tooling is also prepared for this.

## Observatory

Flutter debugging is based on the **Dart Observatory** tool. Dart Observatory is present in the Dart SDK and helps with profiling and debugging Dart applications such as Flutter apps.

When a Flutter app is started in debug mode (remember the JIT compilation from `Chapter 1`, *An Introduction to Dart*), this tool is automatically run, enabling debugging and profiling on the app. By using the `flutter run` command, you will have the `address:port` part of the output after the `Hot Reload` message. This address is the **Observatory UI** address; we can access it through many web browsers* and this is what it looks like:

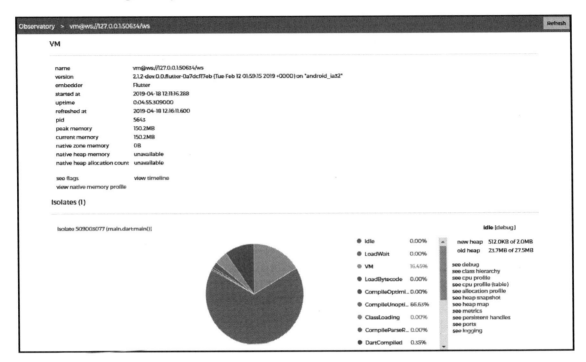

There are some web browser with limitations on displaying the Observatory tool. Please check out the existing issue regarding this: `https://github.com/dart-lang/sdk/issues/34107`.

It prints different information about the app running, such as the Flutter version, used memory, class hierarchy, and logs. Also, an important additional tool can be used, the debug tool:

In this page, as you can see, we have access to all of the debugging functionalities, such as the following:

- Adding and removing breakpoints
- Run step by step, line by line
- Switch and manage isolates

Check all available Observatory UI functionalities and a full usage tutorial at https://dart-lang.github.io/observatory/get-started.html.

When you use some IDE like Visual Studio Code or Android Studio/IntelliJ, you will not be using tools such as the Observatory UI directly. IDEs use Dart Observatory under the hood to expose its functionalities through the IDE interface.

# Additional debugging features

Dart provides additional features to help with advanced debugging with variants of the common tools that can make the debugging process even more useful. These are as follows:

- The `debugger()` statement: Also called programmatic breakpoints, this is where we can add a breakpoint only if an expected condition is true:

```
void login(String username, String password) {
  debugger(when: password == null);
  ...
}
```

In this example, a breakpoint will occur only if the condition in the `when` the parameter is `true`, that is, only if the password argument is `null`. Let's say this is an unexpected value: pausing the execution at this point may help to see why it occurs and how to react to it. This is very useful for tracing unexpected states and logic fails.

- `debugPrint()` and `print()`: `print()` is a method to log information into the flutter log console. When we use the `flutter run` command, its log output is redirected to the console and we can see anything that comes from `print()` and `debugPrint()` calls. The only difference between these calls is that the `debugPrint()` version avoids log dropping by Android kernel (Flutter logs are only a wrapper to `adb logcat`).

> You can read more about Flutter logs at `https://flutter.dev/docs/testing/debugging#print-and-debugprint-with-flutter-logs`.

- `asserts`: `assert()` is used to break app execution when some condition is not satisfied. It is similar to the `debugger()` method, but instead of pausing execution, it interrupts the execution by throwing `AssertionError`.

# DevTools

Dart DevTools is defined in the documentation as follows:

*"A suite of performance tools for Dart and Flutter."*

This is intended to be the next version of the Observatory tools. IDEs are already integrating this suite in their internals, and it is similar to Observatory, as you can see:

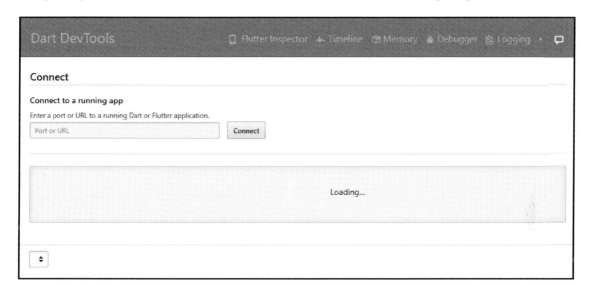

As you can see, it has some tools that can help with performance analysis of Flutter applications, just like Observatory. You can enable/install it by running the following command in a terminal:

```
pub global activate devtools
```

Or, you can run the following:

```
flutter packages pub global activate devtools
```

After that, we can run the tool with this command:

```
pub global run devtools
```

Or, we can use the following:

```
flutter packages pub global run devtools
```

Access the displayed page in a web browser, and you will have something similar to the following screenshot:

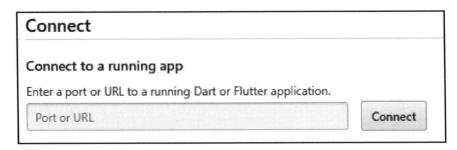

As you can see, we need to provide the port of the running app (the Observatory port, like before) for the DevTool to be able to inspect the application measurements.

Check the DevTools documentation page for details on installation steps for different operating systems and IDEs: `https://flutter.github.io/devtools/`.

Also note that, at the time of writing this book, the DevTools suite is still in release preview and may change by the time you read this.

# Profiling Flutter apps

Flutter aims to provide high-performance apps with high frame rate and smoothness. Like debugging that can help to find bugs and more, profiling is another useful tool that may help developers to find bottlenecks in an application, prevent memory leaks, or improve app performance.

The Observatory tool is, again, the bridge that allows us to inspect Flutter app performance. Like the debugger, this section of the tool is also wrapped into IDEs when we use them.

# The Observatory profiler

As previously seen, Observatory exposes multiple tools to the developer to measure app performance and prevent any possible problems related to it. This is done with the exposition of multiple metrics, as you can see:

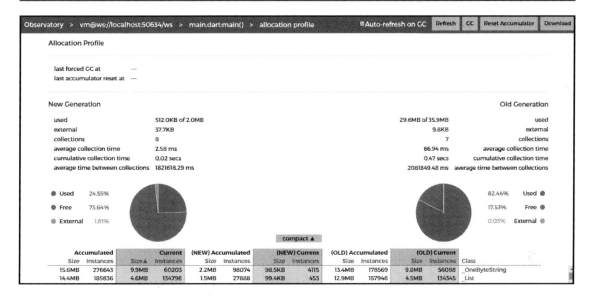

Memory, CPU usage, and other information are available through the monitor so that we can evaluate different aspects of the application.

# Profile mode

When we execute our Flutter application in default *debug* mode with the `flutter run` command, we cannot expect the same performance as the *release* mode. As we already know, Flutter executes in debug mode using the JIT Dart compiler as the app runs, unlike the release and profile modes, where the app code is pre-compiled using the AOT Dart compiler.

To make performance evaluations, we need to make sure the app is running at its maximum capability; that's why Flutter provides different execution methods: debug, profile, and release.

In profile mode, the application is compiled in a very similar way to release mode, and this is clearly understandable, as we need to know how the app will perform in real scenarios. The only overhead added to the app is the required ones to make the profiling enabled (that is, the Observatory can connect to the application process).

Another important aspect of profiling is the necessity of a physical device. Simulators and emulators do not reflect the real performance of real devices. As the hardware is different, app metrics can be influenced and the analysis might be correct.

To run an app in profile mode, we should add the `--profile` flag to the run command (remember, it's only available on real devices):

```
flutter run --profile
```

Running in this mode, we have all of the needed information to inspect the app performance in general. Another useful tool the profile mode enables is the **performance overlay**.

 IDEs also offer profile mode through their particular interfaces, so when you see this mode in the chosen IDE, you know what it means.

## Performance overlay

The performance overlay is visual feedback displayed in the app. It provides multiple helpful performance statics. Specifically, it displays information about rendering time. Here is an example of performance overlay being displayed:

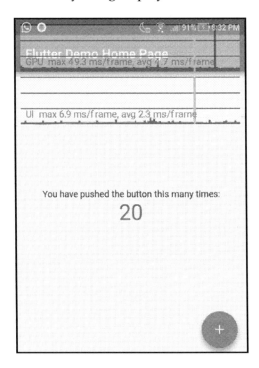

Performance overlay (This is an image of Performance overlay. The other (overlapped) information is not important here.)

Two graphs are displayed representing the time to render frames taken by the two threads, UI and GPU. The current frame is displayed in a vertical green bar. Additionally, we can see the last 300 frames and have an idea about critical rendering stages.

Flutter uses multiple threads to do its job. UI and GPU contain the display work of the framework, and that's why both are shown in the performance overlay. The UI thread is where our Dart code is executed and logic and widget description building occur and where the framework creates a layer tree for the GPU thread to work, where the graphics are brought to life, and where the Skia graphics library runs.

Additionally, to those threads, Flutter also contains the `Platform` thread, where the plugin code runs, and the I/O thread, where expensive I/O tasks are run. Both threads do not appear on the platform overlay.

 You can check some of the possible improvements that performance overlay can help with at `https://flutter.dev/docs/testing/ui-performance#the-performance-overlay`.

# Inspecting the Flutter widget tree

With debugging and profiling, we can discover and resolve many issues and performance problems before they occur in production. Added to that, we can measure an app's cost of execution progressively during development.

Both tools do the job of offering metrics to us and, with that, we can inspect pieces of code carefully, but how about the layout? We can, for sure, measure performance frame by frame based on time of rendering our widget tree, as we have seen before with the help of performance overlay. But how about checking whether our tree is taking more space than needed—that is, has more widgets than needed—or whether a widget is being created at the right time/level.

The Flutter inspector can help with this task. Again, with the great DevTools, we can access this functionality.

# Widget inspector

The widget inspector is another of the great suite of tools that may help the developer with optimization tasks. This tool provides a detailed visualization of the widget tree.

## The Flutter inspector in DevTools

On supported IDEs, the plugin already offers ways to access the widget inspector, using the Flutter widget inspector tool under the hood. It is also accessible in the DevTools suite:

As you can see, the widget tree is presented and we can access all details about widgets. For web developers, this will look very similar to element explorer in web developer tools, like the one in Chrome, for instance.

Like profiler and debugger tools, exploring the widget tree in details can be extremely helpful to find out layout issues that would be difficult without visualization of the tree.

Also, looking at the previous screenshot, we had a small hint to turn on *tracking widget creation*. When we skip this flag, the tool will show a deeper tree than we might expect; this why it exposes intermediate widgets besides the ones that we define in our application. When we enable it, the tree will look much simpler:

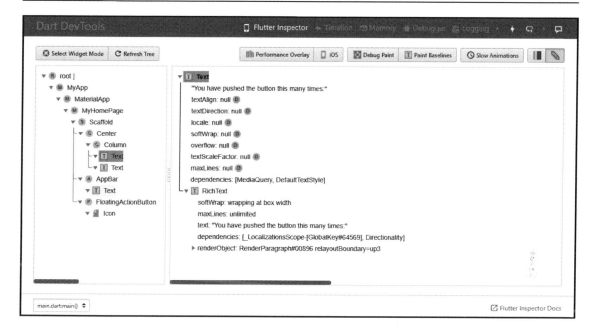

With this, we have a tree that looks much more like the one defined in our code, making it easier to track issues. Also, we have widget property details that also assist in finding small layout problems.

# Preparing apps for deployment

Flutter aims to offer the best possible resources for the developer to work, and so, things such as different builds for development, profiling, and releasing makes sense.

When preparing an app for release, things such as on-the-fly compiling provided by Dart JIT does not make sense; instead, the best thing is to have a smaller, optimized, and performant app provided by the Dart AOT compiler.

Releasing an app on Google Play Store and App Store requires valid publisher accounts. So, refer to the documentation of both platforms to know how to publish to stores after creating a release version of your app.

Google has a one-time $25 registration fee, which you need to pay before you can upload an app. You can sign in at `https://play.google.com/apps/publish/signup/`.

App Store has a $99 membership fee per year. You can find details and sign in at `https://developer.apple.com/support/compare-memberships/`.

# Release mode

In release mode, debugging information is stripped out from the app and the compilation is realized with performance in mind. Remember, in release mode, like the profile, the application can only be run on physical devices, for the same reasons too.

To compile in release mode, we just need to add the `--release` flag to the `flutter run` command and have a physical device connected, and that's all. Although we can do so, we typically do not use the `flutter run` command with the `--release` flag. Instead, we use this flag with the `flutter build` command to have a built app file in the target Android/iOS formats for distribution.

# Releasing apps for Android

In Android, `.apk` is the format expected to be published in the Google Play Store. When we run the `flutter build apk` or `flutter build appbundle` commands, we generate the file ready for deployment.

The Android app bundle format is also supported partially at the time of writing this book.

Before we generate the file for deployment and publishing in any store, we need to make sure all of the information is correct (that is, the name and package), all needed assets are provided and make all platform-specific adjustments.

Let's start by preparing our Favors app for release on Google Play so that we can review all of the final steps to publishing a Flutter app.

# AndroidManifest and build.gradle

In Android, the meta information about the app is provided in both the `AndroidManifest.xml` and `build.gradle` files, so we need to review and make some adjustments in both.

Also, remember to configure the project properly in the Firebase console and add the `google-services.json` file to the project (you can use the same generated for `Chapter 8`, *Firebase Plugins*).

## AndroidManifest – permissions

One important step we need to do is to review the permissions requested in the `AndroidManifest.xml` file. Asking only for the permissions needed is a good and recommended practice, as your app may be analyzed and your publication may be revoked if you request more than truly required permissions.

In our Favors app, this is what the manifest permissions look like:

```
<manifest xmlns:android="http://schemas.android.com/apk/res/android"
    package="com.example.handson">

    <uses-permission android:name="android.permission.INTERNET"/>
    <uses-permission android:name="android.permission.READ_CONTACTS" />
    <uses-permission android:name="android.permission.WRITE_CONTACTS"/>
    <uses-permission android:name="android.permission.CAMERA" />
    <uses-feature
        android:name="android.hardware.camera"
        android:required="false" />
    ...
</manifest>
```

Besides permissions, there is also the `uses-feature` tag (see `Chapter 10`, *Accessing Device Features from the Flutter App*), which can limit installation on devices with a specific feature available (this is not our case), so it's important to review it too.

The `android.permission.INTERNET` permission is used by the Flutter framework with the Observatory tool, so, if your application works offline, you can remove this during release builds (this is not our case, as we use Firebase technologies).

## AndroidManifest – meta tags

Another very important step is to review the meta tags added to the app for working with services such as AdMob or Google Maps. In our Favors app, AdMob was the only key added, so we can review the value to make sure the service will work with the correct key as well:

```
<manifest xmlns:android="http://schemas.android.com/apk/res/android"
    package="com.example.handson">
    ...
    <application>
```

```
        ...
    <meta-data
        android:name="com.google.android.gms.ads.APPLICATION_ID"
        android:value="ADMOB-KEY"/>
    </application>
</manifest>
```

Remember, in AdMob, we can use test keys during development so that our tests are not evaluated as misuse of the API.

## AndroidManifest – application name and icon

Until now, in our tests, when we launch the application, you can see the app icon is a Flutter logo. For release, we need to swap it with our awesome unique icon to make sure our users distinguish our app among millions.

The icon and name are defined in the manifest `application` tag. By default, the icon refers to the default Flutter icon, as you can see:

```
<manifest ...>
    ...
    <application
        android:name="io.flutter.app.FlutterApplication"
        android:label="Hands On: Favors app"
        android:icon="@mipmap/ic_launcher">
    ....
</manifest>
```

So, we make two changes in this tag:

- We change the `label` value to the final name of our app, the name by which our users will recognize our app.
- The `icon` value we can use to switch the app icon (replacing the default Flutter logo):
  - In Android, image resources such as the icon, are located in the `android/app/src/main/res/` directory. Under this directory, there are many folders with variants of a resource, for specific regions, screen sizes, system versions, and so on.

 The icon for the Favors app was generated in the Android Asset Studio tool. It helps us to follow Android guidelines and generate multiple icon variants: `https://romannurik.github.io/AndroidAssetStudio/index.html`.

- We need to replace the `ic_launcher.png` file in each of the `mipmap-xxxdpi` folders to make a full replacement of the app icon.

Check the Material Design guidelines on icons to make sure you create an awesome icon for your app: `https://material.io/design/iconography/`.

After changing the name and replacing the icon, we can review the `build.gradle` file to make the final adjustments for the deployment.

## build.gradle – application ID and versions

The application ID value is what makes an app unique in Play Store and the Android system. A good practice is to use the organization domain as the package and have the app name following it. In our case, we are using `com.example.handson` as the application ID. Make sure to review this value, as it cannot be changed after you upload the app to the store.

You can find this code in the `android/app/build.gradle` file, inside the `defaultConfig` section:

```
defaultConfig {
        applicationId "com.example.handson"
        minSdkVersion 16
        targetSdkVersion 28
        multiDexEnabled true
        versionCode flutterVersionCode.toInteger()
        versionName flutterVersionName
        testInstrumentationRunner "androidx.test.runner.AndroidJUnitRunner"
    }
```

As you can see, we can change more settings than just changing `applicationId`. In Flutter, SDK versions are typically changed in two cases:

- If the framework requirements change
- If we use some library that requires a higher minimum SDK version

We can, for sure, change it to our own required value if we want, but make sure to follow the framework requirements.

## build.gradle – signing the app

The signing step is the final but most important step before releasing an app to the public, even if you do not want to publish in the Google Play Store. It is the signing that confirms the ownership of the application—briefly, whoever has the signature owns the app. You need this so you can publish updates to your app, for example.

Start by taking a look at the buildTypes section of the build.gradle file:

```
buildTypes {
    release {
        signingConfig signingConfigs.debug
    }
}
```

It contains the signingConfig property, pointing to a default signing configuration. We need to change this to our own signing configuration for the reasons mentioned before. We do this by performing these steps:

1.  We generate our developer keystore file (you can use the same keystore for multiple apps). This is done with the following command:

    ```
    keytool -genkey -v -keystore DESTINATION_FILEPATH -keyalg RSA -
    keysize 2048 -validity 10000 -alias key
    ```

    Follow the prompts and this will generate keystore in the DESTINATION_FILEPATH path, for example, <your users dir/my-release-key.keystore>. You should reference this file in the build.gradle file now.

2.  Create an android/key.properties file with the following content:

    ```
    storePassword=<password used for generating key>
    keyPassword=<password used for generating key>
    keyAlias=key
    storeFile=key store file path(i.e. </your users dir/my-release-key.keystore>)
    ```

3.  Then, in build.gradle, we load this new key.properties file and create a new signingConfig class for it:

    ```
    def keystoreProperties = new Properties()
    def keystorePropertiesFile = rootProject.file('key.properties')
    if (keystorePropertiesFile.exists()) {
        keystoreProperties.load(new
    FileInputStream(keystorePropertiesFile))
    ```

```
    }

    android{
      ...

      signingConfigs {
        release {
            keyAlias keystoreProperties['keyAlias']
            keyPassword keystoreProperties['keyPassword']
            storeFile file(keystoreProperties['storeFile'])
            storePassword keystoreProperties['storePassword']
        }
      }
    }
```

4. Just add the snippet before the `android` section and then, declare the signing configuration in the `signingConfigs` subsection. Finally, replace the `signingConfig` property in the `release` option in the previous `buildTypes` section with the new one:

```
    android {
      ...
      buildTypes {
        release {
            signingConfig signingConfigs.release
        }
      }
    }
```

Now, when we use the `flutter build apk` or `flutter run --release` commands, the app will be signed with our own key.

After making these adjustments, we are ready to build and distribute our app. Just a final step: check the app `versionCode` and `versionName` values; they get filled automatically from the `pubspec.yaml` file. So, reviewing this file may be important too.

After building a `.apk` with the `flutter build apk` command, we can install it on a connected physical device with the `flutter install` command. Also, the file to be published in the Play Store is available: `build/app/outputs/apk/app.apk`.

 You can also work on minification and obfuscation of the code to improve the app size and protect against reverse engineering: `https://github.com/flutter/flutter/wiki/Obfuscating-Dart-Code`.

# Releasing apps for iOS

Releasing in iOS has some higher complexity when compared to Android. Although you can test on your own device when developing, making an app public requires you to have a valid Apple Developer account with the ability to publish on App Store, as it's the only supported app publishing channel.

Like Android, first, we need to review some information about the app in the Xcode project settings, like we did in `AndroidManifest.xml`. And after that, we will be able to create an app archive ready for publishing on the App Store.

Also, check the presence of the `GoogleService-Info.plist` file in the `ios/Runner` directory (see `Chapter 8`, *Firebase Plugins*, to remember how to import it inside Xcode).

# App Store Connect

In Android, we do not need to configure anything in the Play Store Console before we have the `apk` ready for publishing. After we have it, we can create a registry on the Play Console; fill the description, details, and marketing settings; then, we upload our `apk` file and publish.

 Remember, you need to be enrolled in a developer program to be able to publish on the App Store. (This also applies to register an app on App Store Connect). Also, check the official guide for more information: `https://help.apple.com/app-store-connect/#/dev2cd126805`.

In iOS, the process is different. The upload and publishing are managed inside Xcode, so to upload the app, we first create a record on the App Store Connect, fill descriptions, and then, on Xcode, we build and upload our iOS app. To register the app, perform these steps:

1. Every iOS application is associated with a Bundle ID, a unique identifier registered to Apple. First, we create a record in App IDs (`https://idmsa.apple.com/IDMSWebAuth/signin?appIdKey=891bd3417a7776362562d2197f89480a8547b108fd934911bcbea0110d07f757&path=%2Faccount%2Fresources%2F&rv=1`), filling the **Bundle ID**, which is the iOS equivalent to Android's `applicationId`.

2. Then, we create an app in the App Store Connect portal selecting the **Bundle ID** we registered in the previous step. (For our Favors app, it's almost the same value as Android's `applicationId`).

After realizing these steps in App Store Connect, we finish the process in Xcode.

# Xcode

In Xcode, we need to make few changes to make the app ready for deployment. We need to change the application icon, public name, and Bundle ID. This is very similar to what we did in Android.

## Xcode – application details and Bundle ID

In the **General** tab of the **Runner** project, we can edit the application **Display Name**, which is the name of our app. We similarly set the Android name `Hands On: Favors app` and set the Bundle ID to `com.biessek.handson.favorsapp`.

Note also the `Version` and `Build` values; they are similar to *version name* and *version code* in Android respectively. For each upload to App Store, be it Store or `TestFlight`, we need to increase the `version` value in the `pubspec.yaml` file.

In the **Deployment Target**, we can set the minimum required iOS version, 8.0 by default—the minimum version Flutter supports.

## Xcode – AdMob

Unlike the configuration in the `AndroidManifest.xml` file, we do not need to update our AdMob ID in iOS. In this case, the ID value is retrieved from the one passed to the `FirebaseAdMob` SDK initialization in Dart itself:

```
FirebaseAdMob.instance.initialize(
  appId: 'YOUR_ADMOB_APP_ID'
);
```

## Xcode – signing the app

Like on Android, we need a way to assert the ownership of the application. Xcode manages it for us; we do not need to touch any file directly. When we register as an Apple Developer and enroll in the Apple Developer Program, we have all of this ready.

After these settings, we can build an iOS version of the app as we did for Android, with the `flutter build ios` command. Then, we need one last step in Xcode to release our app:

1. In Xcode, select **Product** | **Archive** to produce a build archive.
2. Then, select the build archive you just produced with the `flutter build ios` command.

3. Click the **Validate…** button. If any issues are reported, address them and produce another build.

4. After the archive has been successfully validated, click **Upload to App Store…..**

After that, we have an iOS app ready for publishing. We can either publish it on TestFlight (a private test app with trusted users) or in the App Store.

 Read the official documentation to know which one to choose: https://help.apple.com/Xcode/mac/current/#/dev442d7f2ca.

# Summary

In this chapter, we saw an introduction to Flutter widget tests. We saw how they can be used to test widgets individually and how they are structured with the WidgetTester class in the testWidgets function.

We also saw how we can use Flutter tools to explore application performance in details and the available tools to inspect memory and CPU usage such as the Observatory UI and performance overlay. Then, we saw the evolution of tools with the brand new DevTools suite.

Finally, we explored the steps to make our app ready for deployment by checking information and details, changing the app icon visible to the user, and performing platform-specific steps to build an app ready for publishing.

In the next chapter, we will review some important subjects related to native code with platform channels and check how to make your app ready for internationalization.

# 13

# Improving User Experience

If you want your application to reach a high level, you need to keep it open to continuous interaction with user context even though it is not currently running. In addition, developing an internationalized and fully accessible app allows it to grow progressively. In this chapter, you'll learn how to create processes executed in the background, translate your app into the target language, and add accessibility features that improve the usability of the app.

The following topics will be covered in this chapter:

- Accessibility in Flutter
- Adding translations to apps
- Communication between native and Flutter with platform channels
- Creating background processes
- Adding Android-specific code to run Dart code in the background
- Adding iOS-specific code to run Dart code in the background

## Accessibility in Flutter and adding translations to apps

Adding internationalization to a mobile application contributes to growth in the market, reaching a larger public. In the same way, making an app accessible is an important step to reach as many people as possible and with a better experience. Flutter provides ways to make apps more accessible with components focused on users with some form of disability.

# Flutter's support for accessibility

Implementing accessibility correctly in mobile apps enhances the user experience and helps to increase the number of installs and decrease the number of uninstalls. Flutter has components to provide accessibility support:

- **Contrast**: Flutter exposes tools so the developer can colorize widgets appropriately with sufficient contrast.

 Check the W3C recommended contrast specifications: `https://www.w3.org/TR/UNDERSTANDING-WCAG20/visual-audio-contrast-contrast.html`.

- **Large fonts**: In Flutter, text widgets respect this OS setting when determining font sizes. They are scaled up if the user desires it.

 In Android and iOS, we can enable large fonts through accessibility settings in the OS configurations.

- **Screen readers**: **TalkBack** in Android and **VoiceOver** in iOS enable visually impaired users to get spoken feedback about the contents of the screen.

 Flutter provides the `Semantics` widget for the developer to allow the description of the meaning of the widgets so that screen readers can work properly. Check out the widget documentation: `https://api.flutter.dev/flutter/widgets/Semantics-class.html`.

# Flutter internationalization

Flutter provides widgets and classes that help with internationalization and the Flutter libraries themselves are internationalized. This is done with the help of three packages, `intl`, `intl_translation`, and `flutter_localizations`. Let's check out these packages and examine how they help with the internationalization task.

# The intl package

The Dart `intl` package is the basis of translations in Dart, as stated on its page on `pub`:

> *"This package provides internationalization and localization facilities, including message translation, plurals and genders, date/number formatting and parsing, and bidirectional text."*

With this package, we have mechanisms to load translations from `.arb` files. This format is also supported by the **Google Translators Toolkit**. Each `.arb` file contains a single JSON table that maps from resource IDs to localized values.

# The intl_translation package

The `intl_translation` package is based on `intl`. It is needed only in the development phase and contains a tool to generate and parse translations from/to `.arb` files. With this package, we can translate our messages in the `.arb` format and then import them into Dart for using with the `intl` package.

# The flutter_localizations package

The `flutter_localizations` package provides a set of 52 languages (at the time of writing this book) to be used with Flutter widgets. By default, Flutter widgets are only provided with English US localizations, so, to support other languages, the `flutter_localizations` package can be used.

# Adding localizations to a Flutter app

Localization in Flutter is, like any other thing, a widget. We're going to use `flutter_localizations` package to set up translations of a simple app that displays a single message, **Hello Flutter**. We are going to support English, Spanish, and Italian.

# Dependencies

The first step is to add localization dependencies to the `pubspec.yaml` file and fetch them with the `flutter packages get` command:

```
dependencies:
  ...
  flutter_localizations:
    sdk: flutter
dev_dependencies:
  intl_translation: ^0.17.3
...
```

As mentioned before, the first one is the additional Flutter localization package to use its built-in widgets, and the second gives us the tools to generate Dart code with the messages from `.arb` files.

# The AppLocalization class

The next step is to create a class that encapsulates the app's localized values. The `AppLocalizations` class, for example, that would be very similar in all apps, except the string resources involved. This is what it looks like:

```dart
// part of app_localization.dart
import 'l10n/messages_all.dart';

class AppLocalizations {
  static Future<AppLocalizations> load(Locale locale) {
    final String name =
        locale.countryCode == null ? locale.languageCode :
locale.toString();
    final String localeName = Intl.canonicalizedLocale(name);

    return initializeMessages(localeName).then((bool _) {
      Intl.defaultLocale = localeName;
      return new AppLocalizations();
    });
  }

  static AppLocalizations of(BuildContext context) {
    return Localizations.of<AppLocalizations>(context, AppLocalizations);
  }

  String get title {
    return Intl.message(
        'Hello Flutter',
```

```
        name: 'title',
        desc: 'The application title'
    );
  }

  String get hello {
    return Intl.message('Hello', name: 'hello');
  }
}
```

`AppLocalizations` is used to encapsulates the resources. It can be broken down into four main pieces:

- The `load` function: This will load the string resources from the desired `Locale`, as you can see in the parameter.
- The `of` function: This will be a helper like for any other `InheritedWidget` to facilitate access to any string from any part of the app code.
- `get` functions: These will list the available resources translated into our app. Note the `Intl.message` wrapper in the return; that will make the `intl` tool look up this class and populate the `initializeMessages` for us with the translations.
- `initializeMessages`: This method will be generated by the `intl` tool. Note the `import "l10n/messages_all.dart"` file that will be generated in the next steps contains the method that effectively loads the translated messages.

In addition to this class, we need to create another class responsible for providing the `AppLocalizations` resources to the app. This is what it looks like:

```
class AppLocalizationsDelegate extends
LocalizationsDelegate<AppLocalizations> {
  const AppLocalizationsDelegate();

  @override
  bool isSupported(Locale locale) {
    return ['en', 'es', 'it'].contains(locale.languageCode);
  }

  @override
  Future<AppLocalizations> load(Locale locale) {
    return AppLocalizations.load(locale);
  }

  @override
  bool shouldReload(LocalizationsDelegate<AppLocalizations> old) {
    return false;
```

```
            }
        }
```

It also can be broken down into three main pieces:

- The `load` function: Here is the information from the documentation:

    *"The load method must return an object that contains a collection of related resources (typically defined with one method per resource)."*

    We return our `AppLocalizations.load` class.

- `isSupported`: As the name suggests, it returns `true` if the app has support for `receivedlocale`.
- `shouldReload`: Basically, if this method returns `true`, then all of the app widgets will be rebuilt after the loading of resources. You will typically want to return `true` if your app changes `Locale` dynamically.

## Generating .arb files with intl_translation

After defining these classes, we need to create our message translations. As you can see in the `AppLocalizations` class, there are only two string resources to be translated, title and hello. As said before, the translation process is done with `.arb` files. So, we must define `.arb` files for each of the supported languages (English, Spanish, and Italian, in our case), and those files must contain the string resources translated into the target language.

Creating each of these files can be tedious so we can use the `intl_translation` tool, to generate those files. First, we create a directory to store the new files—`lib/l10n`, in this example. Then, we generate the `.arb` files with the following command:

```
flutter pub pub run intl_translation:extract_to_arb --output-dir=lib/l10n
lib/app_localization.dart
```

 The last parameter refers to the file containing the app localization class—`lib/app_localization.dart`, in our case.

This command will generate a file called the `intl_messages.arb` file in `lib/i10n`, and this file serves as a template for our translations:

```
{
  "@@last_modified": "2019-04-22T21:32:20.153408",
  "title": "Hello world App",
  "@title": {
    "description": "The application title",
    "type": "text",
    "placeholders": {}
  },
  "hello": "Hello",
  "@hello": {
    "type": "text",
    "placeholders": {}
  }
}
```

We can create the desired translations based on this file by copying it, renaming it `intl_<language_code>` files, and translating the required resources:

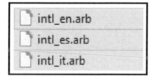

 Check out the GitHub for the source code of all of the files and a full example.

After that, with everything translated, we need to make it ready for use in our application. The process is the inverse of generating `.arb` files:

```
flutter pub pub run intl_translation:generate_from_arb --output-
dir=lib/l10n lib/app_localization.dart lib/l10n/intl_en.arb
lib/l10n/intl_es.arb lib/l10n/intl_it.arb
```

Now we have the generated Dart code containing the translated resources. We will not touch this code directly when we need to add resources; we make it into the `app_localization.dart` and `.arb` files.

Remember, the `AppLocalization` class uses `initializeMessages` from
the `messages_all.dart` file. Now, it's ready to provide localized resources to the app.

## Using translated resources

With all files generated and all resources translated and ready for use, we now need to
properly use them in the application. To do this, we need to set a few properties of the
`MaterialApp` class. This is what our app class looks like:

```
class MyApp extends StatelessWidget {
  // This widget is the root of your application.
  @override
  Widget build(BuildContext context) {
    return new MaterialApp(
      localizationsDelegates: [
        AppLocalizationsDelegate(),
        GlobalMaterialLocalizations.delegate,
        GlobalWidgetsLocalizations.delegate
      ],
      supportedLocales: [Locale("en"), Locale("es"), Locale("it")],
      onGenerateTitle: (BuildContext context) =>
          AppLocalizations.of(context).title,
      theme: new ThemeData(
        primarySwatch: Colors.blue,
      ),
      home: new MyHomePage(),
    );
  }
}
```

We need to set the `localizationsDelegates` and `supportedLocales` properties. You
repeat `supportedLocales` of your delegates and set the `localizationDelegates` array
with `AppLocalizationsDelegate`, plus `GlobalDelegates` from
the `flutter_localizations` package.

From the documentation, note the following:

> *"The elements of the localizationsDelegates list are factories that produce collections of
> localized values. GlobalMaterialLocalizations.delegate provides localized strings and other
> values for the Material Components library. GlobalWidgetsLocalizations.delegate defines
> the default text direction, either left to right or right to left, for the widgets library."*

So, both `GlobalWidgetsLocalizations` and `GlobalMaterialLocalizations` are
likely mandatory if we want to make our app completely localized.

This step loads our resources into our app. Now, to effectively use them, we make use of the `of` method in our `AppLocalizations` class:

```
class MyHomePage extends StatelessWidget {
  MyHomePage({Key key}) : super(key: key);
  @override
  Widget build(BuildContext context) {
    return Scaffold(
      appBar: AppBar(
        title: Text(AppLocalizations.of(context).title),
      ),
      body: Center(
        child: Text(
          AppLocalizations.of(context).hello,
          style: Theme.of(context).textTheme.display1,
        ),
      ),
    );
  }
}
```

With this method, we have access to our instance and all of the `get`s of resources we defined before. That's all to make the app localized, as you can see we get different messages for different device locales:

Now that we have finished with Flutter internationalization, let's move onto communication between native code and Flutter.

# Communication between native and Flutter with platform channels

Flutter has been gaining more and more adopters since 2018 with the release of its first stable version. One of the strongest reasons for this adoption is the facilities provided to develop a beautiful, dynamic, and smooth UI. However, that's not all a mobile application may need; it also has a function to perform and we need to deal with the different host platform's APIs, as many features depend on it, such as the following:

- Bluetooth, camera, sensors, and location
- User permissions
- Notifications
- Storing files and preferences
- Sharing information with other apps

The interchange between the Flutter world and platform needs to be as imperceptible as possible so that the developer does not feel discouraged in using the framework.

Until now, we have used some plugins to implement features that depend on an underlying platform implementation to execute. Plugins and even the application itself may need to communicate somehow with the platform code for all of this to work. All of this is managed by the Flutter engine, so to communicate our Flutter apps code with native Swift/Objective-C and Kotlin/Java code, we will be dealing with **platform channels.**

In Chapter 9, *Developing Your Own Flutter Plugin,* when we saw how to develop our own Flutter plugin, we had an introduction to **method channels**. Method channels are, by definition, a specialization of a Flutter platform channel. So, let's see in detail how all of this works and review method channels as a basis for the few next sections.

# Platform channel

Flutter apps are hosted in a typical native app, that is, when you run a Flutter app, there is a native iOS or Android app running with UI delegations to Flutter. As you already know, Flutter renders all of the UI by itself, and for this to work, the Flutter native layer has all of the code needed to set up an Android `View` or iOS `UIViewController` in which the framework can work.

Some mobile frameworks rely on code generation to make a conversion from some generic top-level language into the native ones, where you almost always write code only in the framework-specific language that later gets converted into native (Kotlin/Java and Swift/Objective-C). This makes it hard for the framework to keep its API as up-to-date as the hosts' platforms, and as Flutter intends to be present in many platforms, it would be even harder for it to accomplish this and evolve at the same time.

To supply this need, Flutter relies on a flexible message passing style, called a platform channel. Let's review its structure:

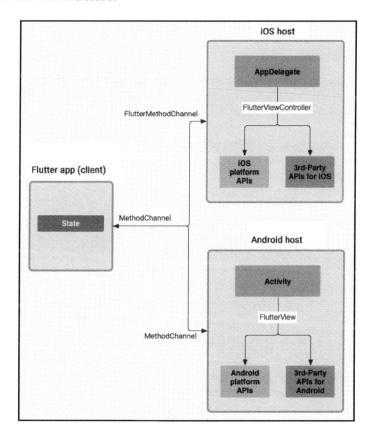

This is the Flutter platform channel architecture view. Official website: `https://flutter.dev/docs/development/platform-integration/platform-channels`.

As illustrated in this diagram, `MethodChannels` are used to send/receive messages. The diagram demonstrates how the platform channels work in general:

- The Flutter app sends messages to the host/native (iOS or Android) portion of the app over a platform channel.
- The host/native portion of the app listens on the platform channel, receives a message, and processes it through its own implementation, using the system-provided APIs and, finally, sends back a result to the calling Flutter portion of the app.

Like plugins, `PlatformViews`, seen previously in `Chapter 11`, *Platform Views and Map Integration*, also relies on the platform channel mechanism to exchange data.

# Message codecs

As we have seen so far, the `MethodChannel` is the main example and most commonly used platform channel because it abstracts many of the complexities of translating data from Dart into native programming languages and vice versa.

There are also other ways of communicating between native and Flutter, such as `BasicMessageChannel`. Check out the official tutorial on platform channels for more details: `https://flutter.dev/docs/development/platform-integration/platform-channels`.

This is made possible with the usage of Flutter standard **message codecs**. Message codecs are responsible for the task of translating data from one language into another. There is a variety of message codes available and we can, if necessary, create our own. They are as follows:

- `BinaryCodec`: These are unencoded binary messages represented using `ByteData`. On Android, messages will be represented using `java.nio.ByteBuffer`. On iOS, messages will be represented using `NSData`.
- `JSONMessageCodec`: These are UTF-8 encoded JSON messages. On Android, messages are decoded using the `org.json` library. On iOS, messages are decoded using the `NSJSONSerialization` library.

- `StringCodec`: These are UTF-8 encoded String messages. On Android, messages will be represented using `java.util.String`. On iOS, messages will be represented using `NSString`.
- `StandardMessageCodec`: This uses the Flutter standard binary encoding. Decoded values will use `List<dynamic>` and `Map<dynamic, dynamic>`, irrespective of content. The message values get translated from Dart types into Android/iOS types.

 Check out the official documentation on the `StandardMessageCodec` class to see how values are mapped from Dart to native and vice versa: `https://api.flutter.dev/flutter/services/StandardMessageCodec-class.html`.

`MethodChannels` uses the Flutter-provided `StandardMessageCodec` under the hood by default to perform the serialization/deserialization of data when we send/receive messages with it.

# Creating background processes

In Chapter 2, *Intermediate Dart Programming*, we saw the Dart approach to concurrent programming: isolates. With this, we can create independent workers that are similar to threads, but do not share memory and communicate with each other only via messages.

In mobile application context, we need to care about concurrency as well. As long operations may cause lag on rendering and so on, Flutter provides an easy way to spawn an isolate, the `compute()` function.

# The Flutter compute() function

The `compute()` method is intended to be a facilitator for the task of spawning a new isolate, sending a message to it, and getting a response back. Its signature goes as follows:

```
Future<R> compute <Q, R>( ComputeCallback<Q, R> callback, Q message, {
String debugLabel })
```

A few parameters describe the request to the new isolate:

- `callback`: This is a top-level function to be executed in the new Isolate. Note `ComputeCallback`. There are generic type annotations `<Q, R>`; the first one, `Q`, denotes the input type of the callback, and `R` denotes the result type of the computation.
  Note from the documentation says:

  > *"The callback argument must be a top-level function, not a closure or an instance or static method of a class."*

- `message`: This is the parameter value of the `Q` type, which will be sent to `callback`.
  Note from the documentation says:

  > *"There are limitations on the values that can be sent and received to and from isolates. These limitations constrain the values of Q and R that are possible."*

- `debugLabel`: This can be used during development, giving a name to the isolate for better differentiation on the Observatory UI tool during profiling.

The `compute()` function is ideal for computations that may take longer than few milliseconds to complete, which may cause some frames to be lost. There are also alternatives for short-term computations. Remember the use of `Futures` in `Chapter 2`, *Intermediate Dart Programming*.

## SendPort and ReceivePort

As pointed out before, the message passed to the `compute()` function and the return value from it must respect some limitations. Those limitations come from the isolates communication layer. Isolates, as said before, communicate with each other through the messages. These messages are sent and received through `SendPort` and `ReceivePort` instances.

To send a message to an isolate port, we first need to obtain a `ReceivePort` instance corresponding to it. The `ReceivePort` class exposes a `sendPort getter` that is bounded to the isolate, so we can send messages to it. How does an isolate get `ReceivePort` from another isolate? It does so through the `IsolateNameServer` class.

## IsolateNameServer

The `IsolateNameServer` class is a global register of Dart isolates, from which we can register and look up for `SendPorts` and `ReceivePorts`. Simply said, an isolate can register its `ReceivePort` through the `IsolateNameServer.registerPortWithName` method and other isolates can obtain the corresponding `SendPort` with the `IsolateNameServer.lookupPortByName()` method.

# A compute() example

As said before, to create an isolate to perform long processes, we use the `compute()` function. We can have any kind of implementation in the isolate callback, which will be passed to the compute function. The only requirement is that it has to be a top-level function. For example, see the following code:

```dart
import 'dart:io';

void backgroundCompute(args) {
  print('background compute callback');
  print('calculating fibonacci from a background process');

  int first = 0;
  int second = 1;
  for (var i = 2; i <= 50; i++) {
    var temp = second;
    second = first + second;
    first = temp;
    sleep(Duration(milliseconds: 200));
    print("first: $first, second: $second.");
  }

  print('finished calculating fibo');
}
```

This method calculates the first 50 Fibonacci numbers and prints to the device logs. As you can see, it contains a `sleep` call, which is a blocking call; this means that no asynchronous operations can be processed in the isolate while it is blocked.

We can execute an isolate to run this callback anywhere in a Flutter application by running the following:

```dart
compute(backgroundCompute, null);
```

This very useful function abstracts all of the setup needed to run and communicate with a new isolate. We dispatch it, with or without any parameters, and retrieve an optional response back.

An important aspect to note, though, is that the new isolate is a child of the main Flutter application isolate and so, if the application gets terminated (that is, when user swipes it out on the applications tray), the child isolate is also terminated.

# Full background process

Although very useful, the `compute()` function may not be the thing we need in all cases. As pointed out before, the child isolate created by the `compute()` function gets terminated whenever the parent isolate terminates.

In some situations, we may want to execute some code totally independent of the main application, as in the following examples:

- We might do so when receiving `push` notifications and updating information. We do not need the application to be running to receive and process remote `push` notifications.
- Another example is when listening for user location changes or entering in geofences.
- Fetching server information from a feed is another example.
- Finally, we might do so when uploading files to the server. Depending on the size of files, operations may need a long time to run and many others.

For use cases where we need a code to run independently of the application UI, we can create **headless isolates**, that is, an isolate that is not bound to the main application isolate and, if the main isolate gets terminated, it does not affect its execution.

Until this point of writing this book, there is no default API for handling those use cases, so plugin authors and developers that need this kind of feature in their application need to deal with low-level foundations of the Flutter engine to create a background isolate and establish communication between layers.

To create a background process, we can split responsibilities in languages and application layers. We also need to check what we can/cannot do with the framework and the underlying platform. Let's take it in order:

1. First, we need to define a Flutter background isolate entry point, similar to the `main()` function of our application. The background isolate needs to have its `main`-like function.

2. With this entry point defined, we can start the background isolate. From the application perspective, we do the following:
   - We dispatch a request through a method call to the native side of our app signaling to initiate the new isolate
   - On the native side, we create the structure needed and run the new isolate independently of the application that made the request
   - With the background isolate ready and running, we notify the native side, so it knows that it can communicate to the isolate

3. From the application, we can start making requests to the native side that will process things related to the Flutter structure and delegate to the background isolate.

This process seems to be a lot more complex than needed, and although not simple, the Flutter community aims to improve this as soon as possible to make the task of background processing in Dart simpler.

Take a look at Flutter issues at: `https://github.com/flutter/flutter/issues` for updates on the background processing alternatives.

The communication can be simplified as follows:

The direct communication between main and background isolates is optional and hard to maintain as we need to take care of running aspects. The most simple way until now is to make requests or, even, use an operating system that triggers to dispatch the background to isolate independent of the main application isolate.

Let's create an example using the same Fibonacci algorithm as before. This time, we start the isolate from the application, just like before, but if we terminate the application (that is, by swiping it out of the applications tray), the logs will still print to the device logs as the process will still be running in the background.

# Init the calculation

From the application, when we click on the calculate button, it should initialize the process we have seen before. The first step is to invoke a method through a method channel. We have created the example in a plugin structure, so it will be easy for you to change it and even use it in your applications. The plugin will be responsible for abstracting the isolate creation process so that it will be transparent to the application. Its only method is calculateInBackgroundProcess, which is called from the application:

```
HandsOnBackgroundProcess.calculateInBackgroundProcess();
```

Check out the hands_on_background_process example on GitHub for the complete source code.

This previous code invokes the plugin method that's responsible for initiating the process that goes as follows:

```
const pluginChannel = MethodChannel('com.example.handson/plugin_channel');

class HandsOnBackgroundProcess {
  static void calculateInBackgroundProcess() async {
    final callbackHandle = PluginUtilities.getCallbackHandle(
        backgroundIsolateMain
    );

    await pluginChannel.invokeMethod(
        "initBackgroundProcess",
        [callbackHandle.toRawHandle()]
    );
  }
}
```

As you can see, first of all, we define a method channel named com.example.handson/plugin_channel for the plugin calls; this is typically the first step in plugins. Then, in the calculateInBackgroundProcess() method, we do the following:

- We get a handle to the new background isolate entry point. We use PluginUtilities.getCallbackHandle utility provided by the framework to get the identifier of the callback to pass to the native side of the application. This way, later, on the native side, we can retrieve this callback and run the background isolate with it as the entry point.
- After getting the handle, we invoke the "initBackgroundProcess" method, passing the handle to it. This method will do the isolate job mentioned before.

Let's take a look at the Dart entry point of the isolate first and then check the code needed to make it work properly.

## The background isolate

The Dart callback passed down to the native part of the plugin through the handle seen before is responsible for calculating the Fibonacci, like before. However, it is not exactly the same:

```
void backgroundIsolateMain() {
  print('background isolate entry point running');
  const backgroundchannel = MethodChannel(
    'com.example.handson/background_channel'
```

```
    );
    WidgetsFlutterBinding.ensureInitialized();

    backgroundchannel.setMethodCallHandler((MethodCall call) async {
      if (call.method == 'calculate') {
        print('calculating fibonacci from a background process');

        int first = 0;
        int second = 1;
        for (var i = 2; i <= 50; i++) {
          var temp = second;
          second = first + second;
          first = temp;
          sleep(Duration(milliseconds: 500));
          print("first: $first, second: $second.");
        }

        print('finished calculating fibo');
        backgroundchannel.invokeMethod("calculationFinished");
      }
    });
    backgroundchannel.invokeMethod("backgroundIsolateInitialized");
  }
```

As you can see, it has some changes:

1. The background isolate starts by setting up a method channel, not the same as before. Now, we create one named `com.example.handson/background_channel`. It is used to establish communication with the native code executed on the background (service on Android and background execution on iOS).

2. Set the handler for the `calculate` method, so that the native code can invoke it to start the calculation. Although it's not really needed in this case (we could start calculation right in the entry point body), it's good for exemplification.

3. After setting up the method channel, we notify the native side with a call to `backgroundIsolateInitialized`. After this, all is ready on the Dart side.

For the Dart side of the background execution, we need to implement just once. Then, for each of the platforms (Android/iOS), we should set up the environment for this isolate to run.

# Adding Android-specific code to run Dart code in the background

In Android, there is the concept of `Services`, which are the ideal way of running application code in the background, independently of the main application execution. So, basically, we need to create a `Service` method, bind the new background isolate, and run.

 Read the official documentation about Android Services: `https://developer.android.com/reference/android/app/Service`.

# The HandsOnBackgroundProcessPlugin class

The first step is to set up the plugin, just like we already did in Chapter 9, *Developing Your Own Flutter Plugin*. It starts with an implementation of the static `registerWith` method that notifies the Flutter engine with the existence of the plugin instance:

```
class HandsOnBackgroundProcessPlugin(
        private val context: Context
) : MethodChannel.MethodCallHandler{
    companion object {
        ...
        @JvmStatic
        fun registerWith(registrar: PluginRegistry.Registrar) {
            val channel = MethodChannel(
                registrar.messenger(),
                "com.example.handson/plugin_channel"
            )
            val plugin = HandsOnBackgroundProcessPlugin(
                registrar.context()
            )
            channel.setMethodCallHandler(plugin)
        }
    }
    ...
}
```

As you can see, it configures the method channel, called `com.example.handson/plugin_channel`, that is used to initialize the calculation through the `initBackgroundProcess` method:

```
override fun onMethodCall(call: MethodCall, result: MethodChannel.Result?)
{
    val args = call.arguments() as? ArrayList<*>
    if (call.method == "initBackgroundProcess") {
        val callbackHandle = args?.get(0) as? Long ?: return
        executeBackgroundIsolate(context, callbackHandle)
    }
}
```

To handle the `initBackgroundProcess` method, it fetches the callback handle coming from Dart. To fetch it properly, it is parsed to the `Long` type (`int` in Dart) according to the `StandardMessageCodec` class.

The execution of the background isolate is done in two steps. The first is done in `executeBackgroundIsolate()`, as follows:

```
. . .
private fun executeBackgroundIsolate(context: Context, callbackHandle:
Long) {
    val preferences = context.getSharedPreferences(
        SHARED_PREFERENCES_KEY,
        IntentService.MODE_PRIVATE
    )
    preferences.edit().putLong(ARG_CALLBACK_KEY, callbackHandle).apply()

    startBackgroundService(context)
}
. . .
```

First, the method stores the handle value in a `SharedPreferences` file. Then, it requests the execution of the background service through the `startBackgroundService()` method:

- Shared preferences are used in Android to store key-value data in a simple and private way. It is used here because we cannot pass parameters to `Service` constructors as they must not get arguments.

You can check out more on shared preferences in the official documentation: `https://developer.android.com/training/data-storage/shared-preferences`.

- `startBackgroundService()` simply makes the request to the Android system to initialize the background service:

```
...
private fun startBackgroundService(context: Context) {
    val intent = Intent(
        context,
        BackgroundProcessService::class.java
    )
    context.startService(intent)
}
...
```

The remaining part of the job is done in the `BackgroundProcessService` class.

# The BackgroundProcessService class

The `BackgroundProcessService` class is the Android service that will be running while our isolate is being executed. As it is in the background, the application may be closed and the isolate will be running normally.

 Again, it is important to check the Android `Service` documentation mentioned before to understand how the life cycle works.

`Service` execution is all managed by the Android system; we do not have full control of it, so we need to react to events provided by the system to execute our isolate based on the `Service` state.

It all starts with the `onCreate` method, when the system creates our `Service` method and we can set up all of the resources needed for it to run. It is a good place to start our background isolate:

```
class BackgroundProcessService : Service(), MethodChannel.MethodCallHandler
{
    override fun onCreate() {
        super.onCreate()
```

```
        createNotification()
        FlutterMain.ensureInitializationComplete(applicationContext, null)
        startBackgroundIsolate()
    }
    ...
}
```

As you can see, it does more than just initialize our isolate. Let's break it down:

1. First, we set up a notification through the `createNotification()` method. The notification is placed on the Android status bar and it makes our service run in the foreground mode. Basically, `Services` that run in the background are more likely to be killed by the system in the case of a lack of resources. Foreground services, in contrast, have a higher priority in the system and are less likely to be terminated in this case.

2. Then, we use the `FlutterMain.ensureInitializationComplete(applicationContext, null)` call, which asserts the Flutter engine is set up and we can use things such as platform channels.

3. Finally, we start the isolate with the `startBackgroundIsolate()` call.

The `startBackgroundIsolate()` method is the main and most complex method in this class. It is responsible for setting up the structure needed for the background isolate to run. It goes as follows:

```
private fun startBackgroundIsolate() {
    val preferences = applicationContext.getSharedPreferences(
        SHARED_PREFERENCES_KEY,
        MODE_PRIVATE
    )
    val callbackHandle = preferences.getLong(ARG_CALLBACK_KEY, 0L)
    if (callbackHandle == 0L) return
    val callback =
    FlutterCallbackInformation.lookupCallbackInformation(
        callbackHandle
    ) ?: return

    sBackgroundFlutterView = FlutterNativeView(this, true)
    val path = FlutterMain.findAppBundlePath(applicationContext)
    val args = FlutterRunArguments()
    args.bundlePath = path
    args.entrypoint = callback.callbackName
    args.libraryPath = callback.callbackLibraryPath

    sBackgroundFlutterView?.runFromBundle(args)
```

```
backgroundChannel = MethodChannel(
    sBackgroundFlutterView,
    "com.example.handson/background_channel"
)
backgroundChannel?.setMethodCallHandler(this)

sPluginRegistrantCallback?.registerWith(
    sBackgroundFlutterView?.pluginRegistry
)
}
```

This method initializes and registers a new background plugin instance in the Flutter
engine just like it's done in normal applications. The process is a little bit trickier, so let's see
how we will go about it:

1. First, we get the Dart callback that is the entry point of the new background
   isolate. To accomplish this, we get the handle from the stored shared preferences
   and use
   the `FlutterCallbackInformation.lookupCallbackInformation` method
   to retrieve the callback information needed to run it.

2. Then, we instantiate a new `FlutterNativeView` method. This view is used to
   have a proper environment for the new isolate to run. In Android, that's how the
   Flutter engine works. Remember, `View` is passed to our Dart side for the
   application work on it. Note the second parameter passed to
   the `FlutterNativeView` constructor, `true`, meaning the view will run in the
   background and does not need a surface to draw on.

3. To finally execute the isolate, we use the `runFromBundle()` method from
   the `FlutterNativeView` instance we saw before. This method needs
   a `FlutterRunArguments` instance to identify what it will run.
   Our `args` variable holds the information we got from `callback`, such as its
   `callbackName` and `callbackLibraryPath`, to find our isolate entry point.

4. After running the background isolate, we create an instance to the background
   method channel named `com.example.handson/background_channel`, just
   like we did in the Dart side.

5. The final step is to register the plugin instance in the Flutter registry with the
   help of the `sPluginRegistrantCallback` property. This property must be
   passed manually to the `Service` class somehow. Why? Flutter
   automatically registers the plugin in the main thread when you use it (remember
   the static `registerWith` method we need to implement for our
   plugins). `PluginRegistrantCallback` is the way we do it manually. Through
   this, we can register a plugin anywhere, such as places where `registerWith` is
   not looked up (our `Service`, in this case).

TIP

Check out the documentation to find out more about threads in Android:
`https://flutter.dev/docs/get-started/flutter-for/android-`
`devs#how-do-you-move-work-to-a-background-thread`.

## The PluginRegistrantCallback property

We pass the `PluginRegistrantCallback` instance to the `Service` class in the example project. We create a descendant of the `FlutterApplication` class, which will serve as our registrant callback to the service:

```
class Application: FlutterApplication(),
PluginRegistry.PluginRegistrantCallback {
    override fun onCreate() {
        super.onCreate()
        Log.w("BACKGROUND", "application")
        BackgroundProcessService.setPluginRegistrant(this)
    }

    override fun registerWith(registry: PluginRegistry?) {
        GeneratedPluginRegistrant.registerWith(registry)
    }
}
```

As you can see, we pass the application instance to the `Service` instance so it will be able to register in the Flutter engine. We also need to set our application class in `AndroidManifest.xml` for this to work:

```
<manifest xmlns:android="http://schemas.android.com/apk/res/android"
    package="com.example.hands_on_background_process_example">
    <application
        android:name=".Application"
        android:label="hands_on_background_process_example"
    >
    ...
</manifest>
```

After setting up the plugin and the background isolate, we need to communicate with it to start the calculations. All we need to do is to handle method calls from the background method channel we have defined:

```
override fun onMethodCall(call: MethodCall, result: MethodChannel.Result?)
{
    if (call.method == "backgroundIsolateInitialized") {
        backgroundChannel?.invokeMethod("calculate", null)
```

```
        } else if (call.method == "calculationFinished") {
            sBackgroundFlutterView?.destroy()
            sBackgroundFlutterView = null
            shutdownService()
        } else {
        } // 'calculate' method from this channel, handled on the Dart isolate.
    }
```

Our `BackgroundProcessService` instance is defined as the method handler of the background method channel calls:

- The method named `backgroundIsolateInitialized` is called from the background isolate when it's ready and, in response to this, we start the calculation invoking `calculate` in the same channel.
- Also, whenever the calculation finishes and the Dart background isolate calls the `calculationFinished` method, our `FlutterNativeView` instance that holds the isolate is destroyed and the service stopped with a call to the `shutdownService()` method, which simply removes the notification defined before and kills the service.

That's all for the Android implementation; with this, even if we terminate our application by swiping it out of the applications tray, the background isolate will be running until it finishes.

# Adding iOS-specific code to run Dart code in the background

Things are different in iOS. Background execution is way more restricted than with Android. The `Service` concept does not exist, and we have a few moments that we can run code in background.

The majority of use cases are covered by `UIBackgroundModes`, where an application can define the supported background modes and then is allowed to run specific kinds of background execution. We can, for example, do the following:

- Have the Audio and AirPlay background mode that sets the app as capable of playing audible content to the user or recording audio while in the background.
- Receive location updates when in the location updates the background mode.
- Newsstand is a download mode, where the application can download and process magazine or newspaper content in the background.

Check the official background execution guide from the iOS documentation: `https://developer.apple.com/library/archive/` `documentation/iPhone/Conceptual/iPhoneOSProgrammingGuide/` `BackgroundExecution/BackgroundExecution.html`.

Much of the work is similar to Android, except for the `Service` part. So, let's start with the plugin definition.

## The SwiftHandsOnBackgroundProcessPlugin class

The registration and setup of the plugin is done in a similar way to the `HandsOnBackgroundProcessPlugin` class. This time, in the `register()` static function, we have the following:

```
public static func register(with registrar: FlutterPluginRegistrar) {
    let channel = FlutterMethodChannel(
        name: "com.example.handson/plugin_channel",
        binaryMessenger: registrar.messenger()
    )
    let instance = SwiftHandsOnBackgroundProcessPlugin(
        registrar: registrar
    )
    registrar.addMethodCallDelegate(instance, channel: channel)
}
```

Like in the Android version, it configures the method channel called `com.example.handson/plugin_channel`, which is used to initialize the calculation through the `initBackgroundProcess` method, as you can see:

```
public func handle(
    _ call: FlutterMethodCall,
    result: @escaping FlutterResult
) {
    if (call.method == "initBackgroundProcess") {
        guard let args = call.arguments as? NSArray else {
            return
        }
        guard let handle = args[0] as? Int64 else {
            return
        }
        executeBackgroundIsolate(handle: handle)
    }
}
```

In this case, as we do not have separation as a service, we start the execution of the background isolate right away from the call.

The execution of the background isolate in the `executeBackgroundIsolate()` method goes as follows:

```
private func executeBackgroundIsolate(handle: Int64) {
    _backgroundRunner = FlutterEngine.init(
        name: "BackgroundProcess",
        project: nil,
        allowHeadlessExecution: true
    )
    guard let info = FlutterCallbackCache.lookupCallbackInformation(
        handle
    ) else {
        return
    }
    let entrypoint = info.callbackName
    let uri = info.callbackLibraryPath
    _backgroundRunner!.run(
        withEntrypoint: entrypoint,
        libraryURI: uri
    )

    _backgroundChannel = FlutterMethodChannel(
        name: "com.example.handson/background_channel",
        binaryMessenger: _backgroundRunner!
    )
    _registrar.addMethodCallDelegate(
        self,
        channel: _backgroundChannel!
    )
    SwiftHandsOnBackgroundProcessPlugin._registerPlugins?(
        _backgroundRunner!
    )
}
```

We can, again, break down the execution into several steps:

1. First, we store an instance of the `FlutterEngine` class in the `_backgroundRunner` property. This instance will be our Flutter plugin that will be the bridge, like `FlutterNativeView` was on Android.

2. Then, we get our entry point from the callback handle through the `FlutterCallbackCache.lookupCallbackInformation()` utility. All of the information is equal to the one we get in Android. Here, we use `entrypoint` and `uri` to run the background isolate through the `_backgroundRunner!.run(withEntrypoint: entrypoint, libraryURI: uri)` call.

3. After running the isolate the final part is very similar to Android. We create the channel named `com.example.handson/background_channel` for the communication and we set its handler as the plugin instance itself.

4. Finally, we register the plugin in the background through the `_registerPlugins` callback, just like `PluginRegistrantCallback` in Android.

 This last step not really needed in iOS. There is *not* another background thread running beside our application. It is moved to a background state but the plugin still getting registered normally. If our application were executed in some `UIBackgroundMode` key like mentioned before, this registration would still be important.

After launching the background isolate, we can, again, handle calls from the background channel:

```swift
public func handle(_ call: FlutterMethodCall, result: @escaping
FlutterResult) {

    if (call.method == "initBackgroundProcess") {
        // ... seen previously
    } else if (call.method == "backgroundIsolateInitialized") {
        self.taskID = UIApplication.shared.beginBackgroundTask {
            self.taskID = .invalid
        }
        _backgroundChannel?.invokeMethod("calculate", arguments: nil)
    } else if (call.method == "calculationFinished") {
        if(self.taskID != nil && self.taskID != .invalid) {
            UIApplication.shared.endBackgroundTask(self.taskID!)
            self.taskID = .invalid
        }
        // end background task
    }
}
```

Although it's different, the basic idea of method handling is similar:

1. When the method named `backgroundIsolateInitialized` is called, we invoke the corresponding `calculate` method, so it performs calculations and logs to the Flutter console. Before that, we register an iOS background task. This will notify the system we need a little bit more time to conclude our work and prevent it from getting finished before expected. Remember, iOS is very restrictive in background tasks.

2. In a call to `calculationFinished`, we simply notify the system our task is finished with `UIApplication.shared.endBackgroundTask(self.taskID!)` and is safe to move our app to the *suspended* state.

It's fundamental for you to understand why and when this can be used: https://developer.apple.com/documentation/uikit/core_app/ managing_your_app_s_life_cycle/preparing_your_app_to_run_in_the_ background/extending_your_app_s_background_execution_time.

Just like in Android, the iOS background plugin is registered as well. We do this with the `_registerPlugins` callback. It's passed down to the plugin over the `setPluginRegistrantCallback()` static function that gets called in the application `AppDelegate` class, very similar to Android:

```
@UIApplicationMain
@objc class AppDelegate: FlutterAppDelegate {
  override func application(
    _ application: UIApplication,
    didFinishLaunchingWithOptions launchOptions:
[UIApplicationLaunchOptionsKey: Any]?
  ) -> Bool {
    GeneratedPluginRegistrant.register(with: self)
    SwiftHandsOnBackgroundProcessPlugin.setPluginRegistrantCallback(
        registerPlugins: registerPlugins
    )
    return super.application(
        application,
        didFinishLaunchingWithOptions: launchOptions
    )
  }
}
```

A little bit different from Android, the `registerPlugins` function is a top-level function, as follows:

```
func registerPlugins(registry: FlutterPluginRegistry) {
    GeneratedPluginRegistrant.register(with: registry)
}
```

As you can see, it is similar to one defined in the Android application, which is used to register the plugins through the `GeneratedPluginRegistrant.register` utility.

 Check out more about threading in iOS: `https://flutter.dev/docs/get-started/flutter-for-ios-devs#threading--asynchronicity`.

After this, our app behaves similarly to Android, and we have printed all of our logs, even in a background state:

```
example — script · flutter logs — 80×24
Runner: flutter: first: 89, second: 144.
Runner: flutter: first: 144, second: 233.
Runner: flutter: first: 233, second: 377.
Runner: flutter: first: 377, second: 610.
Runner: flutter: first: 610, second: 987.
Runner: flutter: first: 987, second: 1597.
Runner: flutter: first: 1597, second: 2584.
Runner: flutter: first: 2584, second: 4181.
Runner: flutter: first: 4181, second: 6765.
Runner: flutter: first: 6765, second: 10946.
Runner: flutter: first: 10946, second: 17711.
Runner: flutter: first: 17711, second: 28657.
Runner: flutter: first: 28657, second: 46368.
Runner: flutter: first: 46368, second: 75025.
Runner: flutter: first: 75025, second: 121393.
Runner: flutter: first: 121393, second: 196418.
Runner: flutter: first: 196418, second: 317811.
Runner: flutter: first: 317811, second: 514229.
Runner: flutter: first: 514229, second: 832040.
Runner: flutter: first: 832040, second: 1346269.
Runner: flutter: first: 1346269, second: 2178309.
Runner: flutter: first: 2178309, second: 3524578.
Runner: flutter: first: 3524578, second: 5702887.
Runner: flutter: first: 5702887, second: 9227465.
```

# Summary

In this chapter, we saw advanced methods to make our application more user friendly and interactive. We started by learning the available tools focused on user accessibility provided by the Flutter framework.

Then, we checked how we can add translations to Flutter apps, by generating `.arb` files, creating multiple translations, importing them to Dart, and applying them to our `MaterialApp` class.

Finally, we took a look at background processing options with Flutter, going from the very useful `compute()` function to a background service on Android and background modes on iOS. We also saw the characteristics and limitations on each platform in this aspect.

In the next chapter, we are going to take a look at widget graphic manipulations and how we can transform widgets and draw custom shapes to the Canvas.

# 14
# Widget Graphic Manipulations

Using widgets as they are by default is sufficient to make a nice-looking Flutter app, but extending the widgets with transformations in layout, such as opacity, rotations, and decorations, can make the UX improve further. In this chapter, you will learn how to add those transformations to a widget. Also, you will learn how to modify a widget by adding graphical transformations to it with the `Transform` class and use the canvas to draw a custom widget.

The following topics will be covered in this chapter:

- Transforming widgets with the Transform class
- Exploring the types of transformations
- Adding transformations to your widgets
- Using custom painters and the Canvas

## Transforming widgets with the Transform class

Sometimes, we need to change a widget's appearance. In response to user input or to make cool effects in the layout, we may need to move the widget around the screen, change its size, or even distort it a little bit.

If you've ever tried to make this in native programming languages, you may have found some difficulties. Flutter, as you remember, is highly focused on UI design and proposes to make the developer's life easier.

# The Transform widget

The `Transform` widget is one of the best examples of the Flutter framework's power and consistency. It's a single-purpose widget that simply applies a graphic transformation to its child and nothing more. Having widgets focused on one single purpose is fundamental to a better layout structure, and Flutter does it very well.

The `Transform` widget, as its name suggests, does a single task: it **transforms** its underlying `child`. Although its task is very complex, it abstracts most part of this complexity to the developer. Let's have a look at its constructor:

```
const Transform({
    Key key,
    @required Matrix4 transform,
    Offset origin,
    AlignmentGeometry alignment,
    bool transformHitTests: true,
    Widget child
})
```

As you can see, besides the typical `key` property, this widget does not need many arguments to do its job. Let's see these arguments:

- `transform`: This is the only mandatory (`@required` annotation) property used to describe the transformation that will be applied to the `child` widget. A `Matrix4` object, this is a four-dimension (4D) matrix that describes the transformation in a mathematical way. There will be more details later.
- `origin`: This is the origin of the coordinate system at which to apply the `transform` matrix. The origin is specified by the `Offset` type, representing, in this case, a point $(x,y)$ in the Cartesian system that is relative to the upper-left corner of the render widget.
- `alignment`: Like `origin`, it can be used to manipulate the position of the applied `transform` matrix. We can use this to specify `origin` in a more flexible way, as `origin` requires us to use real position values. Nothing prevents you from using both `origin` and `alignment` at the same time.
- `transformHitTests`: This specifies whether **hit tests** (that is, taps) are evaluated in the transformed version of the widget.
- `child`: This is the child widget to which the transformation will be applied.

## Understanding the Matrix4 class

In the foundation of geometrical transformations, there is mathematics. In Flutter, transformations are represented in a 4D matrix. Besides methods such as matrix addition or multiplication, the `Matrix4` class contains methods that help with the construction and manipulation of geometric transformations. Some of them are as follows:

- `rotation`: `rotateX()`, `rotateY()`, and `rotateZ()` are some examples of methods that rotate the matrix through a specific axis.
- `scale`: `scale()`, with some variants, is used to apply a scale on the matrix using double values of the corresponding axes (*x*, *y*, and *z*) or through vector representations with the `Vector3` and `Vector4` classes.
- `translation`: Just like before, we can translate the matrix using the `translate()` method with specific *x*, *y*, or *z* values and `Vector3` and `Vector4` instances.
- `skew`: This is used to skew the matrix around the *X* axis with `skewX()` or *Y* axis with `skewY()`.

Check the `Matrix4` official documentation to all of the available possibilities this class offers: `https://api.flutter.dev/flutter/vector_math/Matrix4-class.html`. Remember, it is the basis of the transformations applied with the `Transform` widget.

# Exploring the types of transformations

Although the `Matrix4` and `Transform` widget can already be seen as a simple way, the `Transform` class provides even more facilities to the developer through its factory constructors. There are many of them for each of the possible transformations, making it extremely easy to apply a transformation to a widget without any deeper knowledge of geometric calculations. They are as follows:

- `Transform.rotate()`: Constructs a `Transform` widget that rotates its child around its center
- `Transform.scale()`: Constructs a `Transform` widget that scales its child uniformly
- `Transform.translate()`: Constructs a `Transform` widget that translates its child by an `x`, `y` offset

# Rotate transformation

The rotation transformation appears in situations where we want to simply make our widget rotate. By using the `Transform.rotate()` constructor, we can get effects like this:

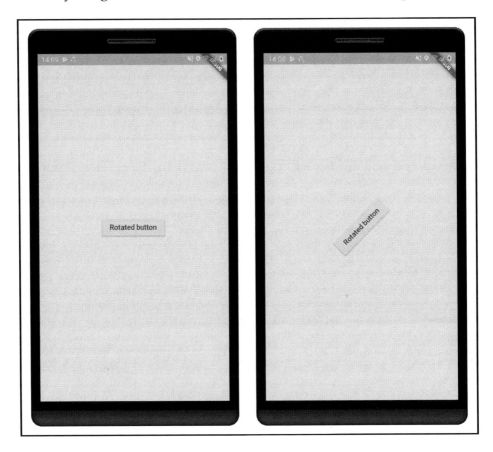

The `Transofm.rotate` constructor variant can be used to achieve this, so let's see what it looks like:

```
Transform.rotate({
    Key key,
    @required double angle,
    Offset origin,
    AlignmentGeometry alignment: Alignment.center,
    bool transformHitTests: true,
    Widget child
})
```

As you can see, it does not differ too much from the default `Transform` constructor. The differences are as follows:

- **Absence of the** `transform` **property**: We are using the `rotate()` variant because we want to apply a rotation, so we do not need to specify the whole matrix to this. We simply use the `angle` property instead.
- **Angle**: This specifies the desired rotation in clockwise radians.
- **Origin**: By default, the rotation is applied relative to the center of the child. However, we can use the `origin` property to manipulate the origin of the rotation, like if we were translating the center of the widget by the origin offset, causing the rotation to be relative to another point if we want to.

# Scale transformation

The scale transformation appears in situations where we want to simply cause our widget to change its size, either by increasing or decreasing its scale. We can get something like this:

This kind of transformation is typically done by using the `Transform.scale()` constructor. Let's see what it looks like:

```
Transform.scale({
    Key key,
    @required double scale,
    Offset origin,
    AlignmentGeometry alignment: Alignment.center,
    bool transformHitTests: true,
    Widget child
})
```

As you can see, just like the `rotate()` factory constructor, this variant does not differ too much from the default one:

- **Absence of the** `transform` **property**: Here, again, we use the `scale` property instead of the whole transformation matrix.
- **Scale**: This is what we use to specify the desired scale in `double` format, `1.0` being the widget's original size. It represents the scalar to be applied to each $x$ and y axis.
- **Alignment**: By default, the scale is applied relative to the center of the child. Here, we can use the `alignment` property to change the origin of the scale. Again, we can combine the `alignment` and `origin` properties to get the desired result.

# Translate transformation

The translate transformation is more likely to appear in animations (see Chapter 15, *Animations*). By using the `Transform.translate()` constructor, we move the widget around the screen:

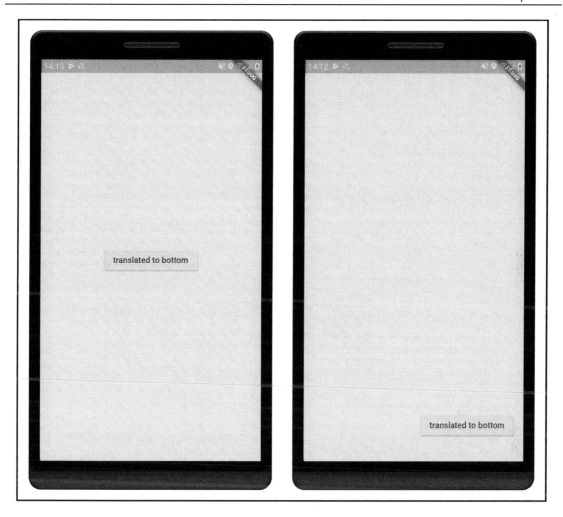

And this is what the `Transform.translate()` factory constructor looks like:

```
Transform.translate({
    Key key,
    @required Offset offset,
    bool transformHitTests: true,
    Widget child
})
```

Here, we have even fewer properties compared to previous transformations. The differences are as follows:

- **The absence of the** `transform` **and** `alignment` **properties**: The transformation will be applied by the `offset` value, so we do not need the transform matrix.
- **Offset**: This time, `offset` simply specifies the translation to be applied on the child widget; this is different from the previous transformations, where it affects the origin point of the applied transformation.

# Composed transformations

We can, and most probably will, combine a number of the previously seen transformations to achieve unique effects, such as rotating at the same time as we move and scale a widget, as in the following example:

Composing transformations can be done in two ways:

- Using the default `Transform` widget constructor and generating our desired transformation using the `Matrix4` provided methods to compose it
- Using multiple `Transform` widgets in a nested way with the `rotate()`, `scale()` and `translate()` factory constructors, achieving the same effect, but causing our widgets tree to be bigger than needed

# Applying transformations to your widgets

As we have seen until now, `Transform` widget can help us to modify the widget's natural appearances. Applying transformations to widgets is as simple as adding a `Transform` widget as the parent of the widget we want to modify. Let's check the alternatives we can use to apply transformations to widgets.

# Rotating widgets

As pointed out before, we can use the `Transform.rotate()` constructor to add a `Transform` widget to the widgets tree responsible for rotating its `child`. We can use something like this:

```
Transform.rotate(
    angle: -45 * (math.pi / 180.0),
    child: RaisedButton(
    child: Text("Rotated button"),
    onPressed: () {},
  ),
);
```

We add a widget that is rotated 315º clockwise (the same as −45º counter-clockwise). The exact same result is achieved using the `Transform` widget's default constructor and a `Matrix4` transformation instead:

```
Transform(
  transform: Matrix4.rotationZ(-45 * (math.pi / 180.0)),
  alignment: Alignment.center,
  child: RaisedButton(
    child: Text("Rotated button"),
    onPressed: () {},
  ),
);
```

The arguments we need to provide in order to get the same result are as follows:

- `transform` with the rotation through the *z* axis
- `alignment` of the transformation

# Scaling widgets

To scale widgets, we use the typical `Transform.scale()`, constructor. To scale up a widget, for example, we can use it as follows:

```
Transform.scale(
  scale: 2.0,
  child: RaisedButton(
    child: Text("scaled up"),
    onPressed: () {},
  ),
);
```

And to get the same result using the default `Transform` constructor, we use the following:

```
Transform(
  transform: Matrix4.identity()..scale(2.0, 2.0),
  alignment: Alignment.center,
  child: RaisedButton(
    child: Text("scaled up"),
    onPressed: () {},
  ),
);
```

In a very similar way to the rotation, we must specify both the origin of the transformation with the `alignment` property and the `Matrix4` instance describing the scale transformation.

# Translating widgets

In a very similar way, we use the `Transform.translate()` constructor by adding a `Transform` widget as a parent of the widget we want to move around:

```
Transform.translate(
  offset: Offset(100, 300),
  child: RaisedButton(
    child: Text("translated to bottom"),
    onPressed: () {},
```

```
  ),
);
```

The default constructor can also be used with `Matrix4` specifying the translation:

```
Transform(
  transform: Matrix4.translationValues(100, 300, 0),
  child: RaisedButton(
    child: Text("translated to bottom"),
    onPressed: () {},
  ),
);
```

We only need to specify the `transform` property with the `Matrix4` instance describing the translation.

# Applying multiple transformations

As previously pointed out, we have two ways to add multiple transformations to widgets. The first is by adding multiple `Transform` widgets above the desired widget:

```
Transform.translate(
  offset: Offset(70, 200),
  child: Transform.rotate(
    angle: -45 * (math.pi / 180.0),
    child: Transform.scale(
      scale: 2.0,
      child: RaisedButton(
        child: Text("multiple transformations"),
        onPressed: () {},
      ),
    ),
  ),
);
```

As you can see, we add a `Transform` widget as a child to another `Transform` widget, composing the transformation. Although simpler to read, this method has a drawback: we add more widgets than needed to the widget tree.

 When we add multiple transformations to a widget at the same time, we have to pay attention to the order of transformations. Experiment by yourself: exchanging the `Transform` widgets' positions will cause different results.

As an alternative, we can use the default `Transform` constructor with the composed transformation with the `Matrix4` object instead:

```
Transform(
  alignment: Alignment.center,
  transform: Matrix4.translationValues(70, 200, 0)
    ..rotateZ(-45 * (math.pi / 180.0))
    ..scale(2.0, 2.0),
  child: RaisedButton(
    child: Text("multiple transformations"),
    onPressed: () {},
  ),
);
```

Just like before, we specify the `alignment` of the transformation as the center of the child widget and then the `Matrix4` instance to describe it. As you can see, it is very similar to the multiple `Transform` widgets version but without nested widgets causing a deeper widget tree.

# Using custom painters and canvas

Flutter aims to provide the best possible tools for the developer to construct application user interfaces with no limitations. By now, you are probably already convinced of this, with the numerous widgets it provides, the facility of extending those widgets, and the universe of possibilities that the framework offers.

The simplicity that Flutter brings to the UI composition does not end with widgets. How about changing the widget look? I'm not talking about extending with a `Transform` widget by translating or rotating it. We can create a widget's with its own unique appearance, its own shape, and its own behaviors. That is possible with the help of three main classes: `CustomPaint`, `CustomPainter`, and `Canvas`.

# The Canvas class

If you've ever programmed some kind of UI in any language, you might have heard or worked with some kind of Canvas. As its name suggests, it provides ways to **paint** things. Canvas can be seen as the **space we work on**, by drawing shapes with our defined styles such as lines, circles, and rectangles.

Flutter Canvas does not work as a literal canvas. Basically, it is just an interface for recording graphical operations to be drawn on the next rendering frame.

## Canvas transformations

All operations we do on Canvas, such as drawing a line or a rectangle, are oriented in a coordinate system, just like any other UI drawing system. This coordinate system has an origin. By default, this is defined by the CustomPaint widget that owns Canvas. The important thing to note is that, because of this characteristic, all of the operations we do on Canvas are affected by its **current transformation**. Whenever we want, we can transform the canvas to affect the subsequent operations.

 Initially, Canvas has no transformation, that is, its transformation matrix are a Matrix4 identity instance.

## Canvas ClipRect

Like transformations, Canvas does have a **current clip region**, meaning that we can clip part of the canvas to be drawn. This is useful when we want just to draw part of a complex shape without caring too much about calculations.

 By default, the clip region of Canvas is infinite, so all of the regions is valid.

## Methods

As pointed out before, Canvas works by recording drawing operations to the next painting frame. To do that, it exposes many methods to allow us to draw various shapes. Let's examine the most common ones:

- drawArc(): Used to draw closed arcs or circle segments
- drawCircle(): Used to draw circles with a determined radius
- drawImage(): Used to draw an image into the Canvas
- drawLine(): Used to draw lines into the Canvas

- `drawRect()`: Used to draw rectangles into the Canvas
- `rotate()`: Adds a rotation transformation to the current Canvas transformation
- `scale()`: Adds a scale transformation to the current canvas transformation
- `translate()`: Adds a translation to the current canvas transformation

 Check out the `Canvas` class documentation for more methods and further details: `https://docs.flutter.io/flutter/dart-ui/Canvas-class.html`.

# The Paint object

The `Paint` object is a description of the style to use when drawing on `Canvas`. It lets us define things such as colors and stroke width. All of the canvas drawing methods retrieve a `Paint` object as the parameter. We can reuse the same `Paint` instance on multiple drawing calls.

# The CustomPaint widget

The `Canvas` object is not available anywhere in Flutter; this can cause confusion. Whenever we want to draw things by hand, we need to use the `CustomPaint` widget. The main purpose of this widget is to provide a `Canvas` object for us to work on.

Having a `Canvas` and a `CustomPaint` widget is not enough to draw on. The purpose of `CustomPaint` is to provide `Canvas` and delegate a `CustomPainter` object that will be responsible for drawing on it.

## CustomPaint construction details

The `CustomPaint` widget simply works as the bridge between the widget tree (by being a widget) and a lower-level painting layer with access to `Canvas`. To create this, we must have a `CustomPainter` instance as it does not make sense to have `CustomPaint` without a painter.

To create a `CustomPaint` widget, we first add it to our widget tree just like we do for other widgets. Let's take a look at its constructor first to understand it:

```
const CustomPaint({
    Key key,
    CustomPainter painter,
    CustomPainter foregroundPainter,
    Size size: Size.zero,
    bool isComplex: false,
    bool willChange: false,
    Widget child
})
```

There are a few properties we need to take a look at to understand how it works:

- `painter`: The painter implementation that draws content on the canvas
- `foregroundPainter`: The painter implementation that draws content on the canvas after the child is painted
- `size`: If the `child` property is not null, the size of the child is used and this value is ignored; otherwise, this specifies the size needed for the draw
- `isComplex` and `willChange`: Hints to the compositor's raster cache, helping with the analysis of rendering costs
- `child`: A child to be below in the widget tree, like any other widget

We can see the painter-related properties in the following screenshot:

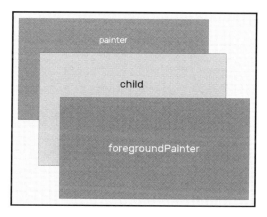

This illustrates the order of drawing: first, the `painter` operations are made, then `child`, and finally, `foregroundPainter` (if any) draws in front of child.

# The CustomPainter object

We know the importance of the `CustomPainter` (or painter) object. As pointed out previously, the painter is responsible for drawing something on `Canvas`. Whenever we want to create our own unique drawing logic, we need to extend the `CustomPainter` class and override two fundamental methods: `paint()` and `shouldRepaint()`.

## The paint method

The `paint()` method is where the `CustomPainter` does its job. It gets called whenever the widget is requested to redraw. This is what it looks like:

```
void paint (
    Canvas canvas,
    Size size
)
```

The only two arguments it receives are as follows:

- `canvas`, where we draw effectively by using its `draw*()` methods
- `size` defines the bounds of the drawing, which we should consider

Paint operations should remain inside the given area. This is what the documentation says:

*"Graphical operations outside the bounds may be silently ignored, clipped, or not clipped."*

## The shouldRepaint method

This is an important method, especially for the Flutter engine. This is what it looks like:

```
bool shouldRepaint (
    covariant CustomPainter oldDelegate
)
```

It receives just the `oldDelegate` argument, which corresponds to the last delegate (`this` `CustomPainter` class instance) that was responsible for painting onto `CustomPaint`. Whenever it returns `false`, then the paint call might be optimized away (this does not mean the paint will not be called). We should compare the old and current delegate to see whether any data related to the paint is different, and then return `true` in this case.

# A practical example

It's time to see how we can use the Canvas and CustomPaint widget to create a widget that has its own painting. In this example, we are going to create chart widgets—a pie and radial chart, to be more specific. Pie charts are a useful kind of circular statistical graphic, which is divided into slices to illustrate numerical proportions.

We are going to start with the pie chart widget, where we retrieve slice values and draw them proportionally in a circle. This is what it is going to look like:

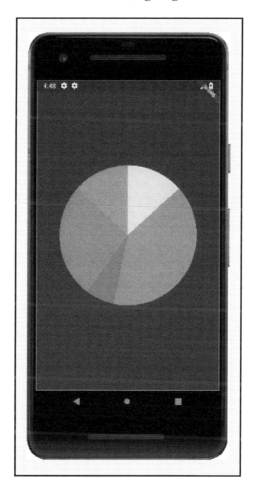

Now, let's define the new PieChart widget with the help of the Canvas and CustomPaint classes.

# Defining a widget

To start with, we typically define a widget, to maintain a minimal level of organization. We define the `PieChart` widget here; this will be a `StatelessWidget` descendant. This widget should abstract the paint layer and expose just what is needed by other widgets. In our case, this is what the `PieChart` properties look like:

```
class PieChart extends StatelessWidget {
  final List<int> values;
  final List<Color> colors;
  ...
}
```

The only properties that describe the widget are `values` and `colors`:

- `values`: This `List` represents each of the section values. Here, we use `int` values for simplicity, but it could be any type to work with any logic.
- `colors`: This `List` contains the colors that should be used to paint each of the sections in the chart.

Now, let's take a look at the `build()` method of this widget:

```
@override
Widget build(BuildContext context) {
  return Row(
    children: <Widget>[
      Expanded(
        child: CustomPaint(
          painter: PieChartPainter(
            values,
            colors
          ),
        ),
      ),
    ],
  );
}
```

There are a few things we need to pay attention to here:

- The CustomPaint widget needs a size to exist, as all of its painting logic should be done in a finite canvas. As we have seen before, the CustomPaint widget defines its size by its child constraints. In our case, we do not have a child, so it needs to be constrained in some way. We could have limited its size by using SizedBox, for example, but it would not be ideal. Instead, we put it inside a Row widget, filling its available horizontal space by surrounding it with an Expanded widget.
- The CustomPaint widget takes our custom painter, PieChartPainter, through the painter property.

That's all that's needed for the widget, as the hard work will be done by the PieChartPainter class.

# Defining CustomPainter

Defining our CustomPainter descendant class is the most important step here. As said before, in this example, we defined a painter that takes a list of int values and, based on that, draws a pie like a circle with proportional slices.

As said before, we need to override two methods from CustomPainter to make this work. Let's see how we define them.

## Overriding the shouldRepaint method

In our example, values and colors describe the drawing, so whenever either of them change, we need to repaint our widget. So, we need to reflect this in the shouldRepaint method, as follows:

```
// part of pie_chart.dart file PieChartPainter class

@override
bool shouldRepaint(PieChartPainter oldDelegate) {
    return !ListEquality().equals(oldDelegate.values, values) ||
      !ListEquality().equals(oldDelegate.colors, colors);
}
```

## Overriding the paint method

The `paint` method is responsible for drawing our chart. This is how we define it:

```
// part of pie_chart.dart file PieChartPainter class

@override
void paint(Canvas canvas, Size size) {
  var center = Offset(size.width / 2, size.height / 2);
  var radius = (size.width * 0.75) / 2;

  Rect chartRect = Rect.fromCircle(
    center: center,
    radius: radius,
  );

  int total = values.reduce((a, b) => a + b);

  _paintCircle(canvas, total, chartRect);
}
```

Let's break it down:

1. First, we need to define our pie extensions. With the given `size` parameter, we can set the `center` of our chart and the radius, which is half of 75 percent of the available space, (var radius = (size.width * 0.75) / 2;), to preserve some space around the chart.
2. Then, we create a `Rect` instance from the given `center` and `radius` properties. This rectangle will be useful when we draw the arcs of each slice (see the `_paintCircle` method explanation later).
3. The `total` value we get by summing up all of the values of the given slice. This will also be useful when we draw each of the slice arcs.
4. Finally, we can draw the pie chart on the canvas.

The `_paintCircle()` method is initially defined as follows:

```
void _paintCircle(Canvas canvas, int total, Rect chartRect) {
  Paint sectionPaint = Paint()..style = PaintingStyle.fill;

  double startAngle = -90;
  for (var i = 0; i < values.length; i++) {
    final value = values[i];
    final color = colors[i];

    double sweepAngle = ((value * 360.0) / total);
```

```
    sectionPaint.color = color;
    canvas.drawArc(
      chartRect,
      startAngle * _toRadians,
      sweepAngle * _toRadians,
      true,
      sectionPaint,
    );

    startAngle += sweepAngle;
  }
}
```

The sections of the chart are drawn sequentially. We need to know in which angle to start a slice and where it goes up to, as a circle has 360º sweep angles. The drawArc method from Canvas is based on specifying a start angle for the arc and its corresponding sweep angle. We can get each of the slice's sweep angles by using a simple **rule of three** calculation based on the total previously calculated.

The rule of three is a mathematical rule that allows us to solve direct and inverse proportion problems.

With this in mind, let's see how we draw each of the slice arcs and form the whole chart:

1. First, we define startAngle. We chose −90º to start drawing the arcs. Using a clock face analogy, this is equivalent to 12 o'clock. If we have chosen 0º to start, this would be equivalent to 3 o'clock or, as stated in the drawArc method documentation:

   *"...zero radians being the point on the right hand side of the oval that crosses the horizontal line that intersects the center of the rectangle and with positive angles going clockwise around the oval."*

2. Finally, we pass through each of the values to draw each of the arcs:

    1. First, we calculate the arc sweep angle, which is nothing more than the angle of an arc in the given circle. As said before, this is obtained from a simple rule of three, where we question: If the total value is equivalent to 360° sweep angle, what is the sweep angle (how much degrees) of the current slice value?

    2. Then, we set the color of our `Paint` object to the current slice color. Our `Paint` object defined before has the `PaintingStyle.fill` style, which means the shape drawn with this paint will be filled with the given color. In our case, that is exactly what we want.

    3. Lastly, we draw an arc that starts at the given `startAngle` property and has `sweepAngle` (check out the following explanation).

Let's see how we can use the `drawArc` method from the `Canvas` class to draw our slices. This is what the `drawArc` method looks like:

```
void drawArc (
    Rect rect,
    double startAngle,
    double sweepAngle,
    bool useCenter,
    Paint paint
)
```

Let's take a look at the values we passed to this function:

- `rect` is used to guide the draw. The arc will be drawn inside the given rectangle, with its sweep angle relative to the rectangle center.
- `startAngle` defines where to start drawing the arc. Remember, 0° is equivalent to 3 o'clock.
- `sweepAngle` defines how much the arc takes from the oval. We calculate this with `total` and each of the slice values.
- `useCenter` helps us to manipulate how the arc is drawn, as mentioned in the documentation:

  *"If its true, the arc is closed back to the center, forming a circle sector. Otherwise, the arc is not closed, forming a circle segment."*

- `Paint` defines how our arc is drawn. Here, we make the arc filled with the `PaintingStyle.fill` style and set its color with the given slice color.

As you can see, we need to convert the angle values into radians before sending them to the `drawArc` function.

# The radial chart variant

To help you to understand the potential of using the `CustomPaint` widgets, let's create another widget, this time to draw a radial chart, like this:

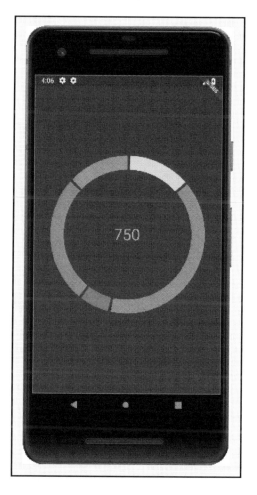

The radial representation is very similar to the pie chart; the only difference is that it has a label in its center showing the total of the values.

# Defining a widget

The RadialChart widget is very similar to the PieChart widget defined before, with the same parameters and the same fundamental objective. The only thing we need to take a look at here is its build() method:

```
// part of radial_chart.dart RadialChart widget

@override
Widget build(BuildContext context) {
  return Row(
    children: <Widget>[
      Expanded(
        child: CustomPaint(
          painter: RadialChartPainter(
            values,
            colors,
            Theme.of(context).textTheme.display1,
            Directionality.of(context),
          ),
        ),
      ),
    ],
  );
}
```

As you can see, the difference is in the value passed to the painter property of the CustomPaint widget. Here, we use a new RadialChartPainter class that has its own paint() implementation. Besides the values and colors, we pass two additional parameters to it:

- TextStyle, which will be used to draw the total value label
- A TextDirection instance that is needed to draw texts in the correct orientation

# Defining CustomPainter

The RadialChartPainter class, like the RadialChart widget, differs in very specific parts from PieChartPainter, which was defined before. At first glance, its paint() method is almost the same as in the from pie chart:

```
// part of radial_chart.dart RadialChartPainter class

@override
void paint(Canvas canvas, Size size) {
  var center = Offset(size.width / 2, size.height / 2);
```

```
var radius = size.width * 0.75 / 2;

Rect chartRect = Rect.fromCircle(
  center: center,
  radius: radius,
);

int total = values.reduce((a, b) => a + b);

_paintTotal(canvas, total, chartRect);
_paintCircle(canvas, total, chartRect);
}
```

As you can see, the only difference is the additional call to _paintTotal(canvas, total, chartRect);.

Before we check this new method, let's first see what changes in the _paintCircle() method:

```
// part of radial_chart.dart RadialChartPainter class
  void _paintCircle(Canvas canvas, int total, Rect chartRect) {
    Paint sectionPaint = Paint()
      ..style = PaintingStyle.stroke
      ..strokeWidth = 30.0;

    double startAngle = -90;
    for (var i = 0; i < values.length; i++) {
      final value = values[i];
      final color = colors[i];

      double sweepAngle = ((value * 360.0) / total);

      sectionPaint.color = color;
      canvas.drawArc(
        chartRect,
        (startAngle + 2) * _toRadians,
        (sweepAngle - 2)* _toRadians,
        false,
        sectionPaint,
      );

      startAngle += sweepAngle;
    }
  }
}
```

As you can see, almost everything is the same, with just a few points to note:

- We have changed our `sectionPaint` style to `PaintingStyle.stroke`; this way, the shape drawn with this paint will not be filled—instead, it will only have its outline drawn. That's why we set the `strokeWidth` property also.
- As you might have noted, before sending the angle values to the `drawArc` function, we first add 2° to the `startAngle` and subtract 2° from the `sweepAngle` value, leaving a little space between the slices to have a better visual result.
- Finally, we pass `false` to the `useCenter` parameter to form not a filled circle, but an arc segment.

That's all we have changed to get a radial chart like this:

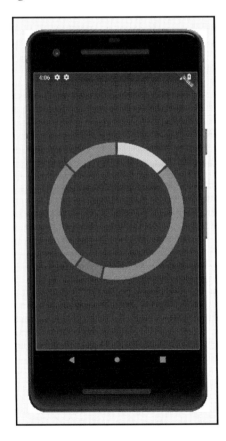

Finally, looking at the text painting, we have the `_paintTotal()` method:

```
void _paintTotal(Canvas canvas, int total, Rect chartRect) {
  final totalPainter = TextPainter(
    maxLines: 1,
    text: TextSpan(
      style: textStyle,
      text: "$total",
    ),
    textDirection: textDirection,
  );

  totalPainter.layout(maxWidth: chartRect.width);
  totalPainter.paint(
    canvas,
    chartRect.center.translate(
      -totalPainter.width / 2.0,
      -totalPainter.height / 2.0,
    ),
  );
}
```

To draw a text into the canvas, we will follow these steps:

1. First, we instantiate a `TextPainter` object, which defines how a text will look when drawn, just like the `Paint` class does for shapes. In our case, we define it to be a **single line** and have its `style` and `textDirection` retrieved from the `RadialChart` widget.
2. Then, we make sure to call the `layout()` function from the `TextPainter` instance. This call will compute the visual position of the glyphs for painting the text.
3. With the known text size, we can position it correctly in the final step. To position the text exactly in the center of the chart, we simply translate the center of the chart rectangle by half of the text size.

That's all for our `CustomPaint` widget. As you may have noticed, our charts look very similar to each other. The biggest difference is in the defined painter. We can abstract these to a single widget, where we can retrieve the desired chart type and just change the painter that we send to the `CustomPaint` widget.

# Summary

In this chapter, we got to know how to change how our widgets look by using the `Transform` class and its available transformations, such as **scaling, translating,** and **rotating**. We also saw how we can compound transformation by using the `Matrix4` class directly.

We learned how the `Canvas` class can be used to take control of the widgets drawn and how we can use this to create our own paintings.

Finally, we saw how the `CustomPaint` widget can be useful to create our own widgets that have not just unique functionalities, but also unique appearances defined by a `CustomPainter` descendant.

In the final chapter, we will check out how to animate widgets, making use of the transformations learned here.

# 15
## Animations

The built-in Flutter animations can be combined and extended to satisfy developer needs in the UX. In this chapter, you will learn a lot more about animations, using Tween animations to manage an animation timeline and curve, and useing `AnimatedBuilder` and `AnimatedWidget` to add and combine beautiful animations.

The following topics will be covered in this chapter:

- Getting to know the basics of Animations
- Using Animations
- Using AnimatedBuilder
- Using AnimatedWidget

# Introducing Animations

In Flutter, animations are widely supported, and the framework provides multiple ways of animating widgets. Also, there are built-in ready-to-use animations that we only need to plug into widgets to make them animate. Although Flutter abstracts many of the complexities that animations involve, there are some important concepts we need to understand before diving into the subject of animations.

# The Animation<T> class

In Flutter, animations consist of status and a value with the T type. The animation status corresponds to its state (that is, if it's running or completed); its value corresponds to its current value, and it is intended to change during the animation execution.

Besides holding that information about the animation, this class exposes callbacks so other classes can know how the animations are running, and the animation's current status and value too.

An `Animation<T>` class instance is only responsible for holding and exposing those values. It does not know anything about visual feedback, what is drawn on screen, or how to draw it (that is, `build()` functions).

One of the most common kinds of animation you will see is the `Animation<double>` type representation, as double value can easily be used to manipulate any kind of values in a sense of proportional space.

The `Animation` class generates a sequence (not necessarily linear) of values between determined minimum and maximum values. This process is also known as **interpolation** and, as said before, this interpolation is not only linear—it can be defined as a step function or a curve. Flutter provides multiple functions and facilities for operating animations. They are as follows:

- `AnimationController`: Despite what its name suggests, it is not used to control animation objects, but helps in the control task of itself, as it extends the `Animation` class and still is an animation.
- `CurvedAnimation`: This is an animation that applies `Curve` to another animation.
- `Tween`: This helps to create a linear interpolation between a beginning and ending value.

The `Animation` class exposes ways of accessing its state and value during a running cycle. Through **status listeners**, we can know when an animation begins, ends, or goes in the reverse direction. By using its `addStatusListener()` method, we can, for example, manipulate our widgets in response to animation start or end events. The same way, we can add value listeners with the `addListener()` method so we get notified every time the animation value changes, and we can rebuild our widgets by using `setState() {}`.

# AnimationController

AnimationController is one of the most used Flutter animation classes. It is derived from Animation<double> class and adds some fundamental methods for manipulating animations. The Animation class is the basis of animation in Flutter; as said before, it does not have any animation control-related methods. AnimationController adds these controls to the animation concept, such as the following:

- **Play and stop controls**: AnimationController adds the ability to play the animation forward, backward, or stop it
- **Duration**: Real animations have a finite time to play, that is, they play for a while and finish, or repeat
- **Allows setting the animation current value**: This causes a stop of the animation and notifies the status and value listeners
- **Allows defining the upper and lower bound of the animation**: This is so that we can know the deemed values before and after playing the animation

Let's check the AnimationController constructor and analyze its main properties:

```
AnimationController({
    double value,
    Duration duration,
    String debugLabel,
    double lowerBound: 0.0,
    double upperBound: 1.0,
    AnimationBehavior animationBehavior: AnimationBehavior.normal,
    @required TickerProvider vsync
})
```

As you can see, some properties are self-explanatory, but let's review them:

- value: This is the initial value of the animation, and it defaults to lowerBound if not specified.
- duration: This is the duration of the animation.
- debugLabel: This is a string to help during debugging. It identifies the controller in debug output.
- lowerBound: This cannot be null; it is the smallest value of the animation in which it is deemed to be dismissed, typically the start value when running.
- upperBound: Also, this cannot be null; it is the largest value of the animation at which it is deemed to be complete, typically the end value when running.

- `animationBehavior`: This configures how `AnimationController` behaves when animations are disabled. If it's `AnimationBehavior.normal`, the animation duration will be reduced, and if it's `AnimationBehavior.preserve`, `AnimationController` will preserve its behavior.
- `vsync`: This is a `TickerProvider` instance the controller will use to obtain a signal whenever a frame triggers.

Check all of the available methods for running animations with the `AnimationController` class: `https://api.flutter.dev/flutter/animation/AnimationController-class.html`.

### TickerProvider and Ticker

The `TickerProvider` interface describes objects capable of providing `Ticker` objects.

`Tickers` are used by any class that needs to know when the next frame is going to be built. They are commonly used indirectly via `AnimationControllers`. When using the `State` class, we can extend with `TickerProviderStateMixin` or `SingleTickerProviderStateMixin` to have `TickerProvider` and use it with `AnimationController` objects.

# CurvedAnimation

The `CurvedAnimation` class is used to define the progression of an `Animation` class as a non-linear curve. We can use this to modify an existing animation by changing its interpolation method. It is also useful when we want to use a different curve when playing an animation forward then in reverse mode, by using its `curve` and `reverseCurve` properties respectively.

The `Curves` class defines many curves ready to use in our animation rather the `Curves.linear` one.

Check out the `Curves` documentation page to see, in detail, how each of the curves behaves: `https://api.flutter.dev/flutter/animation/Curves-class.html`

## Tween

Besides all of these classes, we have one that can help in specific tasks regarding the range of the animation. As we have seen, by default, the simple start and end values of animation are `0.0` and `1.0` respectively. We can, by using `Tweens`, change the range or type of `AnimationController` without modifying it. `Tweens` can be of any type, and we can also create our custom `Tween` class if we want. The point is, `Tweens` returns values at periods between the beginning and the end, which you can pass as props to whatever you're animating, so it's always getting updated; for example, we can change the size of a widget, position, opacity, color, and so on by using specific `Tweens` for each one.

We also have other `Tween` descendant classes such as the `CurveTween` class available so that we can modify an animation curve, or `ColorTween`, which creates interpolation between `Colors`.

## Using animations

When working with animations, we are not going to be always creating exactly the same animation objects, but we can find some similarities in use cases. `Tween` objects are useful for changing the type and range of an animation. We will be, most of the time, composing animations with `AnimationController`, `CurvedAnimation`, and `Tween` instances.

Before we use a custom `Tween` implementation, let's revisit our widget transformations from the last chapter by applying the transformation in an animated way. We will get the same final effect but in a smooth and better way.

# Rotate animation

Instead of changing the button rotation directly, we can instead make it progressive by using the `AnimationController` class:

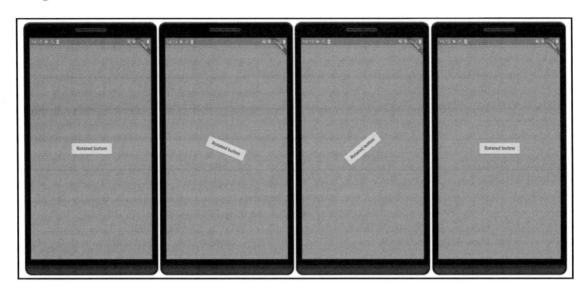

Check out the `hands_on_animations` example on GitHub for the complete examples.

In this example, we are creating our widget in a very similar way to before (in Chapter 14, *Widget Graphic Manipulations*):

```
_rotationAnimationButton() {
  return Transform.rotate(
    angle: _angle,
    child: RaisedButton(
      child: Text("Rotated button"),
      onPressed: () {
        if (_animation.status == AnimationStatus.completed) {
          _animation.reset();
          _animation.forward();
        }
      },
    ),
  );
}
```

As you can see, there are two important things to notice:

- The angle value is now defined with an _angle property instead of directly assigning to a literal
- In the onPressed property, we check whether _animation is completed, and if it is, we repeat it from the beginning

Now, let's see how the animation part is done. So, we need to know how to create our AnimationController object and make it run. Let's take a look at our example class first:

```
class _RotationAnimationsState extends State<RotationAnimations> with
SingleTickerProviderStateMixin {
  double _angle = 0.0;
  AnimationController _animation;
  ...
}
```

A few things are important to notice in this class:

- We have StatefulWidget object called RotationAnimations, to make use of the SingleTickerProviderStateMixin class we've previously seen and provide the required Ticker object for our controller to run.
- Besides that, we have the _angle property, used to define our button's current angle. We can use the setState() method to cause it to be built with a new angle.
- And finally, we have our _animation object, to hold an animation and allow us to manage it.

The initState() function from our State class is the perfect place to set up the animation and start it:

```
@override
void initState() {
  super.initState();

  _animation = createRotationAnimation();
  _animation.forward();
}
```

As you can see, we define our animation through the `createRotationAnimation()` method and make it run by calling its `forward()` function. Now, let's see how the animation is defined:

```
createRotationAnimation() {
    var animation = AnimationController(
      vsync: this,
      debugLabel: "animations demo",
      duration: Duration(seconds: 3),
    );

    animation.addListener(() {
      setState(() {
        _angle = (animation.value * 360.0) * _toRadians;
      });
    });

    return animation;
}
```

We can break up the creation of the animation into two important parts:

- There's the animation definition itself, where we set the animation `debugLabel` property for debugging purposes; the `vsync`, so that it can have a `Ticker` and know when to produce a new animation value; and finally, the animation `duration`.
- The second important step is to listen for the animation value changes. Here, whenever the animation has a new value, we get and multiply it by 360 degrees, so that we get a proportional rotation value.

As you can see, we can generate our desired values based on double animation values, so, most of the time, `Animation<double>` will be enough to play with animations.

If we wanted to, we could add a different curve to the animation by using CurveTween, for example, as you can see in the createBounceInRotationAnimation() method:

```
createBounceInRotationAnimation() {
  var controller = AnimationController(
    vsync: this,
    debugLabel: "animations demo",
    duration: Duration(seconds: 3),
  );

  var animation = controller.drive(CurveTween(
    curve: Curves.bounceIn,
  ));

  animation.addListener(() {
    setState(() {
      _angle = (animation.value * 360.0) * _toRadians;
    });
  });

  return controller;
}
```

Here, we create another Animation instance by using the controller's drive() method and passing the desired curve with a CurveTween object. Notice that we have added listeners to the new animation object instead of the controller, as we want values relative to the curve.

An important point to notice is that we have to dispose of our AnimationController class instance at the end of the lifetime of our State class to prevent leaks:

```
@override
void dispose() {
  _animation.dispose();
  super.dispose();
}
```

This must be done for every kind of animation we do, as we will always be working with AnimationController.

Now, let's see how to create scale animations.

# Scale animation

To create a scale animation and have a better effect than changing the scale attribute directly, we, again, can use the AnimationController class:

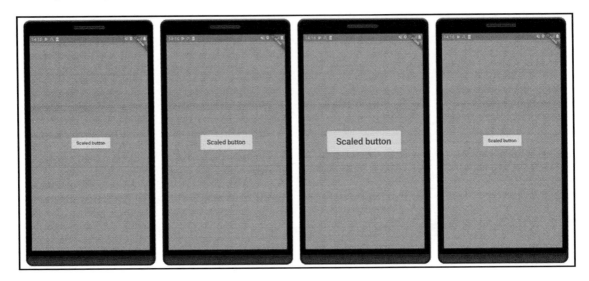

This time, to build our RaisedButton widget with a scale, we define a Transform widget with the well-known Transform.scale constructor:

```
_scaleAnimationButton() {
  return Transform.scale(
    scale: _scale,
    child: RaisedButton(
      child: Text("Scaled button"),
      onPressed: () {
        if (_animation.status == AnimationStatus.completed) {
          _animation.reverse();
        } else if (_animation.status == AnimationStatus.dismissed) {
          _animation.forward();
        }
      },
    ),
  );
}
```

Notice that, now, we use a `_scale` property in place and take a look at the change in the `onPressed` method. Here, we play the animation in reverse mode by using the `reverse()` function of `AnimationController` if it is completed, and play forward if it is at its initial state (that is, after reversing it).

The creation of an `animation` object occurs in a very similar way to rotation animation, but there are slight modifications to the controller construction:

```
createScaleAnimation() {
  var animation = AnimationController(
    vsync: this,
    lowerBound: 1.0,
    upperBound: 2.0,
    debugLabel: "animations demo",
    duration: Duration(seconds: 2),
  );

  animation.addListener(() {
    setState(() {
      _scale = animation.value;
    });
  });

  return animation;
}
```

As you can see, now we change the controller's `lowerBound` and `upperBound` values to make more sense in our case, as we want the button to grow until its size is twice as big, and we do not want it to be smaller than its initial size (`scale = 1.0`). Besides that, we change our animation value listener just to get the value from the animation without any calculations.

# Translate animation

Just like before, we can accomplish a better look in our translation transformation and make it smoother by using `AnimationController`:

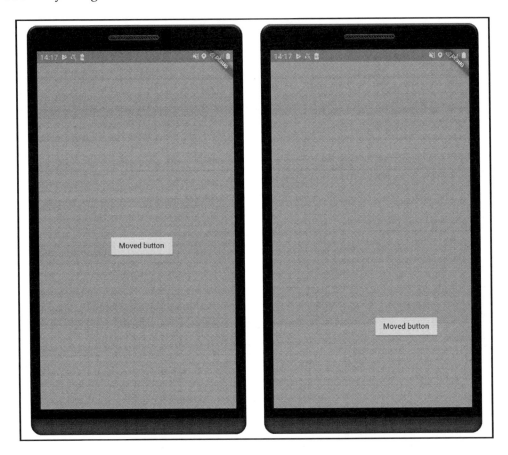

The construction of our widget similar to before; the only exception is the usage of the `Transform.translate()` construction. Now, we have a different value type than `double`. Let's see what we need to change to make an `Offset` animation:

```
createTranslateAnimation() {
  var controller = AnimationController(
    vsync: this,
    debugLabel: "animations demo",
    duration: Duration(seconds: 2),
  );
```

```
    var animation = controller.drive(Tween<Offset>(
      begin: Offset.zero,
      end: Offset(70, 200),
    ));

    animation.addListener(() {
      setState(() {
        _offset = animation.value;
      });
    });

    return controller;
  }
```

As you can see, here, we used a different approach to modify our widget offset. We used a Tween<Offset> instance, passed down to the AnimationController object through the drive() method, just like we did with CurveTween before. This works because the Offset class overrides mathematical operators such as subtraction and addition:

```
// part of geometry.dart file from dart:ui package
class Offset extends OffsetBase {
...
    Offset operator -(Offset other) => new Offset(dx - other.dx, dy -
    other.dy);
    Offset operator +(Offset other) => new Offset(dx + other.dx, dy +
    other.dy);
...
}
```

This makes the calculation of intermediate offsets (animation values) possible and then the interpolation between two Offset values can be achieved.

 Check the source code of the Offset class for details: https://github.com/flutter/engine/blob/master/lib/ui/geometry.dart. Also, note that to create custom interpolations, we typically write custom Tweens; see the next example for more details.

# Multiple transformations and custom Tween

If you remember, we can compose multiple transformations by using the Matrix4 class. For animations, things are similar; we can combine animations, run one after another, and play them—it's all in our hands. To create a composed animation, we can simply create multiple transformation values based on a single Animation object.

By doing that, we can achieve something like this:

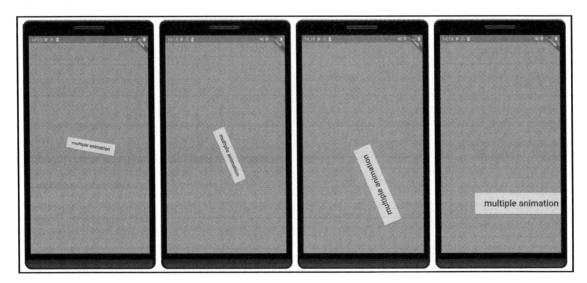

Thinking in a simple way, we can follow these steps:

1. We can simply have multiple values defined in our class, like this:

```
class _ComposedAnimationsState extends State<ComposedAnimations>
    with SingleTickerProviderStateMixin {
  Offset _offset = Offset.zero;
  double _scale = 1.0;
  double _angle = 0.0;
  ...
}
```

2. And whenever the animation value changes, we can calculate our values based on it:

```
animation.addListener(() {
    setState(() {
        _offset = Offset(animation.value * 70, animation.value *
        200);
        _scale = 1.0 + animation.value;
        _angle = 360 * animation.value;
      });
    });
}
```

3. And then, we apply the values we have calculated at each step of animation execution in our `build()` method:

```
_composedAnimationButton() {
  return Transform.translate(
    offset: _offset,
    child: Transform.rotate(
      angle: _angle * _toRadians,
      child: Transform.scale(
        scale: _scale,
        child: RaisedButton(
          child: Text("multiple animation"),
          onPressed: () {
            if (_animation.status == AnimationStatus.completed) {
              _animation.reverse();
            } else if (_animation.status ==
            AnimationStatus.dismissed) {
              _animation.forward();
            }
          },
        ),
      ),
    ),
  );
}
```

This works, and for simple cases it's best to keep like this, as we have fewer objects to take care of and a single animation to play.

To make it more maintainable, however, it's better to separate the value calculation from the animation itself. That's how we can use `Tweens`; remember the `Offset` example, where it is calculated and we simply get the value ready for use.

# Custom Tween

To create a custom `Tween` class, first, we need to define our value object. Here, we have opted for grouping the transformation values:

```
class ButtonTransformation {
  final double scale;
  final double angle;
  final Offset offset;

  // this none getter returns a initial state of transformation
  // with default scale, no rotation or translation
  static ButtonTransformation get none => ButtonTransformation(
```

```
        scale: 1.0,
        angle: 0.0,
        offset: Offset.zero,
      );
  }
```

And then, we extend the `Tween` class with our defined type:

```
class CustomTween extends Tween<ButtonTransformation> {

  CustomTween({ButtonTransformation begin, ButtonTransformation end} ):
  super(begin: begin, end: end,);

  @override
  lerp(double t) {
    return super.lerp(t);
  }
}
```

We need to define our custom `Tween` `lerp()` method (lerp stands for linear interpolation), which is responsible for returning the intermediate `ButtonTransformation` value between `begin` and `end`, based on the `t` value.

By taking a look into the default `Tween` class's `lerp()` implementation, we can see it is very simple:

```
// part of tween.dart Tween class

@protected
T lerp(double t) {
  assert(begin != null);
  assert(end != null);
  return begin + (end - begin) * t;
}
```

It calculates the `lerp()` value by using the +, –, and * operators on the type `T` objects. This means we can simply implement those operators in our `ButtonTransformation` and `Tween` will work as it does with any other type:

```
class ButtonTransformation {
  ...
  ButtonTransformation operator -(ButtonTransformation other) =>
      ButtonTransformation(
        scale: scale - other.scale,
        angle: angle - other.angle,
        offset: offset - other.offset,
      );
```

```
ButtonTransformation operator +(ButtonTransformation other) =>
    ButtonTransformation(
      scale: scale + other.scale,
      angle: angle + other.angle,
      offset: offset + other.offset,
    );

ButtonTransformation operator *(double t) => ButtonTransformation(
      scale: scale * t,
      angle: angle * t,
      offset: offset * t,
    );
}
```

Now, the Tween class is able to generate intermediate ButtonTransformation values as well. We can then use the generated animation values just like before:

```
createCustomTweenAnimation() {
  var controller = AnimationController(
    vsync: this,
    debugLabel: "animations demo",
    duration: Duration(seconds: 3),
  );

  var animation = controller.drive(CustomTween(
      begin: ButtonTransformation.none, // initial state of the animation
      end: ButtonTransformation(
        angle: 360.0,
        offset: Offset(70, 200),
        scale: 2.0,
      )));

  animation.addListener(() {
    setState(() {
      _buttonTransformation = animation.value;
    });
  });

  return controller;
}
```

As you can see, the big difference is in the usage of our CustomTween property. Note that we always need to define begin and end values, as Tweens are based on a range defined by the corresponding interpolation.

With those examples, we have seen how to use and apply the most important animations in Flutter. In the next sections, we will see alternative ways of applying animations to our widgets.

 We can build multiple simultaneous animations using separate `Animation` objects, typically, by setting the same `AnimationController` as their parent. They are guaranteed to be in sync as we will be using the same `Ticker` object.

# Using AnimatedBuilder

Looking at the code that we wrote in the last section, there is nothing wrong with it: it's not too complex or big. However, looking closely, we can see a small problem with it, our button animation is mixed up with other widgets. As long as our code does not scale and get more complex, this is fine, but we know this is not the case most of the time, so we might have a real problem.

The `AnimatedBuilder` class can help us with the task of separating responsibilities; our widget, whether it is `RaisedButton` or anything else, does not need to know it is rendered in animation, and breaking down the `build` method to widgets that each have a single responsibility can be seen as one of the fundamental lemmas in the Flutter framework.

# The AnimatedBuilder class

The `AnimatedBuilder` widget exists so that we can build *complex widgets that wish to include animation as part of a larger build function*. Just like any other widget, it is included in the widgets tree and has a `child` property. Let's check its constructor:

```
const AnimatedBuilder({
    Key key,
    @required Listenable animation,
    @required TransitionBuilder builder,
    Widget child
})
```

As you can see, we have a few important properties here, besides the well-known `key` property:

- `animation`: This is the proper animation as a `Listenable` object. `Listenable` is a type that holds a list of listeners and notify them whenever the object changes. As you may already be thinking, `AnimatedBuilder` will listen for animation updates, so we do not need to do it manually with the `addListener()` method anymore.
- `builder`: This is where we modify the `child` widget based on the animation values.
- `child`: This is the widget that exists regardless of the animation. So, we construct this widget as we would do without the animation.

# Revisiting our animation

To break down our code, modify our animation and make it more maintainable, we start separating what we need for each responsibility. Typically, three things are needed:

- The `animation` itself: Here, we do not need to change anything. Our `AnimationController` will still be the same.
- Add the `AnimatedBuilder` widget to our `build()` method: We will be extracting much of the code related to the animation of the button to make it clear.
- The `child` widget: In our case, it is just `RaisedButton` that changes according to the progress of the animation:

```
class _AnimationBuilderAnimationsState extends
State<AnimationBuilderAnimations>
    with SingleTickerProviderStateMixin {
  AnimationController _controller;
  Animation<ButtonTransformation> _animation;

  @override
  void initState() {
    super.initState();

    _animation = createAnimation();
    _controller.forward();
  }
  ...
}
```

As you can see, we have a few changes here:

- We do not have a `ButtonTransformation` field anymore, as it will be managed in our new widget.
- We separate the `AnimationController` from our `Animation` object. This is very common and better than making type casting everywhere.
- And finally, there's just a small detail in the `createAnimation()` method:

```
createAnimation() {
  _controller = AnimationController(
    vsync: this,
    debugLabel: "animations demo",
    duration: Duration(seconds: 3),
  );

  return _controller.drive(CustomTween(
      begin: ButtonTransformation.none,
      end: ButtonTransformation(
        angle: 360.0,
        offset: Offset(70, 200),
        scale: 2.0,
      )));
}
```

We do not need to listen for animation updates anymore (we do not have an `addListener()` call), as this is done directly by the `AnimatedBuilder` widget.

Then, we modify the `build()` method to use a new widget:

```
@override
Widget build(BuildContext context) {
  return Container(
    color: Colors.grey,
    child: Center(
      child: ButtonTransition(
        animation: _animation,
        child: RaisedButton(
          child: Text("AnimatedBuilder animation"),
          onPressed: () {
            if (_controller.status == AnimationStatus.completed) {
              _controller.reverse();
            } else if (_controller.status == AnimationStatus.dismissed) {
              _controller.forward();
            }
          },
        ),
      ),
    ),
```

```
          ),
        );
      }
```

As you can see, the animation is clearly separated from the creation of `RaisedButton`. We instantiate and pass it to a new widget called `ButtonTransition`, together with our `_animation` object. Let's see this brand new widget:

```
class ButtonTransition extends StatelessWidget {
  final Animation<ButtonTransformation> _animation;
  final RaisedButton child;

  const ButtonTransition({
    Key key,
    @required Animation<ButtonTransformation> animation,
    this.child,
  }) : _animation = animation,
       super(key: key);

  @override
  Widget build(BuildContext context) {
    return AnimatedBuilder(
      animation: _animation,
      child: child,
      builder: (context, child) => Transform(
          transform: Matrix4.translationValues(
            _animation.value.offset.dx,
            _animation.value.offset.dy,
            0,
          )
            ..rotateZ(_animation.value.angle * _toRadians)
            ..scale(_animation.value.scale, _animation.value.scale),
          child: child,
        ),
    );
  }
}
```

Basically, `ButtonTransition` handles the modification of its child (`RaisedButton`) without touching it. The important steps of this `build()` method are as follows:

1. First, we add an `AnimatedBuilder` widget to the widget tree.
2. The `child` class passed to it will be passed back to us in the `builder` method with optimizations in mind. The whole `child` subtree does not need to be rebuilt every time the animation gets updated. Holding it and just placing again helps the framework to rebuild only the needed widgets in the `builder` method.

The documentation says:

*"Using this pre-built child is entirely optional, but can improve performance significantly in some cases and is, therefore, a good practice."*

3. The `builder` method constructs the tree below it with the required animation changes. Note that we do not have to worry about listening to the animation changes; this `builder` method will be called whenever the animation is updated.

Although the final visual result is the same, breaking things down into small parts with single responsibilities is an important concept that improves the maintainability of the code and can lead to better performance.

# Using AnimatedWidget

Separating our animation from widgets with the help of the `AnimatedBuilder` widget is incredibly easy and can bring up may benefits, as we have seen. Flutter offers another interesting alternative that does the same thing as the `AnimatedBuilder` widget with a simpler syntax.

This is common when dealing with a well-structured framework such as Flutter; there is typically more than one way of doing something, and it does not mean that there are significant differences between one way or another. `AnimatedWidget` and `AnimatedBuilder` are great examples of this. Both aim to separate the animation part from the widget building part.

While the `AnimatedBuilder` widget delegates the creation of the widget to a builder method, `AnimatedWidget` defines everything needed with relation to the animation and we simply need to override its `build()` method to reflect animation updates. At the end, `AnimatedBuilder` is itself an `AnimatedWidget` class.

# The AnimatedWidget class

AnimatedWidget is an abstract class and, as we said before, we need to override its build() method directly to reflect animation changes. Its constructor is defined as follows:

```
const AnimatedWidget({
    Key key,
    @required Listenable listenable
})
```

As you can see, the only required property is the Listenable object so that it can listen to animation updates. The whole widget build logic is the responsibility of its descending class.

# Rewriting the animation with AnimatedWidget

Using AnimatedWidget in our case would require us to simply modify our ButtonTransition widget. However, as you remember, there is a concept behind this. To follow this, we need to extend the AnimatedWidget class and transform our widget into an animated button in its build() method.

We start by defining our new AnimatedWidget based widget:

```
class AnimatedButton extends AnimatedWidget {
  final RaisedButton button;

  const AnimatedButton({
    Key key,
    @required Listenable animation,
    this.button,
  }) : super(
          key: key,
          listenable: animation,
        );

  @override
  Widget build(BuildContext context) {
    Animation<ButtonTransformation> animation = listenable;
    return Transform(
      transform: Matrix4.translationValues(
        animation.value.offset.dx,
        animation.value.offset.dy,
        0,
      )
```

```
        ..rotateZ(animation.value.angle * _toRadians)
        ..scale(animation.value.scale, animation.value.scale),
      child: button,
    );
  }
}
```

Now, we have defined our `AnimatedButton` widget derived from the `AnimatedWidget` class. We can highlight two fundamental points here:

- The only thing we need to pass to the super `AnimatedWidget` class is the animation object, so it can listen to animation updates and rebuild itself at the right time.
- In the `build()` method, we access the animation from the `listenable` property of the superclass and use the animation value just like before.

Choosing when to use `AnimatedBuilder` and `AnimatedWidget` may appear confusing at first, but keeping in mind that both can bring up the same benefits helps on this decision. Start by breaking down your widgets with a single responsibility in mind, and taking such decisions will become natural.

# Summary

In this final chapter, we dived into Flutter animations. We learned the fundamental concepts of animation, which are concept mainly defined by the `Animation` class.

We saw important classes the framework provides that `AnimationController`, `CurvedAnimation`, and `Tween`. We also revisited our `Tranformation` examples and added animations to them by using the concepts learned in this chapter. Finally, we saw how to create our own custom `Tween` objects.

Lastly, we saw how to use `AnimatedBuilder` and `AnimatedWidget` to make our animation code cleaner and simpler to understand.

That's all folks. In this book, I have tried to go over some basic but fundamental concepts of this incredible platform. I hope you enjoyed and learned something: that's what motivates us to continue.

# Other Books You May Enjoy

If you enjoyed this book, you may be interested in these other books by Packt:

**React Native Cookbook - Second Edition**
Dan Ward

ISBN: 978-1-78899-192-6

- Build UI features and components using React Native
- Create advanced animations for UI components
- Develop universal apps that run on phones and tablets
- Leverage Redux to manage application flow and data
- Expose both custom native UI components and application logic to React Native
- Employ open-source third-party plugins to create React Native apps more efficiently

**Xamarin.Forms Projects**

Johan Karlsson, Daniel Hindrikes

ISBN: 978-1-78953-750-5

- Set up a machine for Xamarin development
- Get to know about MVVM and data bindings in Xamarin.Forms
- Understand how to use custom renderers to gain platform-specific access
- Discover Geolocation services through Xamarin Essentials
- Create an abstraction of ARKit and ARCore to expose as a single API for the game
- Learn how to train a model for image classification with Azure Cognitive Services

# Leave a review - let other readers know what you think

Please share your thoughts on this book with others by leaving a review on the site that you bought it from. If you purchased the book from Amazon, please leave us an honest review on this book's Amazon page. This is vital so that other potential readers can see and use your unbiased opinion to make purchasing decisions, we can understand what our customers think about our products, and our authors can see your feedback on the title that they have worked with Packt to create. It will only take a few minutes of your time, but is valuable to other potential customers, our authors, and Packt. Thank you!

# Index